HUMAN RESOURCES MANAGEMENET FOR ORGANIZATIONAL SUCCESS

Human Resources Managemenet for Organizational Success

Editor:

Rahmaoui Naima

ArclerPress

www.arclerpress.com

Human Resources Managemenet for organizational Success
Editor: Rahmaoui Naima

© 2017 Arcler Press LLC
708 3ʳᵈ Avenue, 6ᵗʰ Floor
New York
NY 10017
United States of America
www.arclerpress.com

ISBN: 978-1-68094-497-6

Library of Congress Control Number: 2016951356

Arcler Press LLC publishes wide variety of books and eBooks. For more information about Arcler Press and its products, visit our website at www.arclerpress.com

About the Editor
Rahmaoui Naima

Naima obtained her academic Master degree from economics university in 2012,her interests financial corporations,and marketing ,she's currently working as a financial manager.

Contents

List of Contributors

John W. Boudreau
Department of Human Resource Studies Center for Advanced Human Resource Studies
Cornell University, Ithaca, NY 14853-3901

Irfan Ullah
Iqra University, Islamabad, Pakistan

Robina Yasmin
Iqra University, Islamabad, Pakistan

Deepak K. Datta
University of Kansas

James P. Guthrie
University of Kansas

Patrick M. Wright
Cornell University

Jaap Paauwe
Erasmus University Rotterdam

Jean Paul Boselie
Erasmus University Rotterdam

Patrick M. Wright
Department of Human Resource Studies Center for Advanced Human Resource Studies
(CAHRS) School of ILR Cornell University

Rebecca R. Kehoe
Department of Human Resource Studies Center for Advanced Human Resource Studies
(CAHRS) School of ILR Cornell University

Dr. Danial Saeed Pirzada
Associate Professor, Center for Advanced Studies in Engineering,19-Ataturk Avenue,
G-5/1, Islamabad, Pakistan

Farah Hayat
Ph.DScholar, Center for Advanced Studies in Engineering, 19-Ataturk Avenue, G-5/1,
Islamabad, Pakistan

Amjad Ali Ikram
M.Sc Engineering Management, Center for Advanced Studies in Engineering, 19-Ataturk Avenue, G-5/1, Islamabad, Pakistan

Muhammad Ayub
M.Sc Engineering Management, Center for Advanced Studies in Engineering, 19-Ataturk Avenue, G-5/1, Islamabad, Pakistan

Kamran Waheed
M.Sc Engineering Management, Center for Advanced Studies in Engineering, 19-Ataturk Avenue, G-5/1, Islamabad, Pakistan

Mansoor Hussain
M.phil scholar, Army Public College of Management and Sciences (APCOMS),Rawalpindi,Pakistan, University of engineering and technology (UET) Taxila, Pakistan Corresponding Address: CB-194, Lane-3 Sherzaman Colony Tulsa Road Lalazar, Rawalpindi, Cantt ,Pakistan

Mushtaq Ahmad
Army Public College of management and sciences (APCOMS) Rawalpindi,Pakistan University of Engineering and Technology(UET), Taxila Pakistan

Mubeen Mujahid
MS & Research Scholar, Department of Management Sciences, The Islamia University of Bahawalpur, Pakistan

Syeda Nudrat Sameen
MS & Research Scholar, Department of Management Sciences, The Islamia University of Bahawalpur, Pakistan

Hina Naz
MS & Research Scholar, Department of Management Sciences, The Islamia University of Bahawalpur, Pakistan

Farkhanda Nazir
MS & Research Scholar, Department of Management Sciences, The Islamia University of Bahawalpur, Pakistan

Sobia Manzoor
MS & Research Scholar, Department of Management Sciences, The Islamia University of Bahawalpur, Pakistan

Is'haq Ibrahim Bani Melhem
Department of Economics and Muamalat, Universiti Sains Islam Malaysia, Nilai, 71800, Malaysia

Dr. Charles Kombo Okioga
Kisii University, Kenya

Anthony Igwe
Department of Management, University of Nigeria, Enugu Campus, Enugu, Nigeria

J. U. J Onwumere
Department of Banking and Finance, University of Nigeria, Enugu Campus, Enugu, Nigeria

Obiamaka P. Egbo
Department of Banking and Finance, University of Nigeria, Enugu Campus, Enugu, Nigeria

Rukevwe Juliet Ogedegbe
Ajayi Crowther University, Department of Business Administration, Ogbomosho Road, Oyo .Oyo State, Nigeria

Salman Hussainm
AIOU, Islamabad, Pakistan

Shah Muhammad
AIOU, Islamabad, Pakistan

Zia-ur-Rehman Majed Rashid
AIOU, Islamabad, Pakistan

Nasser Fegh-hi Farahmand
Department of Industrial Management, Tabriz Branch, Islamic Azad University, Tabriz, Iran PO box 6155, Tabriz, Iran

Preface

Human Resource Management (HRM) is the integrated use by an organization of systems, policies and management practices to recruit, develop and retain employees who will help the organization meet its goals. HRM plays an important role in assuring employee satisfaction, improving performance and productivity. This can further an organization's competitive advantage, and directly contribute to the organization's success.

HRM provides managers with skills and tools to enhance their own performance and the performance of their employees. By using these tools and working closely with HR professionals, managers can help build their employees' capabilities and strengthen employee commitment to the organization. This in turn will strengthen individual and organizational performance, and further the organization's ability to meet its goals according to performance objectives and standards. That's why HRM gained its importance over last few decades. Managers now can realize that the effectiveness of HR function has a substantial impact on the bottom line performance of the organization. In this book we're gonna learn the organizations success relates with it's Human Resource management function. The first chapter links the Human Resources and Organization Success. The second chapter Reviews the influence of Human Resource Practices on Internal Customer Satisfaction and Organizational Effectiveness chapter 3 unswers the question : Does IndustryMatter in HRM and Firm Productivity? chapter 4 reviews the HRM and Performance chapter 5 examines the Human Resource Practices and Organizational Commitment. Chapter 6 discusses the impact of the Human Resources on the Risk Management and the Company Performance , chapter 7 reviews the mostly discussed research areas in Human Resource Management (HRM), Chapter 8 discusses the importance of human resource management in Adding Value to Organizational Success in Gaining Competitive Advantage. Chapter 9 reviews the impact of Human Resources on the Risk Management and the Company Performance. The contribution of Human Resource strategies to the Organizational Success has been discussed in the chapter 10. The chapter 11 describes the effective Human Resource Management As Tool For Organizational Success, chaper 12 reviews the achievement of the Organisational Objectives through Human Resource Management Practices, chapter 13 analyzes the Effects of HR System on Organizational Performance. Finally chapter 14 reviews the Organizational Supporting by Human Empowerment. I hope this book is good source for researcher in Human Resource Management and organizational success fields.

Editor

Rahmaoui Naima

1

CHAPTER

HUMAN RESOURCES AND ORGANIZATION SUCCESS

John W. Boudreau

Department of Human Resource Studies Center for Advanced Human Resource Studies Cornell University, Ithaca, NY 14853-3901

This paper has not undergone formal review or approval of the faculty of the ILR School. It is intended to make results of research, conferences, and projects available to others interested in human resource management in preliminary form to encourage discussion and suggestions.

Fortune magazine's November 1994 cover story tells us the six reasons "Why Companies Fail"[1]:

(1) Identity Crisis: Top managers don't have a "mental model" of the organizations key competencies, so they succumb to management fads, creating "change fatigue", and the work force resists their initiatives (examples include Josten's and Subaru).

(2) Failures of Vision: Managers prepare only for the most obvious future business obstacles, failing to create strategies flexible enough to "deal with the wildest-case scenario" (examples include the Commerce Clearing House and Quotron Systems, both of whom failed to anticipate how computer technology breakthroughs would fundamentally change their business).

(3) The Big Squeeze: Managers take on excessive debt, assuming that present business success will continue, or to discourage predatory raiders. The result can be reduced capability to weather business downturns, resulting in divestitures and layoffs, or even bankruptcy.

Citation: Boudreau, J. W. (1996). Human resources and organization success, http://digitalcommons.ilr.cornell.edu/cahrswp/174

(4) The Glue Sticks and Sticks: Organization traditions, once a source of strength, become obstacles to innovation and new thinking. Curing the problem often requires tough decisions about which organizational leaders should leave, and how to create and make room for those who can think differently. Managers at Digital Equipment Corporation (DEC), once the premier provider of networked systems, now struggle to trim a massive work force, and revitalize former flexibility and inventiveness.

(5) Anybody Out There?: Stick close to your customers, an often quoted mantra that is more difficult to follow in practice. One key, a well-trained sales force that can build expertise about key customers or markets, plus a system to motivate them to gather and communicate information about changing tastes, and dissatisfaction among clients. Managers must find a way to create "players", instead of "cheerleaders". High-profile examples include Cross penmakers, Merry-Go-Round fashion retailers, and General Motors.

(6) Enemies Within: Managers who fail to consider the "human factor", risk creating uncooperative or even hostile workers, who often have the means to scuttle even the best-laid business strategies. By the time employees join unions, go out on strike, or engage in sabotage, it's probably too late to deal constructively with the problem. Encouraging risk-taking while penalizing good-faith failures, or admonishing cost-reductions while taking record bonuses can sap employees' loyalty and commitment, and perhaps their willingness to perform.

How can managers prevent their company (or division, region or product line) from having these problems? How could tools such as financial planning, marketing, operations research, and accounting help them cope? Do they offer a complete answer?

HUMAN RESOURCES ARE EVERY MANAGER'S JOB

The pitfalls described above cannot be avoided without managing people well. In fact, as we shall see, evidence suggests that organizations can create sustained and consistent competitive advantage only by mastering the management of their people, or "human resources." Every person who works in organizations plays a role in managing people. This is especially true for those of you who aspire to create, manage, and lead future organizations. Certainly, tools from marketing, finance, operations and other management disciplines will be required. In fact, principles from these areas can even be applied to managing people better. Moreover, even applying the traditional tools will require greater awareness of their impact and relationship to people. Judy Lewent, one of today's "hottest" executives, and CFO of Merck & Co. says even financial analysis should serve to encourage the right behaviors in people, "finance departments can take the nuances, the intuitive feelings that really fine business people have and quantify them"[2]. This paper introduces human resource management, and shows why it is so important in modern organizations. It will help you understand how human resource management affects your future, and that of your organization. Human resources are every manager's job, both the general manager and the human resource professional. The job of enhancing the value of people in organizations is everyone's job, not the job of "human resource specialists" or the "human resource department". To emphasize that point, let's examine the challenges faced by organizations, that show how important human resource management is to all organization members.

CHANGING ORGANIZATIONS MAKE HUMAN RESOURCES MORE IMPORTANT

It's almost trite to say that organizations are changing rapidly, perhaps more rapidly than ever before. One study of hundreds of business suggests that 37% of organizations are "transforming" through quality initiatives and fundamental changes in the way work is done[3]. One pattern in these changes is the increasing importance of people issues that require managers to understand how people contribute to organizational success. Here, we highlight the key role that managing human issues plays in mastering this organizational ambiguity.

Organization Design

The very concept of an organization has fundamentally changed. If an organization ever could be represented by a chart with boxes and lines, that idea is probably passe. Some have suggested using a grid or "matrix", to emphasize that each person in the organization must consider at least two intersecting roles, such as plant manager and regional product team leader. However, even a matrix implies defined organizational boundaries, a concept that also appears rather dated. At Hewlett-Packard, some internal enterprises buy millions of chips from suppliers because H-P's chips are too expensive[4]. Perhaps the appropriate metaphor is a spinning top, built on a base of solid independent businesses, with stability provided by cooperation, teamwork and planning, thrust provided by management "vision and style", and an organizational culture that prevents the parts from spinning off[5]. Successfully creating teamwork, vision, and culture requires that today's managers understand how to manage people well.

Organizational Goals

Organizations have always strived to provide value to their constituents, to survive, and to adapt. Today, many claim that reaching those goals requires a keener focus on "softer" factors. Leading writers argue that the companies that will survive are those with strong "cultures", driven by leaders who relentlessly pursue a "vision", through "simple structures", providing "world-class training", that value "people skills", and that foster "entrepreneurship"[6]. Charles Handy, a leading business futurist, suggests that key challenges facing future managers include: Shorter and more intensive work lives, the demise of corporate pension plans, motivating employees in the manner of not-for-profit organizations, loyalty to the team rather than to the organization, and increasing responsibility for education beyond schools[7]. Managers who master these trends will significantly affect their success in an increasingly global and volatile world. Activities such as employee education, organizational design, pensions and loyalty are no longer the exclusive domain of the "human resources department", they are integral parts of every manager's job, and they are the focus of this book.

Re-Engineering

Re-engineering, redesigning work to streamline processes and combine fragmented tasks for more efficiency, has become a mantra for many organizations. Reengineering efforts have often proceeded from an operational or financial model, resulting in enlarging the work of employees, cutting entire administrative processes, and generally finding ways to do more with less[8]. Astounding returns are possible, but so are increasing work loads, and wrenching decisions about who stays and who must go[9]. After publishing their book, "Reengineering the Corporation", authors Michael Hammer and James Champy note that up to 70% of reengineering efforts fail[10]. They say that "the redesign, as brilliant as it may be, doesn't get results because of managerial thought and ideology."[11] Perhaps managers need to be "reengineered", to better understand the effects of reengineering on careers, burnout, and the new social contract between employees and organizations[12]. As Michael Hammer puts it,

"The biggest lie told by most organizations is that 'people are our most important assets.' Total fabrication. They treat people like raw material. If you're serious about treating people as an asset, we're looking at a dramatic increase in investment in them."[13]

Managers must understand what it means to "invest in people" to create social contracts, and how those investments pay off, so that organizations can better reconcile and integrate the claims of shareholders, customers, and employees.

Learning Organizations

How do modern business leaders ensure that their organizations remain flexible innovative, and energized? How can managers help their organizations avoid the tendency to become complacent? For many, the "learning organization" concept offers the answer. Is managing people well important to such an organization? Senge says that human resource management is key to knowing who the organization's innovators are, and to diagnosing what's needed to make learning spread, and how to make every aspect of the organization a learning opportunity[14]. Such tasks are clearly too important to be left to the organization's "training department." Every employee and manager must understand how people learn, if a learning organization is to become a reality.

"Virtual" Organizations

Organizational boundaries are blurring. The line between an organization and its suppliers, customers, and consultants is less defined. In the early 1980's, few believed Charles Handy's prediction that, by the year 2000, half the working population would make a living outside traditional organizations. Yet, today up to 35% of U.S. workers are unemployed, temporary, part-time, or contractual, and the numbers may be even higher in Europe[15]. Employees at General Electric Corporation often spend over 50% of their time sharing management ideas with suppliers, to help suppliers improve their business, so they can provide GE the lowest possible price and highest quality. Thus, suppliers, customers, and the government become direct participants in the organization's activities. In such a "virtual" organization, relationships and intellectual capital are keys to productive value and success. Continuous learning and development must extend beyond the traditional organization boundaries, as managers focus on developing an array of alliances, both inside and outside the organization. For example, Charles Handy proposes the organizations must either ensure that employees can find work after they leave the company, or suffer heavy taxes from Governments. At British Petroleum, the implication is that business managers must take direct responsibility for employee development. "Gone are the days when a line manager would sift through a list of courses. Instead, we are moving toward providing development which is designed for individuals, to enhance their skills and personal portfolio"[16]. Understanding how people are motivated, and how they develop, is a key to nurturing competitive advantage in such an environment. The "virtual" organization fundamentally changes the meaning of ideas such as it performance", "communication", and "competition", and requires a keen understanding of the human consequences of work relationships.

Organizational Ownership

Employee ownership is nothing new. It was the original organizational design. Families owned and ran the means to produce food and shelter. Modern organizations frequently focus on "shareholders" as the real owners of the organization's capital and economic returns. Classic business theory suggests that firms exist to enhance shareholder value, but the notion of ownership is changing, as more organizations provide stock to employees. Some organizations have become fully employee-owned. UAL Corp., parent of United Airlines, awarded various employee groups 55% of the company's stock in exchange for a $4.9 billion package of labor concessions, such as wage levels and work flexibility[17]. When employees own the company, human resource management issues become stockholder issues. Managers aspiring to lead such organizations must understand human resource management as a fundamental business discipline, and integrate it with other business disciplines. As Stephen M. Wolf, outgoing UAL Chairman notes, "our fleet is in place, the route structure is in place, our service strategy is in place. But there was one piece of the puzzle missing: Our labor costs were not competitive."[18] Human resource management comprises the tools that managers must understand to control such costs.

Globalization

Major companies frequently operate across national boundaries. The hard data suggests that this will become a requirement for survival in the future. Companies in all size categories and in all industries grew faster, and had higher sales and profits if they had global activities. In fact, sales for companies with no foreign activities grew at only half the average of the group[19]. Major organizations use communication technology to form "virtual teams" that work together simultaneously across national boundaries. Many organizations have actually relocated major headquarters functions to different countries[20]. While globalization presents significant challenges for managing financial, marketing and production processes, some of the thorniest issues revolve around managing people. Up to 40 percent of expatriate American managers do not even complete their foreign assignments due to poor performance or inability to adjust, and up to 80 percent perform below par in foreign assignments[21]. Conservatively, such failures cost $100,000, so it's not hard to see that improving the success rates can significantly affect the bottom line. Moreover, the key business challenges abroad often stem from the availability of human capital, as much as financial and physical capital. Motorola has provided thousands of dollars in scholarships at Tianjina and Nankai Universities in China, in an effort to increase the supply of desperately-needed well-educated workers[22]. Japan's labor system of employment guarantees still survives, but the 1994 recession forced both Japanese and foreign managers doing business there to realize the significant business implications of traditions such as lifetime employment and wage inflexibility[23]. Coca-Cola, with businesses in 25 divisions, 6 regional groups and more than 195 countries, credits innovations in managing its international work force as a key to continued success. Pay and benefits are coordinated across countries, right down to the income tax. Workers pay "hypothetical income taxes" based on the U.S. system, and Coca-Cola pays their actual foreign taxes, adjusting for tax credits, etc[24]. In many ways, it is the nature of the global workforce that will determine competitive advantage for future organizations[25].

The "New" Work

People do their jobs differently now, as organizations increasingly strive to increase quality, speed, innovation and responsiveness. Tasks that used to take months now take days. "Soft factories" have emerged. When a customer orders a pager from Motorola, typically via 800 phone lines or e-mail, the specifications are immediately downloaded at the factory in Florida, where robots pick out the appropriate components, and humans assemble the devices. No matter how unusual the order (Sizzling Yellow color, goes ding-dong, etc.), the pager is often ready in 80 minutes and arrives at the customer's door that day. IBM workers build 12 products at once, assisted by their individual personal computer that automatically tracks the parts to be assembled, and provides on-line assembly assistance if the worker gets in trouble. Robots, once believed to be destined to replace humans, have instead been relegated to simple jobs, and software, computers, and humans have emerged as key manufacturing factors[26]. In Japan, the factory of the future resembles the craft shops of the past. Small and oddly-shaped assembly pods have replaced linear mass-production conveyor belts. New production methods emphasize "individual workers' skills rather than production teams"[27]. Human factors also seem significant in exploiting new technology. It appears that computer technology's benefits have been slow to materialize, despite exponential increases in computer speed and power, because managers were slow to change work practices, and to tailor software to worker needs[28]. Successful managers must understand human factors at work, if they are to maximize the payoff from new work designs, technologies and production practices. Human resource management is what helps managers make good decisions about these issues.

GOOD MANAGERS NURTURE HUMAN RESOURCES WELL

Human resource skills are essential to future managerial success, as you can see from observing what the best top managers say about their most critical challenges.

Increasingly, successful CEO's describe their success in terms of skillful management of people. Jack Welch, CEO of GE, describes his "lessons for success", including "The only way I see to get more productivity is by getting people involved and excited about their jobs", "Anybody who gets this [CEO] job has got to believe in the gut that people are the key to everything and "If you're not thinking all the time about making every person more valuable, you don't have a chance."[29] Harvard management experts admonish future top managers to move "beyond strategy to purpose", proposing that only organizations with purpose can develop employees' broad perspectives and can convert employees from mere contractors to committed members. Tetsuya Katada, the third president of Komotsu, one of Japans largest heavy-equipment makers, remade the company, with the objective of "revitalizing its human resources"[30]. Among the lessons learned from giant companies that continue to thrive like startups: Hire Carefully and Teach Continuously[31]. Henry Schact, CEO of Cummins Engine, credits his organization's success in part to embracing work teams, creating a clear path for management succession, and offering 100 hours of training to workers annually[32]. Should top managers be involved in such "mundane" activities as recruiting new employees? Microsoft, with over 15,000 employees, hires software writers "like we're a ten-person company hiring an 11th", with Bill Gates wooing senior engineers, and requiring even experienced software developers to go through five or six hours of intense interviews[33]. Desi DeSimone, CEO of 3M offers "ten commandments" for nurturing a creative company, including "create a culture of cooperation", "stage a lot of celebrations", "be honest and know when to say no", and "make the company a lifetime career"[34]. At Southwest Airlines, a "principle driving force for changes occurring in the Airline industry", CEO Herb Kelleher is well known for his performance at company festivities, and boasts a work force that is twice as productive as many rivals. Kelleher works to instill what he calls "an insouciance, an effervescence", and admiring competitors say "At other places, managers say that people are their most important resource, but nobody acts on it. At Southwest, they have never lost sight of the fact."[35] Perhaps Hewlett-Packard's CEO, Lewis Platt, put it best, "As CEO, my job is to encourage people to work together, but I can't order them to do it"[36]. Today's managers need not master the technical details of people management, but must become informed consumers, capable of analyzing fads from facts.

THE THEORY: HUMAN RESOURCES CREATE SUSTAINABLE COMPETITIVE ADVANTAGE

Examples aside, are there good general reasons to expect that managing people better will enhance organizational outcomes? The answer is yes. While there is much to learn, there is also much that is known about human behavior at work. Here, we will summarize theories about how organizations benefit when people are well-managed. These theories emphasize the effects of human resources on the organization. They focus on how the human resource practices affect both the attributes of people (such as their knowledge and skill), their drive to use those attributes, and the results of their behaviors[37]. Stakeholder Value, and Sustainable Competitive Advantage Before we explore why human resources add value, it is appropriate to define what we mean by value to organizations. We will take a broad view in this book, focusing on various "stakeholders".

Stakeholders are the groups and individuals who establish organizational goals. External stakeholders are not organizational members, and include customers, suppliers, communities, regulators, unions and investors. Internal stakeholders are organizational members, and include employees and managers."[38]

The value of this perspective is seen in examples above. Each example illustrates an organizational issue that requires skillful management of people. Yet each organizational issue has competing and diverse interests. This may be more obvious in not-for-profit organizations, or highly-visible public-service organizations, it is just as true in business organizations as well. Managers who fail to take the broad view risk optimizing one factor while courting disaster on another. Even considering the diverse views of stakeholders, all organizations strive to grow and survive, and to create a purpose that is unique over time. This unique purpose that lasts over time has been called "sustainable competitive advantage"

Sustainable competitive advantage occurs when an organization is implementing a value creating strategy not simultaneously being implemented by any current or potential competitors, and when other organizations are incapable of duplicating the benefits of that advantage."[39]

Sustainable competitive advantage may sound like a very aggressive and militaristic term, but in fact it applies as well to philanthropic and public organizations as it does to businesses or armies. To survive and grow, any organization must acquire and use resources in unique and valuable ways or, over time, other organizations will. Consider the case of the U.S. Postal Service, which remains one a cornerstone of U.S. society, but is no longer the delivery method of choice, for example, when speed is of the essence. DHL, UPS and Federal Express now serve that role, because they have found ways to create unique value, relative to the U.S. Postal Service.

Sustainable competitive advantage derives from a "resource-based" view of organizations. Resources include physical capital, human capital, and organizational capital. This view assumes that organizations can influence the quality of the resources available to them, and that these resources do not move easily between organizations. Organizations have a unique competitive advantage when they find ways to increase the quality of their resource, or to use their resources more effectively than others. This advantage is sustainable when it can't be easily copied.

Specifically, sustainable competitive advantage is caused by resources that:

1.   Add value to the organization,
2.   Are unique or rare among competitors,
3.   Cannot be perfectly imitated by others
4.   Cannot be substituted by resources that others possess[40]

Can people be managed to create sustainable competitive advantage? Yes. In fact, many argue that people may be the most promising source of competitive advantage for today's organizations. Think about it for a moment: The complex relationships among people within and outside your organization can be quite valuable, as the examples above have shown. Moreover, because such relationships are complex, and often depend on the unique culture and history of the organization, it is very difficult to copy them. To overcharacterize, competitors can purchase the same plants and equipment, acquire the same stocks and debt instruments, and match the pricing and distribution practices as your organization, because these are all observable. However, it is particularly difficult to peer inside your organization to decipher exactly how you create capability and motivation among your employees[41]. Employees don't show up on the financial statements, and their contributions are often quite subtle. Obviously, skillful managers must find competitive advantage in all the resources they use, but people certainly rank high among those resources. Of course, that same complexity means that managers face a significant challenge to manage people in a way that enhances, rather then detracts from the organization. So, in this book we will try to introduce you to theories and ideas to help you do that. Next, we briefly review how general theories of management and business suggest that managing people well creates value.

Economics

Economic theory has long suggested that people, or "human capital" matters in organizations, though much of economic theory focused on the costs of labor, or the behavior of wages in response to the demand and supply of labor, or the skill and productivity of workers[42]. For example, these "human capital" theories suggest that organizations will pay to train workers, and offer higher wages to workers, when their skills are uniquely useful to the organization, but organizations will not pay for skills that could be transported elsewhere.

Theories of "internal labor markets" and the economics of industrial organizations takes a broader view, suggesting that "employment contracts", or bargains between employers and employees are not simply fashioned by external markets, but are created by employers to help coordinate, monitor and motivate employees. They are influenced not only by considerations of economic efficiency, but also by political, cultural and institutional forces[43]. One interesting variant of these ideas is "agency theory", which views work relationships as contracts between a "principal" who delegates work to an "agent". Designing an appropriate contract is the key to ensuring that the principal's work gets done, even when the agent can't be directly supervised[44]. Managers must understand how to design work and construct incentives that enable and motivate employees to achieve the goals of "principals", such as shareholders and Boards of Directors. These theories all suggest that a well-educated and trained labor force is key to competing on any basis other than cutting costs, and that to make such workforce requires coordinating human resource policies such as how employees are chosen, how they are paid, and how their work is designed.

Political Science

National norms and political conditions pose particular challenges to managers attempting to maximize the value of their people. For example, when external economic shocks occur, countries with highly coordinated national systems of negotiated employment contracts (such as Sweden and Germany) respond better, and produce less unemployment compared to countries with more independent and decentralized systems (such as the U.S.)[45] Powerful European unions constrain managers' ability to compete with pay cuts and layoffs. This may seem a disadvantage, but research shows that such constraints cause employers to compete on product quality, and to organize the work so that higher-paid workers are more productive. In fact, German managers say that works councils are actually a positive factor for the competitiveness of their organizations[46].

Psychology

Perhaps the science most closely linked to human resource management is psychology. Psychological theories of motivation, attitudes, and learning suggest that organizations can significantly affect the capability and willingness of employees to behave in certain ways. There is convincing evidence that workers respond in predictable ways when they are selected, paid, evaluated and trained, and managers who understand these patterns can improve their ability to achieve goals through people. Later chapters in this book will describe many of these theories, and show how they can help managers understand the consequences of decisions about managing people at work. In fact, some industrial psychology models even propose ways to translate the effects of human resource programs into dollars, so they can be compared with the anticipated dollar-valued return from other investments. These models suggest that the return on investments in people is often quite lucrative[47].

THE EVIDENCE: MANAGING HUMAN RESOURCES AFFECTS THE BOTTOM LINE

We have seen that organizational changes make human factors increasingly important, that top managers manage human resources well, and that management theory suggests that well managed human resources can make a difference. Even the business press has embraced the idea that "intellectual capital" may be a company's "most valuable asset. "[48] Are there real tangible examples of human issues directly affecting the bottom line? Let's take a few examples of the cost side of human resources. How organizations choose workers can have significant legal implications, as Target Stores learned after settling for more than $1.3 million (plus court costs) a case brought by security-guard job applicants claimed privacy violations when a selection test asked them about their sexual orientation and religion[49]. Bridgestone/Firestone, Inc. was fined nearly $7.5 million after a worker died as a result of safety violations[50]. For three months, among 440 unskilled blue-collar workers and low-level clerical employees in financial services, the costs of discretionary absence were estimated to be $3,223[51]. For organizations have thousands of employees, whose absence patterns span many years, multiplying by a factor of 10 or even 100 may better reflect the true impact.

On a more positive note, human resource management can also improve performance. Companies with high-performance management systems averaged 10.2% return on equity, compared to 4.4% for companies without such systems[52]. Individual human resource activities can payoff handsomely. At Adolph Coors Company showed a 124% to 833% return on investment from its wellness promotion activities[53]. Helene Curtis company's flexible work time program increased the number of new mothers returning to work from 69% to 93%, saving the company $360,000 in one year[54]. McDonnell Douglas Corporations programs assisting employees with psychological problems and chemical dependency produced savings of $6 million, over four years. Beyond single programs it appears that integrated human resource strategies may be even more lucrative than merely the sum of the parts. Research shows that automobile assembly plants, steel mini-mills and a diverse sample of U.S. firms perform significantly better when they combine flexible production arrangements, team-based work systems and "sophisticated" or "high-commitment" human resource practices such as performance-based pay and extensive training[55]. Even the business press has embraced the idea that "intellectual capital" may be a company's "most valuable asset."[56] Managing human resources affects many organizational constituents, so merely looking at the bottom-line effects may not always tell the whole picture. However, there is no doubt that those who manage people issues well see the benefits in financial terms. They may be as obvious as a reduction in payroll or training costs, or they may be more subtle, such as long-run increases in efficiency and creativity that make investments in technology and marketing pay off. It is not always easy to tease out the independent effects of managing people well, but the effects are there, and managers can ignore them at their peril, or exploit them for their benefit.

THE PROPER DOMAIN OF HUMAN RESOURCES

What is the domain of human resource management? Managing people well influences every aspect of organizations. Still, because human resource management involves the employment relationship, its goals and activities focus there. Exhibit 1-1 shows how 1,200 experts from 12 countries rated the HR goals and practices that would help them achieve competitive advantage in the 21st century. U.S. experts placed high priority on "rewarding employees for customer service", Germans and French rated "rewarding employees for customer service" as the top priority, while Japanese gave top priority to "communicating business directions, problems and plans."[57] When countries are statistically grouped by their priorities, the Anglo-Saxon countries of United Kingdom, Australia, Canada and the U.S. form a group, with Germany and Italy located close by. France and Korea each form their own cluster, the fourth cluster is the Latin countries of Brazil, Mexico and Argentina, and the fifth cluster includes only Japan. The major differences seem to be that Japanese experts placed lower priority on promoting a culture of empowerment than did the U.S. and Latin country experts, both Japan and France placed lower priority on promoting diversity and cultural equality, and the U.S. placed significantly higher emphasis on flexible work practices than France or Brazil[58]. Traditionally, those who study and practice human resource management focus on the activities of managing people. The activities are important, but the activities are merely means to an end. Managers must focus on the results, not just the activities, or else human resource management becomes merely a set of administrative decisions, disjointed and insignificant.

HUMAN RESOURCES AND ORGANIZATIONAL PERFORMANCE

Exhibit 1-2 contains the model that summarizes what we have seen. Human resources are part of a system, with each part of the system interacting with the others. The Environment provides context, opportunities and constraints. The Organization which combines many resources to survive, grow, and create value for constituents. The Human Resources represent the employees of the organization, and the results they create through the employment relationship. The vertical arrows spanning the levels represent relationships. Relationships may be exchanges, or mutual influence. Each component of the model has relationships with the others. For example, for business Organizations to survive they must receive materials, capital and labor from the Environment, and in turn they must provide payments, return-on-investment, and rewards. Just as real, but perhaps less obvious, Organizations receive Cultural inputs such as social values, norms, and history, and in turn their behavior affects society's values, norms and history. Within the Organization, the Human Resources are influenced by the Organization's Culture, Structure, Products and Strategy. In turn, the Human Resources support these Organizational components by returning value through such things as performance, attitudes, loyalty and creativity.

Within the Human Resources box are the three components of Human Resource value:

1. Opportunity, which is the necessary circumstances for employees to create value for the organization;

2. Capability, which is the capacity of employees to create value; and

3. Motivation, which is the drive or force employees feel to contribute to organizational value.

All three components must be present for human resources to contribute to organizational value. For example, many businesses traditionally organized work to minimize the demands on workers, and to make them interchangeable. Today, we see a resurgence of teams, individual accountability, and reliance on front-line employee ideas and suggestions. It seems quite likely that employees were always somewhat capable and motivated to creatively contribute through teams and suggestions, but because the work was not organized properly, they had no Opportunity. Or, consider organizations that redesign the work to require teamwork and creativity, and have highly intelligent and experienced workers, but recognize and reward workers only as individuals. Here, there is Opportunity and Capability, but the Motivation is lacking. Thus, Human Resources are enhanced when managers find ways to build Opportunity, Capability, and Motivation. The enhanced Human Resources bring greater value to the Organization, which supports the Organization's ability to bring greater value to its Environment. In turn, the Organization receives necessary inputs from the Environment, and can use those inputs to further increase the value of Human Resources.

Exhibit 1-1: Highest-Rated HR Goals

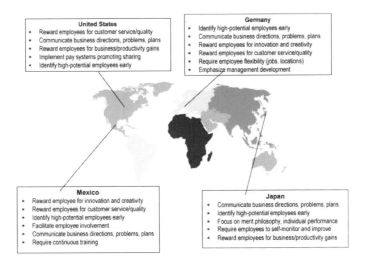

United States
* Reward employees for customer service/quality
* Communicate business directions, problems, plans
* Reward employees for business/productivity gains
* Implement pay systems promoting sharing
* Identify high-potential employees early

Germany
* Identify high-potential employees early
* Communicate business directions, problems, plans
* Reward employees for innovation and creativity
* Reward employees for customer service/quality
* Require employee flexibility (jobs, locations)
* Emphasize management development

Mexico
* Reward employee for innovation and creativity
* Reward employees for customer service/quality
* Identify high-potential employees early
* Facilitate employee involvement
* Communicate business directions, problems, plans
* Require continuous training

Japan
* Communicate business directions, problems, plans
* Identify high-potential employees early
* Focus on merit philosophy, individual performance
* Require employees to self-monitor and improve
* Reward employees for business/productivity gains

Exhibit 1-2: Human Resources and Organizational Performance

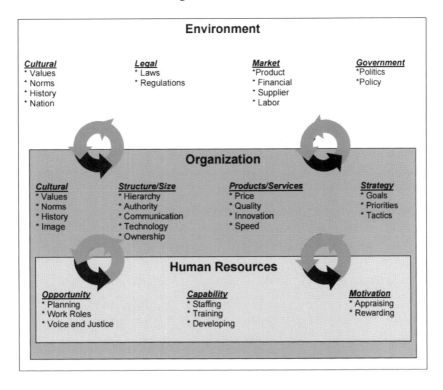

Environment

Cultural
* Values
* Norms
* History
* Nation

Legal
* Laws
* Regulations

Market
* Product
* Financial
* Supplier
* Labor

Government
* Politics
* Policy

Organization

Cultural
* Values
* Norms
* History
* Image

Structure/Size
* Hierarchy
* Authority
* Communication
* Technology
* Ownership

Products/Services
* Price
* Quality
* Innovation
* Speed

Strategy
* Goals
* Priorities
* Tactics

Human Resources

Opportunity
* Planning
* Work Roles
* Voice and Justice

Capability
* Staffing
* Training
* Developing

Motivation
* Appraising
* Rewarding

REFERENCES

1. Kenneth Labich, "Why Companies Fail", Fortune, November 14, 1994, pp. 52-68.

2. Nancy A. Nichols, "Scientific Management at Merck: An Interview with CFO Judy Lewent". Harvard Business Review, January-February, 1994, pp. 89-99.

3. Paul Osterman, "How Common is Workplace Transformation and Who Adopts It?", Industrial and Labor Relations Review, vol. 47, no. 2, January, 1994, pp. 173-188.

4. William E. Halal, "From Hierarchy to Enterprise: Internal Markets are the New Foundation of Management". Academy of Management Executive, vol. 8, no. 4, 1993, pp. 69-83.

5. Sumantra Ghoshal & Henry Mintzberg, "Diversifiction and Diversifact", California Management Review, 37, no. 1, Fall, 1994, pp. 8-27.

6. Brian Dumaine, "Why Great Companies Last", Fortune, January 16, 1995, p. 129; John Rau, "Nothing Succeeds Like Training for Success", The Wall Street Journal, September 12, 1994, p. A16.. "Workplace Innovation", Work In America, vol. 18, no. 11, November, 1993, p. 3.

7. Carla Rapoport, "Charles Handy Sees the Future", Fortune, October 31, 1994, pp. 155-168.

8. Michael Hammer & James Champy, Reengineering the Corporation: A Manifesto for Business Revolution (New York, NY: Harper Business, 1993).

9. Robert W. Keidel, "Rethinking Organizational Design", Academy of Management Executive, vol. 8, no. 4, 1994, pp. 12-27.

10. Thomas A. Stewart, "Reengineering: The Hot New Managing Tool," Fortune, August 23, 1993, pp. 41-48.

11. Hal Lancaster, "Re-Engineering Authors Reconsider Re-Engineering", The Wall Street Journal, January 7, 1995, p. BI.

12. Michael Hammer & James Champy, Reengineering Management, 1994

13. Hal Lancaster, "Re-Engineering Authors Reconsider Re-Engineering", op cit.

14. Charlene Marmer Solomon, "HR Facilitates the Learning Organization", Personnel Journal, November, 1994, pp. 56-64.

15. Carla Rapoport, "Charles Handy Sees the Future", Fortune, October 31, 1994, pp. 155-168.

16. Carla Rapoport, op. cit., p. 164.

17. Kenneth Labich, "Will United Fly?", Fortune, August 22, 1994, pp. 70-77. Greg Steinmetz and Michael J. McCarthy, "UAL Buyout Plan Is Opposed By Big Holder", The Wall Street Journal, June 8, 1994.

18. Kenneth Labich, ibid.

19. Charles Taylor and Gail D. Fosler, "Tile Necessity of Being Global", Across the Board, February, 1994, pp. 40-43.

20. "Ford's Reorganization", The Economist, January 7, 1995, pp. 52-53.

21. Nick Forster, "International Managers and Mobile Families: The Professional and Personal Dynamics of Trans-National Career Pathing and Job mobility in the 1990s, " The International Journal of Human Resource Management, vol. 3, no. 3 (December, 1992), pp. 605-623. J. Black and Mark Mendenhall, "Cross-Cultural Training Effectiveness: A Review and a Theoretical Framework for Future Research," Academy of Management Review, vol. 15, no. 1 (1990), pp. 113-36.

22. Marcus W. Brauchli, "Class Issue", The Wall Street Journal, November 15, 1994, p. Al.

23. Michael Williams, "Japan's Labor System Survives Recession", The Wall Street Journal, November 8, 1994, p. A19.

24. Dawn Anfuso, "HR Unites the World of Coca-Cola", Personnel Journal, November, 1994, pp. 112-121.

25. "The New Global Workforce", Business Week, November 18, 1994, pp. 110-132.

26. Gene Bylinsky, "The Digital Factory", Fortune, November 14, 1994, pp. 92-110.

27. 27. Michael Williams, "Back to the Past", The Wall Street Journal, October 24, 1994, p. Al.

28. Timothy F. Bresnahan and Shane Greenstein, "The Competitive Crash in Large-Scale Commercial Computing", National Bureau of Economic Research, Working Paper # 4901, 1994.

29. "Jack Welch's Lessons for Success", Fortune, January 25, 1993, pp. 86-93. Excerpt from Noel Tichy, Control Your Destiny or Someone Else Will, 1993.

30. Christopher A. Bartlett and Sumantra Ghoshal, "Changing the Role of Top Management: Beyond Strategy to Put-pose", Harvard Business Review, November-December, 1994, pp. 79-88.

31. Wendy Zellner, Robert D. Hof, Richard Brandt, Stephen Baker and David Greising, "Go-Go Goliaths", Business Week, February 13, 1995, pp. 64-69.

32. Kevin Kelly, "A CEO Who Kept His Eyes on the Horizon", Business Week, August 1, 1994, p. 32.

33. Alan Deutschman, "The managing Wisdom of High-Tech Superstars", Fortune, October 17, 1994, pp. 197-205.

34. Thomas J. Martin, "Ten Commandments for Managing Creative People", Fortune, January 16, 1995, pp. 135-136.

35. Kenneth Labich, "Is Herb Kelleher America's Best CEOT'", Fortune, May 2, 1994, pp. 43-52.

36. Alan Deutschman, "How H-P Continues to Grow and Grow", Fortune, May 2, 1994, pp. 90-100.

37. George T. Milkovich and John W. Boudreau, Human Resource Management (7th ed.), (Burr Ridge, IL: Richard D. Irwin, 1994). Patrick M. Wright, Gary C. McMahan and Abagail McWilliams, "Human Resources and Sustained Competitive Advantage: A Resource-Based Perspective", International Journal

of Human Resource Management, vol. 5, no. 2, May, 1994, pp. 302-326. Jeffrey Pfeffer, "Producing Sustainable Competitive Advantage Through the Effective Management of People", Academy of Management Executive, vol 9, no. 1, 1995, pp. 55-72. "Competitive Advantage Through People", California Management Review, Winter, 1994, pp. 9-28. Susan E. Jackson and Randall S. Schuler, "Understanding Human Resource management in the Context of Organizations and their Environments", Annual Review of Psychology, 1995 (forthcoming). Lee D. Dyer, Thomas A. Kochan and Rosemary Batt, "International Human Resource Studies: A Framework for Future Research", Working Paper #92-23, Center for Advanced Human Resource Studies, Cornell University, Ithaca, New York, 1992.

38.   Milkovich and Boudreau, 1994, op. cit., p. 214.

39.   J. Barney, "Firm Resources and Sustained Competitive Advantage", Journal of Management, 1991, vol. 17, pp. 99-120. S. Lippman and R. Rumelt, "Uncertain Imitability: An Analysis of Interfirm Differences in Efficiency Under Competition", Bell Journal of Economics, 1982, vol. 13, pp. 418-38. Wright, et al., 1994, op. cit.

40.   Barney, 1991, op. cit., p. 102.

41.   Wright, et al., 1994, op. cit. Pfeffer, 1994, op. cit. Jackson and Schuler, forthcoming, op. cit.

42.   Walter Oi, "Labor as a Quasi-Fixed Factor", Journal of Political Economy, vol. 70, December, 1962, pp. 538-555. Gary Becker, Human Capital: A Theoretical and Empirical Analysis with Special Reference to Education. 1964 (New York: National Bureau of Economic Research).

43.   Dyer, et al., 1992, op. cit., p. 16. Joseph Stiglitz, "Symposium on Organizations and Economics", Journal of Economic Perspectives, vol. 5, no. 2, 1991, pp. 15-24. Herbert Simon, "Organizations and Markets", Journal of Economic Perspectives, vol. 5, no. 2, pp. 25-44. Clark Kerr, "The Balkanization of Labor Markets", In E. Wight Bakke, Ed., Labor Mobility and Economic Opportunity. 1954 (Cambridge, MA: Harvard University Press). Peter Doeringer and Michael Piore, Internal Labor Markets and Manpower Analysis. 1971 (Lexington, MA: D.C. Heath). Paul Osterman, Employment Futures: Reorganization, Dislocation, and Public Policy 1988 (Oxford: Oxford University Press).

44.   K.M. Eisenhardt, "Agency Theory: An Assessment and Review", Academy of Management Review, 1989, vol. 14, pp. 57-74.

45.   Newell and J. Symons, "Wages and Employment in the OECD Countries". London School of Economics Centre for Labour Economics, Discussion paper #219, May, 1985.

46.   Dyer, et al., 1992, op. cit, p. 20-21. Wolfgang Streek, "Industrial Relations and Industrial Change: The restructuring of the World Automobile Industry in the 1970s and 1980s. Economic and Industrial Democracy, 1987, vol. 8, pp. 437-462. Lowell Turner, Democracy at Work? Labor and the Politics of New Work Organization 1990 (Ithaca, NY: Cornell University Press). Kirsten Wever, "German Managerial Ideology", Unpublished manuscript, Northeastern

University School of Management.

47. John W. Boudreau, "Utility Analysis for Decisions in Human Resource Management," In Marvin D. Dunnette & Leatta M. Hough (Eds.) Handbook of Industrial and Organizational Psychology, (2nd ed.), Vol. 2. Palo Alto: Consulting Psychologists Press, pp. 621-745.

48. Stephanie Losee, "Your Company's Most Valuable Asset: Intellectual Capital", Fortune, October 3, 1994, pp. 68-74.

49. BNA Employee Relations Weekly, July 19, 1993, at 803.

50. Kefin G. Salwen, "Fines of Nearly $7.5 Million Are Levied After Worker Death at Bridgestone Unit", The Wall Street Journal, April 19, 1994, p. A5.

51. Joseph N. Martocchio, "The Financial Cost of Absence Decisions", Journal of Management, vol. 18, no. 1, 1992, pp. 133-152.

52. "Performance Management: The Bottom Line", HRM News, November 25, 1994, p. 2.

53. Daniel K. Bunch, "Coors Wellness Center -- Helping the Bottom Line", Employee Benefits Journal, March, 1992, pp. 14-18.

54. "HR Management: Measuring HR Efforts Pays Off", Human Resource Management News, January 2, 1995, p. 1.

55. John Paul MacDuffie, "Human Resource Bundles and Manufacturing Performance: Organizational Logic and Flexible Production Systems in the World Auto Industry", Industrial and Labor Relations Review, vol. 48, no. 2, January, 1995, pp. 197-221. Jeffrey B. Arthur, "Effects of Human Resource Systems on Manufacturing Performance and Turnover", Academy of Management Journal, vol. 35, no. 3, 1994, pp. 670-687. Mark A. Huselid, "The Impact of Human Resource management Practices on Turnover, Productivity and Corporate Financial Performance", Academy of Management Journal, forthcoming.

56. Stephanie Losee, "Your Company's Most Valuable Asset: Intellectual Capital", Fortune, October 3, 1994, pp. 68-74.

57. Priorities for Competitive Advantage, an IBM study conducted by Towers-Perrin, 1992.

58. Paul Sparrow, Randall S. Schuler, Susan E. Jackson, "Convergence or Divergence: Human Resource Practices and Policies for Competitive Advantage Worldwide", International Journal of Human Resource Management, forthcoming.

THE INFLUENCE OF HUMAN RESOURCE PRACTICES ON INTERNAL CUSTOMER SATISFACTION AND ORGANIZATIONAL EFFECTIVENESS

Irfan Ullah and Robina Yasmin

Iqra University, Islamabad, Pakistan

ABSTRACT

It is generally believed that the impact of Human Resource Practices on internal customer satisfaction can create comparative advantage for the organizational performance. The main objective of this study was to find out the impact of Human Resource Practices on internal customer satisfaction and organizational effectiveness. The impact of human resource practices on the overall performance of organizations has been a leading subject of research and the results have been encouraging, indicative of positive relationship between Human Resource practices and organizational effectiveness. Data was collected through personally administered questionnaire-based survey from 290 banking personnel of Pakistan. Structural equation modeling was used to examine the anticipated model. The results showed that some Human Resource Practices appear to be linked to internal customer satisfaction and organizational effectiveness. The implications for practitioners were to modify and emphasize certain human resource practices, and to emphasize the role of internal customers for organizational effectiveness enhancement. These findings revealed the importance of internal customers in enhancing employee morale, organizational commitment, employee productivity, turnover rate and the organization's ability to attract talent.

Citation: Irfan Ullah andRobina Yasmin,2013,The Influence of Human Resource Practices on Internal Customer Satisfaction and Organizational Effectiveness,Journal of Internet Banking and Commerce, ISSN: 1204-5357

INTRODUCTION

The human being is the most important asset for organizations. In the age of competitiveness, organization cannot be able to bear the loss of prospective human resource. It is realistic challenge for Human Resource professionals to make it possible by exploiting the human potential in a mode to make them educated employee and creative for business and society as well. Organizations devote considerable resources to attract, develop, and inspire capable individuals. These firms do not want their proficient employees to leave (Cascio 2000; Glebbeek & Bax, 2004). Much concern has been exposed for the deliberate participation of the Human Resource and its impact on organizational effectiveness (Lahteenmaki et al, 1998; Rangone, 1999; Analoui, 2002). The contest has directed to the establishment of a resource-based model of human resource management (Boxall, 1996), recognizing human resource as being accountable for increasing organizational effectiveness (Kakabadse & Kakabadse, 2000) and a rational cursor for the improved organizational success (Analoui, 2002). The resource-based shift toward strategic management regards human resource as a matchless source of competitive benefits of the organization (Baird & Meshoulan, 1998; Lahteenmaki et al, 1998). It has been recommended that there is a relation between an organizational effectiveness and the utilization of its human resources (Lorange & Murphy, 1984; Boxall, 1991; Lundy, 1994; Storey, 1998: Guest, 2002: Hansson & Jensen, 2004: Caliskan, 2010).

Customer and their expectation are important subject to organizations and businesses. To survive in highly viable marketplace, businesses require offering goods and services that need extremely satisfied and loyal customers. The satisfied customers are probable to return to those who facilitated them, whereas dissatisfied customers are expected to exit in a different place. The retention of satisfied customers is vital to the survival of an organization (Jones & Sasser, 1995). Accordingly, firms have challenges to produce demand for their goods or services through excellent customer support. To conquer persistent excellence, external customer support needs internal structures, which are lined up to serve the external customer, with each internal subsystem through adding value to others in the firm because the other subsystems were its customers (Deming, 1986; Pransky et al., 2005; Urbano & Yordanove, 2008). The concept of an internal customer advocates that every employee is both a seller and a buyer to other people within the organization (Money & Foreman, 1995).

The value of service distributed to external customer is often established by the value of service that internal customer – employees – provide each other (Cook, 2000). If any business desires to improve the quality of its service, it desires to conquer the "them and us☐ attitude established in several organizations among administration and employees. The value of service provided to employees in a company often establishes how well the external customer is served up (Osman, et al, 2004). The appropriate use of human resource develops the performance of an organization. Without employee assistance, it is not possible to find out whether human resource practices are constructive to workforce, or whether these merely append to workload of workforce and anxiety intensity (Pass, 2002). Organizations contribute major resources to create a center of attention, and motivate capable groups that may not leave them later, particularly in a rigid marketplace (Cascio 2000; Glebbeek & Bax 2004). If these capable people leave the organization soon, the result will be interruption to the regular functions and lesser performance of an organization (Huselid 1995; Kacmar et al. 2006; Morrow & McElroy 2007).

Organizational departments provide services to their customers, such as management information system, HRs and purchase section, maintain the workforce (Marshall et al., 1998). There are two thoughts, which have been discussed in relationship to internal customer satisfaction. These thoughts are from total quality management and from marketing. Comparison between these thoughts showed that service of internal customer is different from internal marketing, because the earlier spotlights on how the people serve up the business, while the second emphasizes how a business serves the people. Human resource practices on their behalf attempt to transfer organizational routine and traditional practices into the shape and need of current scenario. Human resource practices and internal customer satisfaction strongly influence different problems of the organizations. These problems consist of turnover, safety, productivity, effectiveness, and product and service quality. By satisfying and empowering workforce, organizations would be capable to resolve these problems (Appelbaum et al. 2000; Connor & Becker, 2003; Singh, 2004; Haines, Jalette, & Larose, 2010) This research investigates the relationship between human resource practices, internal customer satisfaction and organizational effectiveness. It aims to observe the impact of these practices on internal customer satisfaction and organizational effectiveness.

LITERATURE REVIEW AND RESEARCH MODEL

Resource- based view narrates that practices, competencies, skills or strategic assets of an organization are a foundation of aggressive benefit (Mabey et al., 1998). These resources are rare, valuable, and non-alternatable (Barney, 1991).

Human Resource Practices

Practice is the process of an organization by which available resources are developed, combined, and transformed into value offerings (Teece, Pisano & Shuen 1997). Practice is a talent of an organization to set up its real or insubstantial assets, to execute the duty, and a commotion to advance productivity (Amit & Schoemaker, 1993).

HR practice is supported going on carrying, increasing or replacing knowledge in the organization (Saa-Perez & Garcia-Falcon, 2002). The HR Practices are deep-rooted in the skill to recombine and reconstitute the resources of the organization. Background specificity, tacitness and temporality are their solution possessions (Bhatt, 2000). For an organization to sustain in competitive environment effectively, the researchers have exclaimed that human resource practices repeatedly perform comparative activities (Arthur, 1994; Delery & Doty, 1996). If it is the holder, a set of appropriately extended human resource practices may offer a significant basis of sustained aggressive improvement. Prior investigations have revealed numerous human resource practices, for instance, Huselid (1995) observed how persons selection, performance evaluation, inducement reward, job design, complaint actions, information sharing, behavior judgment and labor-management participation influence performance of a company. Likewise, Delery and Doty (1996) observed that the mainly significant human resource practices consist of the usage of internal career path, formal training and development system, result-oriented evaluation, performance based reward, job safety, worker voice and extensive job description. Moreover, Pfeffer (1998) recognized seven human resource practices, involving job protection, selective employment, self-managed groups, provision of high salary contingent on firm performance, widespread training, decline of position dissimilarity, and information sharing.

Moreover, several diverse categorizations of human resource practices have been devised into more common human resource magnitude. For example, Cunningham and Rowley (2010) clustered human resource practices into organization planning, recruitment, compensation, development, performance evaluation and communication. In the meantime, Schuler and Jackson (1996) analyzed five elements: performance appraisal, recruitment and selection, planning, compensation and development. Ulrich and his classmates (1989) established a model comprising of selection, strategic planning, training and development, organization development and transform, performance appraisal, a compensation system, and organizational behavior and theory. Human resource practices have been progressively more controlled through the prospects of stakeholder incorporating recruitment and selection, training and development, performance management, employee participation, and compensation that are adopted as elements of human resource practices in this research. The existence of these best practices reveals the rank of human resource expert knowledge and resource allocation competence.

Recruitment and Selection

Recruitment is the process to identify and attract a group of prospective individuals from outside and within the company to assess for employment. When these individuals are acknowledged, the procedure of selecting suitable individuals for job can commence. This means gathering, quantifying, and estimating information about the qualifications of individuals for particular positions. Companies utilize these approaches to enhance the probability of appointing persons who possess the right expertise and capabilities to be winning in the target post. Selection is a procedure of selecting such applicants who have the exact and necessary qualification to realize the requirement of the leaving jobs and prospect job opportunities.

Selection is the main and foremost aspect, which plays a significant part in the excellence, survives. Administration must be more vigilant while hiring new candidates for specific work selection. The major purpose of recruitment and selection is to select the right individual for the right post (Dale, 1999). The penalties of bad selection may very disastrous for the organization. The individual, who is unable to understand the aims and philosophy of the firm, may cause to have bad impact on customer satisfaction, relationship with suppliers and production. Maslow's need hierarchy theory describes the importance of financial rewards (Maslow, 1943). The wrong compensation would demotivate. Good compensation would maintain performance levels, not increase them.

The available rewards must be in a 'currency' that the individual values, and if this were money, so be it (Herzberg, Mausner & Snyderman, 1959; Peters, 2005).

Training and Development

Training and development formulates a significant role in organization. Training and development can advance the level of self-awareness of a person, enhance talent of an individual and enhance the motivation of an employee (Wexley & Latham, 2002). Because the activity of an organization turns into more knowledge-driven, training and development performs an eternally supplementary significant function to meet the education desires of persons as well as tactical essentials of the organization (Harrison & Kessels, 2004). Training and development smooth the progress of superior altitudes of inspiration and inventiveness in support of workforce (Marchington & Wilkinson, 2002). From the viewpoint of an organization, training and development is the key relationship involving the human resource policy of an organization and in general company policy (Mabey, Salaman & Storey, 1998). Cast-off in a planned way, training and development can provide organization a viable circumference in the comfortable and release of goods and services (Mabey et al, 1998).

Performance appraisal

Performance appraisal is important in the organizational setting. According to Jennifer and Jones (1996), it gives two major functions; it enhances high level of job satisfaction and organizational performance, and it provides accurate information to be used in decision-making.

The primary goal of performance appraisal is to assist business in executing administrative decisions pertaining to promotions, dismissals, layoffs and salary increases. For instance, the current job performance of a worker is often the most important reflection for determining whether to promote the individual. Managers must identify that a worker's development is a continuous series of defining performance objectives, presenting training essential to accomplish the objectives, appraising performance as to the achievement of the objectives and then setting new, and higher objectives.

Compensation benefits

Milkovich and Newman (1999) defined compensation as all types of monetary incomes and substantial remunerations that a worker receives as a component of employ agreement. A more precise meaning is given by Flippo (1984 p. 281), who has described compensation as the satisfactory and reasonable compensation of employees for their contribution to organizational goals.

The writer has recognized three components of compensation as base pay (to attract eligible entrants); variable pay (to stimulate work performance) and additional extreme benefits (to retain capable employees). Steven, Appelbaum and Mackenzie (2000) also gave explanation that other results are more positive, on the other hand the challenge of aligning a company's inducement compensation essentials to generate the behaviors that assist the accomplishment aspect in improving a firm's strategic effectiveness. A satisfied internal customer would be an efficient and effective service giver who would chase a customer centric pattern (Comm & Mathaisel, 2003). Founded on these results, scholars have started to highlight internal customer satisfaction with intend of achieving an organizational perception of what comprises quality in the business.

Compensation (Wages, rewards, medical and transport facility) is a key concern in HR administration. These are basic requirements and provide workforce remuneration for working (Bohlander, Snell & Sherman, 2001). It is exposed that recompense remuneration stimulate as well as direct manners in the direction of accomplishment of an exacting task (Milkovich & Newman, 2002).

Employee Participation

Participation by various names includes collective management, worker empowerment, worker involvement, participatory decision-making, discrete management, open-book administration, or industrialized equality (Steinheider, Bayerl, & Wuestewald, 2006). The fundamental conception entails any power-sharing arrangements in which place of work manipulate is allocated among persons whose are not equal in hierarchical levels. Such types of Power-sharing arrangement might involve several worker participation designs consequential in co- determination of running circumstances, problem resolving, and decision-making (Locke & Schweiger, 1979). Participation also involves, Information sharing with workers, employee suggestion program, Self-directed work groups, Problem-solving teams and flexible job design (Haines, Jalette, & Larose, 2010).

An employee suggestion program comprises worker analysis feedback. Information sharing contains, for instance, with respect to company's effectiveness, colleagues' salary, technical or managerial transformation etc. This means that workers have some feedback on strategies. Problem-solving teams are teams whose tasks are restricted to definite parts, for example quality or workflow. Self-directed work groups are semiautonomous work teams or mini-enterprise work teams that have an elevated altitude of liability for an extensive series of decisions. Flexible job design comprises job rotation, job enrichment/redesign (broadened job definitions), and job enrichment (increased proficiency diversity or autonomy of work). Firms gain from the supposed inspirational influences of workers in Participatory decision-making. When workforce involves themselves in the process of decision making, they enhance appreciative and awareness among social groups and seniors, and improve employees value in the firm (Probst, 2005). When every person in a business involves in the process of decision-making, business communication is supplementary efficient and each generates more well organized outcomes (Walker, 2007). If employees are involved in the process of decision-making, then they ultimately attain organizational goals that influence them. In this procedure, participation may be exercised as a device that develop business relations, discover motivation of workforce and enhance the pace of information transmission across the company.

Work Environment

employee turnover, job satisfaction, employee turnover, job involvement and organizational commitment (Jong & Hartog, 2010). In the study of Zeytinoglu and Denton (2005), it has been revealed that work environment is one of the aspects that influence employees' choice to stay with the business. Fay, Bjorkman and Pavlouskaya (2000) exclaimed that it is very essential to identify the rising wants of people to keep them dedicated and provide the work atmosphere when needed. Individuals like working, and attempt to work in those companies that present constructive work atmosphere where they consider they are making diversity and where most individuals in the company are capable and pulling together to move the business forward (Milory, 2004). Workplace design has a deep influence on employees and tends to stay with work as long as satisfied (Brown & Metz, 2009). To retain employees, the workplace design should generate atmosphere that is supportive for employees of poor eyesight, supply tools that require less strength and appropriate position for old employees (Samantha & Dahling, 2009).

Internal Customer Satisfaction

The value of service conveyed to external customer is often identified by the value of service that internal customers give each other, (Connor, 2003). It is very essential to keep in mind that, every person within a firm offers a service. There are internal as well as external customers. Internal customer is the employee in a company who is responsible to manufacture products. Every employee obtains materials or services from other employee in the procedure of manufacturing their own products. It is essential that, in order to satisfy external customers, internal customers be delighted first. Customer service guides to customer satisfaction whereas internal customer service guides to employee satisfaction. In Total Quality Management systems, all employees are persuaded to observe each other like vital customers during the manufacture and service delivery procedures (Marshall & Miller, 1991). In an organization, all employees are both the receivers and providers of products or services. George (1994) exclaims that as several workers do not make contact with external customers directly, so what they act or do not manipulates the excellence of service rendered. In order to deal with this matter, the employees of such types want to acknowledge value and treat other workers as internal customers.

On the other hand, it is essential to recognize that internal customers are as diverse and varied in their personnel distinctiveness as external customers.

While the common people may be a confusing generalization, similarly it is significant to recognize and react optimistically to diversity in the interior customer foundation (Joanna, Riordan, Peter & Humphreys, 2003). It is also declared that it is essential to recognize diverse forms of internal customer service associations, some of which might be very vital and work important in their disposition rather than others. Moreover, it is essential not to suppose that internal and external consumer service associations are openly comparable in nature. For instance, internal customers are compensated customers of the services they utilize. Because they are generally more knowledgeable and educated about the services offered than external customers. Consequently, they might be added challenging consumers than normal customers (Joanna et al., 2003).

Organizational Effectiveness

Organizational effectiveness capture organizational performance advantage the countless internal performance results generally linked with more effective or efficient processes and other external measures that transmit to deliberations that are broader than those merely linked with economic evaluation (either by managers, shareholders, and customers), for example corporate social responsibility (Richard et al., 2009).

Organizational effectiveness is an intangible notion and is principally not possible to measure. Rather than measuring organizational effectiveness, the firms tend to determine proxy measure that will be utilized to signify effectiveness. Proxy measures utilized might involve such matters like number of individuals served, kinds and sizes of population fragments served, and the demand within those fragments for the services the firm provides.

Organizational effectiveness refers to how a business accomplishes its tasks effectively. Organizational effectiveness procedures are apprehensive with considerating the inimitable potentials that firms build up to guarantee the achievement. This contains determining the worth of human resources of organization (Jamrog & Overholt, 2004). In the past, researchers had a tendency to employ the phrase 'organizational performance' to signify monetary and economic measures for example, revisit on investment, earnings per share, profitability, and almost immediately (Harel et al., 2003). Accordingly, company performance might be evaluated in conditions of their involvement to biased psychosomatic well being (commitment, attachment and happiness), relatively in provisions of purposive criterion (Jansen et al., 2001), because the company utilizes not just one element of a an individual but moderately the entire individual, as well as professional, personal and societal traits (Harnesk, 2004).

This study used a different inconsistent appraise to detect by this newer meaning of organizational effectiveness, which integrates the HR phases of organizational effectiveness: employee self-esteem, efficiency, turnover rate attraction of talent and organizational commitment.

Conceptual Model

Human resource practices donate to employee satisfaction and organizational ability, which in line persuade customers and shareholders satisfaction. Anyone could evaluate human resource practices through studying the customers of an organization. For instance, Tsui (1990) observed how administrators, managers and line managers ranked the significance and usefulness of human resource function. Ulrich (1997) recommended performing a human resource assessment as element of a balanced scorecard advance to appraising the effectiveness of human resource function. One phase of this audit is the customer value study, in which workers, as end users of The Human Resource program and practice, point out their assessments of the value of this practice.

Total Quality Management philosophy narrates that internal customer satisfaction is one of the vital matters. Through internal customer satisfaction, hr practices have an optimistic effect on organizational objectives. There is pragmatic proof to sustain this argue. For example, the key forecasters of the enhancement in the overall effectiveness of human resource were modifications in internal customer satisfaction altitude (Teo & Crawford, 2005). According to Molina and Ortega (2003), more training may definitely influence on organizational effectiveness through elements like internal customer satisfaction and external customer faithfulness. Moreover, Hoque (2003) recommended that by implementing a balanced scorecard an organization that has implemented Total Quality Management could enhance employee satisfaction and consequently effectiveness of an organization. Wright et al. (1994) also narrated that HR practices entrenched in human resource system of an organization may influence employee performance by manipulating worker expertise and motivation.

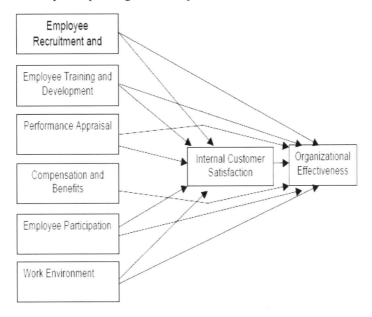

Figure 1: Theoretical model.

Researchers have also observed the association between internal customer satisfaction and diverse HR results. For example, Matzler et al. (2004) originated that internal customer satisfaction compels efficiency. Vora (2004) studied vital elements to generate an atmosphere for internal customer satisfaction, directing to enhance internal customer morale to attain enterprise -wide victory in an international market. Maylett (2009) exclaimed that organizations have to devise different employee retaining policies, comprising compensate increases, additional benefits, profit sharing and compensated time off, in order to reduce turnover rate of employees.

HRM can directly manipulate firm effectiveness in the appearance of high performance job practice. This scheme has developed into attach within the human resource management text at the hypothetical stage. Pfeffer (1994) and Guest (2002) recommended that universal Human resource practices must be considered as predecessor to firm effectiveness. Several researchers have emphasized human resource as a determining factor of organizational performance (Morrow et al., 2007), and an association between core competencies and organizational performance is projected, principally with a particular focus on the association between human resource capability and organizational effectiveness. Numerous researches have constantly originated a statistically considerable correlation between human resource and organizational effectiveness, which incorporates employee efficiency, turnover, confidence, organizational environment, organizational loyalty and job satisfaction (Chang & Chen, 2002; Pfeffer, 1994; Arthur, 1994; Huselid, 1995; Lindberg, 2006; Chang & Huang, 2010). Accordingly, the subsequent hypotheses are projected:

Hypothesis 1: Employee Recruitment and Selection practice have a positive impact on internal customer satisfaction.

Hypothesis 2: Employee Training and Development practice have a positive impact on internal customer satisfaction.

Hypothesis 3: Performance Appraisal practice has a positive impact on internal customer satisfaction.

Hypothesis 4: Compensation and Benefit practice have a positive impact on internal customer satisfaction.

Hypothesis 5: Employee Participation practice has a positive impact on internal customer satisfaction.

Hypothesis 6: Work Environment has a positive impact on internal customer satisfaction.

Hypothesis 7: Internal customer satisfaction has a positive impact on organizational effectiveness.

Hypothesis 8: Employee Recruitment and Selection practice has a positive impact on organizational effectiveness.

Hypothesis 9: Employee Training and Development practice has a positive impact on organizational effectiveness.

Hypothesis 10: Performance Appraisal practice has a positive impact on organizational effectiveness.

Hypothesis 11: Compensating and Benefit has a positive impact on organizational effectiveness.

Hypothesis 12: Employee Participation has a positive impact on organizational effectiveness.

Hypothesis 13: Work Environment has a positive impact on organizational effectiveness

METHODOLOGY

Instrument

The research was carried out using a questionnaire-based survey. The questionnaire was adopted from the literature of Chang and Huang (2010), Singh (2004), Moos (1994) and Haines, Jalette, and Larose, (2010). The instruments that were utilized by this questionnaire were a five-point Likert scale. The questionnaires were distributed among different banks in Islamabad and Rawalpindi and had two different parts. The first part of the questionnaire comprised of demographic information. The second part included the questions related to different independent variables (employment recruitment and selection, training and development, performance appraisal, compensation and benefits, employment participation), mediate variable (internal customer satisfaction), and the dependent variable (organizational effectiveness). All of these questionnaires were measured on a five-point Likert scale.

Measures: Human resource practices:

Six human resource practices were included: employee recruitment and selection, employee training and development, performance appraisal, compensation, and employee participation. Each HR practice was calculated using different sub items. The items of recruitment and selection, employee training and development, performance appraisal, compensation and benefits were adopted from the scale of Singh (2004). The scale of Haines, Jalette, & Larose (2010) was used to measure employee participation. The scale of Moos (1994) was used to measure work environment. Based on the scale exercised by Singh (2004), Moos (1994) and Haines, Jalette, and Larose (2010), to appraise human resource practices through the amount of their application, the HR managers and line managers were requested to point out the frequency of human resource practices execution on a five-point Likert scale having range from 'Strongly agree' (5) to 'Strongly disagree' (1).

Internal customer satisfaction

Thirteen items were used to measure internal customer satisfaction. The scale of Chang & Huang (2010) was used for measuring internal customer satisfaction. Respondents were requested to signify the level of their satisfaction with recruitment, selection, training for newcomers, and training for current employees, career planning, promotion system, performance management, compensation, benefits, and participation. The responses were measured by means of a five-point Likert scale having range from 'strongly agree' (5) to 'strongly disagree(1)'.

Organizational effectiveness

To measure organizational effectiveness a scale composed of five items was used. The scale of Chang & Huang (2010) was used for measuring organizational effectiveness. Respondents were requested to compare employee morale, attraction to talent, employee productivity, organizational commitment and employee turnover rate with competing organizations. A five-point Likert scale was used to evaluate the response ranging from 'much better than competitors' (5) to 'much worse than competitors' (1).

Pilot testing

Pilot testing is essential to check questionnaire reliability, questionnaire items and language used in the items (Ticehurst & Veal, 2000). There are several advantages of carrying out pilot testing before doing actual survey. For instance, to test the questionnaire wording, to check sequence of items, achieving familiarity with respondent, and estimating response rate of the targeted sample. Primarily, for evaluating reliability of the questionnaire, Cronbach's alpha was analyzed. For pilot testing, 60 questionnaires were distributed to different banks. With the help of pilot testing researcher was able to adjust questionnaire and its language accuracy. Pilot testing permits to test several phases of a questionnaire with regard to simplicity of completion and usefulness of data collection.

Reliability

Reliability of the scale variables varied from .657 to .781. This depicts that each variable had internal consistency among items used to measure that particular variable (Field, 2006). Overall reliability of measurement scales was .701. Reliability results greater than 0.6 were considered acceptable (Jolibert & Jourdan, 2006). Therefore, the survey questionnaire was reliable for examining the impact of Human resource practices on internal customer satisfaction and organizational effectiveness.

Table 1: Reliability of Scale items

Variable	Cronbach's Alpha	Items
Recruitment and selection	.696	4
Employee training and Development	.710	6
Compensation and benefits	.657	5
Performance Appraisal	.762	6
Employee Participation	.775	8
Work Environment	.702	9
Internal customer satisfaction	.781	13
Organizational effectiveness	.704	5

MAIN STUDY

Population and Sample

Population is a set of all elements (Gilbert, 2001). From the population, sample was selected to collect data that can be representative of the whole target population.

Sampling is important for an empirical study that uses a positivistic approach (Hussey, 1997). It is a fraction of subjects drawn from a population. Sampling offers detailed information that deal with small number of units (Sekaran, 2006). This study was carried out in banking sector of Pakistan.

The target respondents for this study were Human Resource managers and Line mangers. The reason for selecting this population stands on the fact that they are professionally working and experiencing these practices. They are also aware about the importance of implementation of such practices. Banking sector of Pakistan is comprised of 36 commercial banks (including 25 local private banks, 4 public sector commercial banks and 7 foreign banks) and 4 specialized banks. This study was conducted in twin cities of Rawalpindi and Islamabad. Almost all the major Pakistani banks have their branch offices in these cities duly controlled by their regional offices. The data was collected about the employees of public banks i.e. National Bank of Pakistan, First Women Bank and privatized banks which included Muslim Commercial Bank Limited, United Bank Limited, Allied Bank Limited, and Habib Bank limited, operating commercially in the aforesaid selected areas. Random sampling techniques were adopted. The sample was mainly categorized into six banks, which consist of 120 branches including their controlling offices in the twin cities. 400 questionnaires were distributed among human resource managers and line managers of various units of banks in Pakistan. Of these questionnaires, 290 questionnaires were returned. The sample size of above-mentioned respondents meets the minimum obligation of diverse statistical analysis for example regression analysis, factor analysis, and analysis of diverse and ultimately of structural path.

Procedure

The questionnaire was personally distributed among human resource managers and line managers of banking sector of Pakistan. Before giving the questionnaire to the respondents, all the questions were explained to the respondents so that they could easily fill up the questionnaire. The feedback of the respondents was quantitatively analyzed. Different numbers were specially assigned to the options on the nominal scale and to the options on the five point Likert scale. After assigning the numerical values, they were specially added to the Statistical tool for management Sciences Software (SPSS). To review the characteristics of respondents and collected data descriptive statistics were performed and to test hypothesis regression test was applied. This study employed descriptive statistics, factor analysis, and regression. Descriptive statistics was used for gaining a descriptive overview of collected data. This study used the structural equation modeling method to institute the model. Regression analysis was used to identify the relationship of HR practices, internal customer satisfaction and organizational effectiveness.

Confirmatory factor analysis

Table 2 demonstrates the estimates of the variable of the study such that the estimates, which were significant, were considered well for further model fit.

Table 2: Estimates of constructs of study

Constructs	Items		Estimates
Recruitment and Selection	RS1	Recruitment and selection	.548
	RS2	Recruitment and selection	.512
	RS3	Recruitment and selection	.823
	RS4	Recruitment and selection	.675
	TD1	Training & Development	.751
	TD2	Training & Development	.559
Training and Development	TD3	Training & Development	.598
	TD4	Training & Development	.834
	TD5	Training & Development	.466
	TD6	Training & Development	.451
	PA1	Performance Appraisal	.838
	PA2	Performance Appraisal	.485
Performance Appraisal	PA3	Performance Appraisal	.673
	PA4	Performance Appraisal	.961
	PA5	Performance Appraisal	.775
	PA6	Performance Appraisal	.693
	CB1	Compensation and Benefits	.765
	CB2	Compensation and Benefits	.850
Compensation and Benefits	CB3	Compensation and Benefits	.949
	CB4	Compensation and Benefits	.875
	CB5	Compensation and Benefits	.903

	EP1	Employee Participation	.519
	EP2	Employee Participation	.853
	EP3	Employee Participation	.973
	EP4	Employee Participation	.799
Employee Participation	EP5	Employee Participation	.864
	EP6	Employee Participation	.527
	EP7	Employee Participation	.483
	EP8	Employee Participation	.519
	WE1	Work Environment	.517
	WE2	Work Environment	.491
	WE3	Work Environment	.548
	WE4	Work Environment	.621
Work Environment	WE5	Work Environment	.602
	WE6	Work Environment	.454
	WE7	Work Environment	.615
	WE8	Work Environment	.673
	WE9	Work Environment	.545
	ICS1	Internal Customer Satisfaction	.916
	ICS2	Internal Customer Satisfaction	.830
Internal Customer Satisfaction	ICS3	Internal Customer Satisfaction	.805
	ICS4	Internal Customer Satisfaction	.621
	ICS5	Internal Customer Satisfaction	.581
	ICS6	Internal Customer Satisfaction	.432
	ICS7	Internal Customer Satisfaction	.665
	ICS8	Internal Customer Satisfaction	.558
	ICS9	Internal Customer Satisfaction	.610
	ICS10	Internal Customer Satisfaction	.589
	ICS11	Internal Customer Satisfaction	.636
	ICS12	Internal Customer Satisfaction	.524
	ISC13	Internal Customer Satisfaction	.831
	OE1	Organizational Effectiveness	.517
	OE2	Organizational Effectiveness	.528
Organizational Effectiveness	OE3	Organizational Effectiveness	.861
	OE4	Organizational Effectiveness	.556
	OE5	Organizational Effectiveness	.788

RESULTS

Analysis of Demographics

The sample included 290 respondents who were working in different departments of different branches in the banking sector of Pakistan. Table 3 illustrates the composition of respondents. According to table, there were 290 respondents, out of them 87 were female and 203 were male. That is, sample consists of 30% of female and 70% of male respondents. Age distribution of respondents is presented in table. The table explains that most of respondents were in age category of 31-40, 42.8% of respondents. 15.9% were in age category of 21-30. In the age category of 41-50, there were 41.4% respondents. Married and unmarried both respondents were included into the sample. Marital status of respondents of the sample is illustrated in the table. Table shows that 56.9% respondents were married and 43.1% were unmarried employees. Employees were asked to indicate their highest education qualification. Collected data on the highest education qualification is presented in the table. According to the given data in the table, Graduation has recorded as the highest education qualification of most of the respondents in the sample. That is, 48.6% employees were Graduate. 30.7% were Master, 19% were MS/M. Phil and 1.7% were Ph. Ds. Table indicates that most of the respondents had more than ten year experience in the present bank. As a percentage, 34.5 % had more than ten years of service in the present bank and 26.2% had 6-10 years service.

Table 3: Frequency distribution of demographic profile of the respondents

Demographic	Category	Frequency	Percent
Gender	Male	203	70.0
	Female	87	30.0
Age	21-30	46	15.9
	31-40	124	42.8
	41-50	120	41.4
Marital Status	Married	165	56.9
	Unmarried	125	43.1
Qualification	Graduate	141	48.6
	Master	89	30.7
	MS/M. Phil	55	19.0
	PhD	5	1.7
Service Period	1-2	64	22.1
	3-5	51	17.6
	6-10	76	26.2
	More than ten years	99	34.1
Total		290	100

Note. N=290.

Hypothesis Testing

The result in table 4 reports regression path, regression estimates, standard error, critical ratio, significance values, and label of hypothesized relationship. The result describes positive and significance impact of recruitment and selection on internal customer satisfaction (β=.56, P< 0.05, Hypothesis 1). It shows that recruitment and selection intensifies internal customer satisfaction by 56% approximately. The critical ratio (CR=6.647) reveals that recruitment and selection is considered as an important determinant of internal customer satisfaction. The analysis further demonstrates that employee training and development (β=.61, P< 0.05, Hypothesis 2), performance appraisal (β=.59, P< 0.05, Hypothesis 3), compensation (β=.51, P< 0.05, Hypothesis 4), employee participation (β=.64, P< 0.05, Hypothesis 5), and work environment (β=.57, P< 0.05, Hypothesis 6) have positive and significant impact on internal customer satisfaction. As predicted, internal customer satisfaction is positive and significantly related to organization effectiveness (β=.76, P< 0.05, Hypothesis 7). To test the effect of human resource practices on organizational effectiveness, all HR practices were found to have a positive and significant impact on organizational effectiveness. The analysis further demonstrates that employee recruitment and selection (β=.42, P< 0.05, Hypothesis 8), employee training and development (β=.56, P< 0.05, Hypothesis 9), performance appraisal (β=.44, P< 0.05, Hypothesis 10), Compensation and benefits (β=.64, P< 0.05, Hypothesis 11), employee participation (β=.57, P< 0.05, Hypothesis 12), and work environment (β=.49, P< 0.05, Hypothesis 13) have positive and significant impact on organizational effectiveness.

Table 4: Regression paths of research model, estimates, critical ratio and P-value

Hypotheses	Effects			Estimate	S.E.	C.R.	P	Remarks
H1	Satisfaction	<---	Staffing	.557	.084	6.647	***	Supported
H2	Satisfaction	<---	Training	.607	.114	5.318	***	Supported
H3	Satisfaction	<---	Appraisal	.586	.074	5.651	***	Supported
H4	Satisfaction	<---	Compensation	.509	.067	5.231	***	Supported
H5	Satisfaction	<---	Participation	.636	.094	6.736	***	Supported
H6	Satisfaction	<---	Workenv	.568	.053	16.877	***	Supported
H7	Effectiveness	<---	Satisfaction	.761	.056	16.665	***	Supported
H8	Effectiveness	<---	Staffing	.418	.051	5.421	***	Supported
H9	Effectiveness	<---	Training	.561	.056	14.665	***	Supported
H10	Effectiveness	<---	Appraisal	.440	.046	7.019	***	Supported
H11	Effectiveness	<---	Compensation	.638	.058	5.850	***	Supported
H12	Effectiveness	<---	Participation	.571	.055	6.306	***	Supported
H13	Effectiveness	<---	Workenv	.491	0.49	5.924	***	Supported

Note: ***p< .05

Putting the entire model simultaneously, the result shows that employee participation is the most important determinant (β=.64) of internal customer satisfaction, followed by employee training (β=.61), performance appraisal (β=.59), work environment (β=.57), employee recruitment and selection (β=.56) and compensation (β=.51). They share almost the same influence in terms of enhancing internal customer satisfaction. On the other hand, internal customer satisfaction exerts the greatest impact on organizational effectiveness (β=.76), while the subsequent predictors of organizational effectiveness are compensation (β=.64), employee participation (β=.57), employee training and development (β=.56), work environment (β=.49), performance appraisal (β=.44) and recruitment and selection (β=.42). Compensation exerts the greatest effect on organizational effectiveness and the least impact on internal customer satisfaction among the six human resource practices.

Table 5: Structure Equation model fit Measures of constructs of the study

Constructs	Chi	D.F	Chi/D.F	GFI	IFI	CFI	NFI	AGFI	RMSEA
Model	92.537	23.13	4	.914	.923	.922	.918	.910	.056
Traditional Cut off Criteria			≤5	≥0.90	≥0.90	≥0.90	≥0.90	≥0.90	≤0.08

Note. D.F — Degree of Freedom, GFI — Goodness of Fit Index, IFI — Incremental Fit Index, CFI —Comparative Fit Index, NFI — Normated Fit Index, AGFI—Adjusted Goodness of Fit Index, RMSEA—Root Mean Square Error of Approximation

The results in the Table 5 signify model fitness index, as significant regression paths necessarily means model is fit, researcher have to go through model fit index provided by AMOS output. Table 5 reveals seven (7) model fitness criteria. The model chi Square (Chi) and associated significant value indicates that this criterion fulfills the minimum requirement of model fitness, as the significant value is less than level of significance (P < 0.05) indicating discrepancies factors in the model (Tabachnick & Fidell, 2007). Another fitness measure is goodness of Fit index (GFI), by convention the value of GFI equal to or greater 0.90 is acceptable (Schumacker & Lomax, 2004). This criterion fulfills the minimum acceptance level of Model Fit (GFI> 0.90) and AGFI is variant of goodness of fit, which adjusted goodness of fit index for degree of freedom. . Further criteria includes CFI (comparative fit index) is revised form of NFI (norm fit index). The suggested value for NFI and CFI is equal or greater .90 (Hooper et al, 2008). RMSEA (root mean square error of approximation) tells about optimally chosen parameters would fit the population co-variance Matrix (Byrne, 1998). RMSEA value below 0.08 shows good fit of the model. Based upon the aforementioned criteria, model fit indices fulfill the criteria of Model fitness.

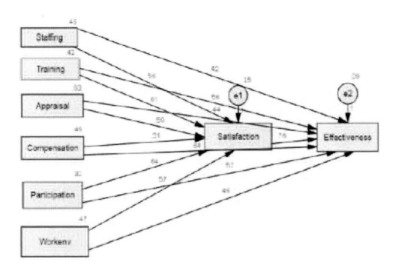

Figure 2: Path diagram.

DISCUSSION

The paper contributes to understanding of influence of HR practices on internal customer satisfaction and organizational effectiveness in Pakistan. The results of the study presented empirical support for the existence of a positive and statistically significant influence of HR practices on internal customer satisfaction organizational effectiveness in Pakistan. Our study of Banking Sector in Pakistan presented support for the hypothesized positive effects of HR practices on organizational effectiveness. The results indicate statistically significant relationship of recruitment and selection, training and development, performance appraisal, compensation and rewards, and employee participation with organizational effectiveness. Together with earlier studies on HR practices, the result of present study indicate that extensive use of an integrated approach to efficient HR practices yield positive results in term of their effects on organizational effectiveness. In context of Pakistan, it would be pertinent to substantiate these results through empirical studies of other industries of the economy

Recruitment and selection may consequence commencing the various accents of Human Resource experts as well as executives. The focal point of Human Resource experts is to see whether the recruitment map fits recruitment effectiveness, company policy and the fit between the business and candidates. It is also apprehensive regarding the multi-methods, as well as applicable, consistent assortment devices. From the users' point of view, line executives may be bothered supplementary regarding the duration of time essential for hiring the exact individual, with the supportive capability as well as solidity of newcomer. Hence, the capabilities of Human Resource departments have established by the recruitments and selections have no influence on internal customer satisfaction Attitudes and dedication of employees are improved, once internal customers are satisfied with HR practices, selection, recruitment, promotion, compensation, benefits, and training of employees. This satisfaction increases employee behaviors and reduces turnover rate. This constructive circle also helps in enhancing the capability of an organization to draw talent (Jyothi & Venkatesh, 2006).

The results of studies illustrate that employer-provided training might in fact rise intended earnings rate (Batt, 2002; Kalleberg & Lincoln, 1996). Therefore, the easiness of association rationalization appears supplementary appropriate than the firm dedication case toward description of the manipulation of employer-provided training on intended turnover. The alternates that entail lessening in training reserves or employ faculty from rivals might have bad penalty. For example, the place of work might languish or practice retribution from rivals (Gardner &Timothy 2005). As regards compensation and benefit, frontline executives are pleased when HR department expresses potentials in marketplace study, compensate for- concert scheme, job appraisal and aggressive compensation packages in labor marketplace. A market study tails external equity whereas job evaluation tails internal equity. Equity theory recommends that an individual estimate himself with others. Rewards may improve the financial well-being of people through wages, bonuses, or profit sharing, or indirectly, through employer-subsidized benefits for instance retirement plans, paid vacations, paid sick leaves, and purchase discounts (Sue Shellenbarger, 1999). Consequently, the reward issue cannot be disregarded, as it will generate a "situation in which the anticipation or the actual goal-directed behavior of an individual or group are infertile or are about to be fruitless (Steers & Black, 1994). Rewards promote efforts, performance and there is lot of support that they often do (Gibbons, 1997).

Regular monitoring of the performance and constant feedback about performance is essential to get the desired results. Researchers established that employees' participation in setting performance goals, clarity about performance standards, flexibility of the system to respond to the changing needs, and employee right to appeal against performance evaluation are vital attributes of an effective performance appraisal that contributes toward superior performance by workforce (Islam & Rasad 2006; Sidin et al., 2003; Webb, 2004; Wu, 2005). Employee participation is characterized by wide ranging HRM related activities primarily focused on employee management. These practices include employees sharing schemes, cooperatives, industrial democracy, unions, employees' involvement, HR and high commitment work practices, team working, collective bargaining, employee empowerment, employee partnership in providing input in strategic decision making, and employees' right of information sharing at all levels (Summers & Hyman, 2005). The results of present study concur with results of earlier studies that HR practice of employee participation is positively and significantly associated with organizational effectiveness (Amable, 2003; Hall & Soskice, 2001; Hartcourt & Wood, 2007; Rizov & Croucher, 2008).The results of study demonstrated that perceived adequacy or inadequacy of work environment, both physical and psychosocial, extends noticeable effect on employees' job satisfaction and performance, and perception of effectiveness of an organization. The employees who perceive and feel the work environment as to be adequate, safe and congenial, develop positive attitude towards various job components, which ultimately results in higher job satisfaction and job involvement among these employees. Sayeed and Mehta (1981) reported positive correlation between Q.W.L. and employees' job satisfaction. The positive relationship between adequate and favorable work environment and performance noted in the present study may be attributed to the physical convenience, facilities and comfort, feeling of safety and security, and congenial and motivating climate prevailing in the work environment. After pioneer formulations of Frederik Taylor in second decade of twentieth century, numerous empirical investigations revealed that adequacy or appropriateness of various features of physical condition at work, such as; illumination, temperature, noise and atmospheric conditions help in enhancing industrial productivity. Fine and Kobrik (1978) noted negative effect of high temperature on performance of mental as well as physical task. Increasing illumination level has also been found to result in some improvement in performance. The studies have also demonstrated positive relationship between perceived work environment and organizational effectiveness (Hansson & Jensen, 2004; Pransky et al., 2005; Lindberg, 2006). The observation may be attributed to the fact that adequate and favorable features of physical and social environment of the organization are major constituents and as well as determinants of overall effectiveness of the organization.

CONCLUSION

Placing the entire hypothesis simultaneously, the consequence of standardized whole belongings illustrates so as they share nearly the similar impact in provisions of enhancing internal customer satisfaction. Conversely, internal customer satisfaction exercises the greatest impact lying on organizational usefulness, whereas the consequent predictor of organizational effectiveness is compensation. Compensation has the highest impact on organizational effectiveness, the slightest effect on internal customer satisfaction.

Compensation is the slightest significant manipulate for employees on their satisfaction. It might reveal the detail to facilitate workforce have previously acknowledged the reward presented prior to joining the organization. On the contrary, these are provided by supplementary HR practices in anticipation that these turned out to be the members of organization. Accordingly, compensation is not the only factor influencing satisfaction. Conversely, compensation influences organizational effectiveness generally among six HR magnitudes. It illustrates that compensation is the ultimate result efforts of employees, and so directly manipulates organizational effectiveness (Haines, Jalette, & Larose, 2010).

MANAGERIAL IMPLICATION

Overall, the consequence of this research is reliable in the midst of the projected speculation. Moreover, this assumed model is a fine robust. The learning reveals a few important inferences. Those inferences are argued by changing and highlighting definite Human Resource practice, as well as by giving focus on the function of internal customers for organizational usefulness improvement. Concerning the Human Resource practices, a few HR practices based on customer necessities might require to be evaluated. For instance recruitment and selection the robust between employment map and company policy, employment usefulness, different employment techniques, consistent and compelling assortment procedures, as well as the robust flanked by candidates and the organization with which the Human Resource expert is apprehensive might contain minor precedence than supplementary aspects for example the duration of occasion essential for hiring the right individual, the collaboration capability of newcomers and solidity which may be means apprehensions for interior customers.

Further Human Resource practice may contribute a significant part into improving organizational effectiveness. For instance, majority of the employees have issues regarding compensation and benefits. Human Resource experts should assign huge hard work to signifying their competence in work valuation, market analysis, a pay-forperformance scheme, aggressive compensation & benefits within the labor marketplace. All These pains may help to oblige the customers, as well as strengthen the potentials in order to improve organizational effectiveness.

Human Resource experts must identify and stay close up to their customers to improve the satisfaction of internal customers. Conversely, Human Resource experts might exercise diverse techniques to study about the organization and its customers. For instance, they may drive HR experts to technological conventions, attract talented people like, marketer, investor, engineer and R& D expert to convene with Human Resource groupings, make sure that Human resource experts connect trade groups, and give out to Human Resource experts photocopy of tactical policy, technological information and buyer evaluation of goods and services. Moreover, at workforce meeting, the company plan may be talked about as often as recompense, evaluation, and T& D. These negotiations may necessitate that customers are recognized, occupied, and essential to the function of the Human Resource division.

Alternatively, HR expert is accountable for running groups interconnected performs as well as tend to take care of employee troubles. Moreover determining Human Resource performs, Human Resource expert can entail front line executive into Human Resource tasks. Several of these practices and troubles may be successfully grasped by frontline executive due to having nearer relationships and better considerate of worker desires and troubles. The primary role of HR experts should be as serving managers advance management excellence and helping them hold with employee troubles. Human Resource experts can better develop service excellence by highlighting the meticulous function of boss in-group organization.

RECOMMENDATIONS

Subsequent to extensive discussion and comprehensive analysis, this study suggests a number of recommendations for business leaders and banking industry of Pakistan for designing human resource practices. Based on results, the study recommends that the victory of banks is reliant on the Human Resource practices, procedures, applications, and implementation towards their internal customers. It is acknowledged that the association with employees' satisfaction is believed one of the most important drivers of the perceived internal service quality and it is strongly related to employee retention but unfortunately, this association in its real spirit is hardly taken notice of. Hence, it is essential for the bank management that they must satisfy the internal customers first to make them extremely motivated with good working morale, and they will effort more effectively and efficiently. The facets of jobrelated attitudes improved while the quality of Human resource practices enhance. The study recommends that the human resource development departments should evaluate and increase the motivation, training, and retention of good employees. The employees' selection and their compensation and rewards, their training and development, and participation all are the most imperative human resource practices in increasing the employees' satisfaction and the retention of potential workforce.

The study further recommends that to deliver outstanding internal service quality to the employees and endeavor for company characteristic, the internal customer satisfaction is very important. These all aspects may be attained if the management takes extra care as developing the human resource practices launching from selection and recruitment, identifying the employees with their core capability and arranging remarkable work environment. Therefore, it is suggested that it must be encouraging to facilitate the employees to deliver what is projected of them. Management should treat internal customers since they would like them to treat their external customers. Satisfy employees, prepare them, respect them, and make champion of them because the mode human resources are treated by the organization has a direct influence on the way those human resources treat the business' customers. If the businesses treat the employees properly, they will treat the customers' correctly.

LIMITATIONS AND DIRECTIONS FOR FUTURE RESEARCH

This study has several limitations, which should be incorporated in future research. The anticipated model focuses on only a small number of important variables influencing organizational effectiveness. To study the sound effects of several further variables, the structural equation modeling method may be used. Therefore, future research can consider different sophisticated models. Here in this research, Organizational effectiveness incorporates behavior and attitude variables. Attitude-behaviorperformance judgment may be exercised for developing further imminent in the black box. Many clusters of internal customers might be examined, for the moderate association; these internal customers may be Managers, Chief Executive Officers and employees. Having possession of the diverse disposition of their everyday jobs, this is rational to believe that the link connecting Human Resource Practices and organizational effectiveness through internal customer satisfaction may fluctuate according to the objective customers. This study did not include external customer satisfaction in the theoretical model test because of particular concentration on internal customer and organizational effectiveness with respect to human resource management. External customer satisfaction should be incorporated in future research.

REFERENCES

1.   Amit, R., & Schoemaker, P. J. H. (1993). Strategic assets and organizational rent. Strategic Management Journal, 14, 33–46.

2.   Analoui, F. (2002). The Changing Patterns of Human Resource Management (eds). Aldershot: Ashgate.

3. Analoui, F. (1999). Effective human resource development: a challenge for developing countries (Eds). Aldershot: Ashgate.

4. Arthur, J. (1994). Effects of human resource systems on manufacturing performance and turnover. Academy of Management Journal, 37, 670–687.

5. Baird, L. & Meshoulan, I. (1998). Managing two fits of strategic human resource management, Academy of Management Review, 13, 116-128.

6. Barney, J. B. (1991). Firms' resources and sustained competitive advantages. Journal of Management, 17, 99–120.

7. Batt, R. (2002). Managing Customer Services: Human Resource Practices, Quit Rates, and Sales Growth. Academy of Management Journal, 45, 587-97.

8. Bhatt, G. D. (2000). A resource-based perspective of developing organizational capabilities for business transformation. Knowledge and Process Management, 7, 119–129.

9. Bohlander, G., Snell, S. & Sherman, A. (2001). Managing Human Resources. Cincinnati, OH: South-Western College Publishing.

10. Boxall, P. (1996). The strategic HRM debate and the resource-based view of the firm. Human Resource Management Journal, 6, 59-75.

11. Boxall, P. (1991). Strategic HRM: beginning of a new theoretical sophistication? Human Resource Management Journal, 2, 60-79.

12. Byrne B, M (1998). Structural Equation Modeling with LISREL, PRELIS and SIMPLIS: Basic Concepts, Applications and Programming. Mahwah, New Jersey: Lawrence Erlbaum Associates.

13. Caliskan, N. E. (2010). The impact of strategic human resource management practices on organizational performance . J. Nav. Sci. Engg, 6(2), 100-116.

14. Cascio, Wayne F. (2000). Costing Human Resources: The Financial Impact of Behavior in Organizations. Cincinnati: South-Western.

15. Chang, P. L., & Chen, W. L. (2002). The effect of human resource management practices on firm performance: empirical evidence from high-tech firms in Taiwan. International Journal of Management, 19 (4), 622-38.

16. Chang, W.-J. A., & Huang, T. C. (2010). The impact of human resource capabilities on internal customer and organisational effectiveness. Total Quality Management , 21 (6), 633–648.

17. Comm, C. L. & Mathaisel, D. F. X., (2000). Assessing Employee Satisfaction in Service Firms: An Example in Higher Education. The Journal of Business and Economic Studies 6(1), 43-53.

18. Connor, P. E., & Becker, B. W. (2003). Personal value systems and decision-making styles of public managers. Public Personnel Management, 32, 155–181.

19. Cook, S. (2000). Customer Care & How to Create an Effective Customer Focus, Third Edition, Kogan Page Limited.

20. Cunningham, L.X. & Rowley, C. (2010). Small and medium-sized enterprises in China: A Literature review of human resource management and suggestions for

further research. Asia Pacific Business Review. 16(3). 319-337.

21. Delery, J., & Doty, D. (1996). Modes of theorizing in strategic human resourcemanagement: Test of universalistic, contingency, and configuration performance predictors. Academy of Management Journal, 39, 802–835.

22. Deming, W.E. (1986), Out of the Crisis, Massachusetts Institute of Technology, Cambridge, MA.

23. Field, A. (2006). Discovering Statistics Using SPSS, Second Edition edn, SAGE Publications, London.

24. Flippo, E. B. (1984). Personnel Management. Mcgraw-Hill College.

25. Gardner, Timothy, M. (2005). Inter-firm Competition for Human Resources: Evidence from the Software Industry. Academy of Management Journal, 48 (2), 237–56.

26. Gibbons R., (1997). Incentives and careers in organizations. In advances in Economic theory and Econometrics, Vol. II, Kreps D. and Wallis K, ed. Cambridge University press, U.K.

27. Glebbeek, Arie C., & Erik, H. B. (2004). Is High Employee Turnover Really Harmful? An Empirical Test Using Company Records. Academy of Management Journal, 47 (2), 277–86.

28. George, S. (1994). The Capabilities of Market-Driven Organizations. Journal of Marketing, 58, 37 -51.

29. Gilbert, N. (2001). Researching Social Life, 2nd edn, Sage, London.

30. Guest, D. E. (2002). Human resource management: When Research Confronts Theory. International Journal of Human Resource Management. 12(7), 1092-1106.

31. Haines, V. Y., Jalette, P. & Larose, K. (2010). The influence of human resource management practices on employee voluntary turnover rates in the Canadian nongovernmental sector. Industrial and Labor Relations Review, 63(2), 228-246.

32. Hansson T, Jensen I. Swedish Council on Technology Assessment in Health Care (SBU). Chapter 6. Sickness absence due to back and neck disorders. Scand J Public Health Suppl. 2004; 63, 109-51.

33. Harel, G.H., Tzafrir, S.S., & Baruch, Y. (2003). Achieving organizational effectiveness through promotion of women into managerial positions: HRM practice focus. International Journal of Human Resource Management, 14, 247–263.

34. Harnesk, R. (2004). Partnership with internal customers: A way to achieve increased commitment. The TQM Magazine, 16, 26–32.

35. Harrison, R., & Kessels, J. (2004). Human resource development in a knowledge economy: An organizational view. New York: Palgrave Macmillan.

36. Herzberg, F., Mausner, B., & Snyderman, B. B. (1959). The motivation to work. New York: John Wiley & Sons.

37. Hooper D, Coughlin, J. & Mullen, M. R. (2008). Structural Equation Modeling:

Guidelines for Determining Model Fit. Elect. J. Bus. Res. Methods. 6 (1): 53 – 60.

38. Hoque, Z. (2003). Total quality management and the balanced scorecard approach: A critical analysis of their potential relationships and directions for research. Critical Perspectives on Accounting, 14, 553–566.

39. Huselid, M.A. (1995). The impact of human resource management practices on turnover, productivity, and corporate financial performance. Academy of Management Journal, 38, 635–672.

40. Hussey, J. & Hussey, R. (1997), Business Research, A practical guide for undergraduate and postgraduate students, Palgrave, New York.

41. Islam, R. Rasad, S.M. (2006). Employee performance evaluation by the AHP: A case study. Asia Pacific Management Review, 11 (3), 163-176.

42. Jamrog, J. J., & Overholt, M. H. (2004). Measuring HR and organizational effectiveness. Employment Relations Today, 31(2), 33–45.

43. Jansen, P., Van der Velde, M., & Telting, I. A. (2001). The effectiveness of human resource practices on advancing men's and women's ranks. Journal of Management Development, 20, 318–330.

44. Joanna, O., Riordan, Peter, C. & Humphreys, (2003). Developing an Effective Internal Customer Service Ethos. Institute of Public Administration 57-61. Lansdowne Road Dublin 4. Ireland.

45. Jolibert, A., & Jourdan, P. (2006). Marketing Research - Méthodes De Recherche Et D'études En Marketing. Paris: Dunod.

46. Jyothi, P. and Venkatesh, D.N. (2006). Human Resource Management, New Delhi: Oxford University Press.

47. Kacmar, K. Michele, Martha, C., Andrews, David, L. Van Rooy, R. Chris Steilberg, &Stephen Cerrone. (2006). Sure Everyone Can be Replaced…But at What Cost? Turnover as a Predictor of Unit-Level Performance. Academy of Management Journal, 49(1), 133–144.

48. Kakabadse A. & Kakabadse, N. (2000). Leading the pack: future role of IS/IT professionals. The Journal of Management Development. 19, 97-155.

49. Kalleberg, A. L. & Moody, J. W. (1994). Human Resource Management and Organisational Performance, American Behavioural Scientist, 37, 948-62.

50. Lahteenmaki, S., Storey, J. & Vanhala, S. (1998). HRM and company performance: The use of measurement and the influence of economic cycles. Human Resource Management Journal, 8, 51-65.

51. Lindberg, P. (2006). The work ability continuum Epidemiological studies of factors promoting sustainable work ability. Thesis for doctoral degree. Karolinska Institute.

52. Locke, E. A., & Schweiger, D. M. (1979). Participation in decision-making: One more look. Research in Organizational Behavior, 1, 265–339.

53. Lorange, P. & Murphy, D. (1984). Bringing human resource strategy into strategic planning: systems design considerations. In Strategic Human Resource

Management.

54. C. Fombrun et al (Eds). New York: Wiley. Lundy, O. (1994). From personnel management to strategic human resource management. The International Journal of Human ResourceManagement. 5, 687-717.

55. Mabey, C., G. Salaman, & J. Storey. (1998). Strategic human resource management: A reader. London: Sage.

56. Marchington, M., & A. Wilkinson. (2002). People management and development: Human resource management at work. London: Chartered Institute of Personnel and Development.

57. Margret Dale. (1999). The Art of HRD, Successful Recruitment and Selection. London: Kogan Page.

58. Matzler, K., Fuchs, M., & Schubert, A. K. (2004). Employee satisfaction: Does Kano'smodel apply? Total Quality Management & Business Excellence, 15, 1179–1198.

59. Marshall, G. W., Baker, J., & Finn, D. W. (1998). Exploring internal customer service quality. Journal of Business & Industrial Marketing, 13, 381–392.

60. Maslow, A. H. (1943). A theory of human motivation. Psychological Review, July 1943. 370-396.

61. Maylett, Tracy (2009). 360-Degree Feedback Revisited: The transition from development to appraisal. Compensation and Benefits Review, September/ October 41(5), 52–59.

62. Milkovich & Newman, (2002). Compensation, 7th ed, The McGrew-Hill Companies, Inc.

63. Molina, J. A., & Ortega, R. (2003). Effects of employee training on the performance of North- American firms. Applied Economics Letters, 10, 549–552.

64. Money, A. & Foreman, S. (1995). Internal Marketing: Concepts, Measurement and Application. J Mark Manage.

65. Morrow, Paula, & James McElroy. (2007). Efficiency as a Mediator in Turnover-Organizational Performance Relations. Human Relations, 60 (6), 827–849.

66. Osman, M. R., Rosnah, M. Y., Ismail, N., R. Tapsir & M. I Sarimin (2004). Internal Customer Satisfaction In ISO 9001 Certified Manufacturing Companies. International Journal of Engineering and Technology, 1 (2), 179 – 187.

67. Pass, S. (2002). Human resource management and competitive performance in the manufacturing sector: The missing link. Management Research News, 25(10), 150–153.

68. Peters, M. (2005). "Entrepreneurial skills in leadership and human resource management evaluated by apprentices in small tourism businesses." Education & Training. 47 (8/9) 575- 591.

69. Pfeffer, J. (1998). Seven practices of successful organizations. California Management Review, 40, 96–124.

70. Pransky G, Gatchel R, Linton S. J., Loisel, P. (2005). Improving return to work

research.J Occup Rehabi, 15 (4), 453 7.

71. Probst, T. M. (2005). Countering the Negative Effects of Job Insecurity Through Participative Decision-making: Lessons From the Demand–Control Model. Journal of Occupational Health Psychology, 10, 320–329.

72. Rangone, A. (1999). A resource based approach to strategy analysis in small-medium sized relationship to business-unit performance. Strategic Management Journal. 9, 43-60.

73. Richard et al. (2009). Measuring Organizational Performance: Towards Methodological Best Practice. Journal of Management, 2 (2), 334-350.

74. Saa-Perez, P. D., & Garcia-Falcon, J. M. (2002). A resource-based view of human resource management and organizational capabilities development. International Journal of Human Resource Management, 13, 123–140.

75. Sasser, W. E. & Arbeit, S. (1976). Selling jobs in the service sector. Business Horizons, 9 (3), 125-140.

76. Schuler, R. S., & Jackson, S.E. (1996). Human resource management: Positioning for the 21stcentury (6th ed.). St Paul, MN: West.

77. Schumacker, R. E., & Lomax, R. G. (2004). A Beginner's Guide to Structural Equation Modeling. Mahwah, NJ: Lawrence Erlbaum.

78. Sekaran, U. (2006). Research Methods for Business: A Skill Building Approach, 4th edn, John Wiley and Sons, New Delhi.

79. Sidin, S. M, Hussin, S. R. & Soon, T. H. (2003). An exploratory study of factors influencing the college choice decision of undergraduate students in Malaysia. Asia Pacific Management Review, 8 (9), pp. 259-280.

80. Steers, R. & Black, J. (1994). Organization Behavior, 5th ed, Harper Collins. Steinheider, B., Bayerl, P. S., & Wuestewald, T. (2006, June). The Effects of Participative Management on Employee Commitment, Productivity, and Community Satisfaction in a Police Agency. Paper presented at the annual meeting of the International Communication Association, Dresden InternationalCongress Centre, Dresden, Germany. Retrievedfromhttp://www.allacademic.com/meta/p93097_index.html

81. Steven H. Appelbaum & Mackenzie. L. (2000). Compensation in the Year 2000: Pay forPerformance?. Health Manpower Management 22(3), 31–39.

82. Storey, J. (1998). Do human resources really have a role in strategy? Financial Times Mastering Management, 9, 14-18.

83. Sue Shellenbarger, (1999). Employees who value time as much as money now get their Reward. Wall street journal, B-1.

84. Tabachnick, B. G., & Fidell, L. S. (2007). Using multivariate statistics (5th ed.). Upper Saddle River, NJ. Pearson International.

85. Teo, S., & Crawford, J. (2005). Indicators of strategic HRM effectiveness: A case study of an Australian public sector agency during commercialization. Public Personnel Management, 34, 1–16.

86. Teece, David J., Gary Pisano & Amy Shuen (1997). Dynamic Capabilities and Strategic Management. Strategic Management Journal, 18 (7), 509–535.

87. Ticehurst, G. W. & Veal, A. J. (2000). Business research methods: a managerial approach, Longman, French Forest, NSW.

88. Tsui, A. (1990). A multiple constituency model of organizational effectiveness: An empirical examination at the human resource level. Administrative Science Quarterly, 35, 458–483.

89. Ulrich, D. (1987). Organizational capability as a competitive advantage: Human resource professionals as strategic partners. Human Resource Planning, 10(4), 169–184.

90. Urbano, D. & Yordanova, D. (2008). Determinants of the adoption of HRM practices in tourism SME's in Spain: An exploratory study. Service Business. 2, 167-185.

91. Vora, M. K. (2004). Creating employee value in a global economy through participation, motivation and development. Total Quality Management & Business Excellence, 15, 793–806.

92. Webb, J. (2004). Putting Management Back into Performance: A Handbook for Managers and Supervisors, Australia: Allen & Unwin.

93. Walker, G. B. (2007). Public participation as participatory communication in environmental policy decision-making: From concepts to structured conversations. Environmental Communication, 1, 99–110.

94. Wexley, K. N., & G. P. Latham. (2002). Developing and training human resources in organizations. Upper Saddle River, NJ: Prentice Hall.

95. Wright, P.M., McMahan, G. C., & McWilliams, A. (1994). Human resources and sustained competitive advantage: A resource-based perspective. International Journal of Human Resource Management, 5, 301–326.

96. Wu, H. L. (2005). A DEA approach to understanding the performance of Taiwan's steel industries 1970-1996. Asia Pacific Management Review, 10 (6), 349-356.

HRM AND FIRM PRODUCTIVITY: DOES INDUSTRY MATTER?

Deepak K. Datta[1], James P. Guthrie[1] and Patrick M. Wright[2]

[1]University of Kansas
[2]Cornell University

Recent years have witnessed burgeoning interest in the degree to which human resource systems contribute to organizational effectiveness. Pfeffer (1994, 1998), for example, argues that success in today's hyper-competitive markets depends less on advantages associated with economies of scale, technology, patents, and access to capital and more on innovation, speed, and adaptability. Pfeffer further argues that these latter sources of competitive advantage are largely derived from firms' human resources. Based on these and similar arguments, Pfeffer (1994, 1998) and others (e.g., Becker, Huselid & Ulrich, 2001; Kochan & Osterman, 1994; Lawler, 1992; 1996; Levine, 1995) strongly advocate greater firm investments in high performance or high involvement human resource practices. We believe these sentiments to be true in the main; however, we also believe that these investments may be relatively more beneficial in some contexts relative to others. More specifically, as emphasized in the strategic management and industrial organization literatures (e.g., Porter, 1980; Dess, Ireland & Hitt, 1990), a firm's industry (or industries) is an important part of the milieu within which organizational policies and practices are framed and executed. We believe this to also be the case for HR policies and practices. This remains largely speculative, however, because of a lack of empirical research on how industry conditions influence the efficacy of alternative HR practice configurations. This study seeks to fill this important void in the strategic HR literature by examining how industry characteristics moderate the value of human

Citation: Datta, D. K., Guthrie, J. P. & Wright, P. M. (2003). HRM and firm productivity: Does industry matter? http://digitalcommons.ilr.cornell.edu/cahrswp/25/

capital and, by extension, the importance and value of utilizing high performance work practices (HPWPs) in organizations.

The paper is structured as follows: after a brief discussion of recent developments and themes in the strategic human resource management (SHRM) literature, we provide arguments highlighting the importance of industry relative to HR systems. Following this, we draw on the organization theory, industrial organization economics, strategic management and SHRM literatures to argue that HPWPs may be more valuable in the context of particular industry conditions. We then present and discuss results of an empirical test of these arguments.

THEORETICAL PERSPECTIVES

HRM in Context Along with Pfeffer (1994, 1998), a number of authors have argued that recent systemic changes in firms' labor and product/service markets have elevated the importance of human resource issues and practices (e.g., Becker et al., 2001; Lawler, 1996; Schuler, 1990). Against this backdrop, researchers and practitioners have been exhorted to adopt a more strategic perspective on human resource management. Wright and McMahan (1992: 298) define strategic human resource management as "the pattern of planned human resource deployments and activities intended to enable an organization to achieve its goals." Researchers in the HR field have traditionally concentrated on technical innovations in practices, focusing on the effects of selection, training, appraisal and rewards on individual-level outcomes of job satisfaction or performance. Further, these subdiscipline innovations have occurred in relative isolation from one another (Wright & McMahan, 1992). SHRM addresses issues at a more 'macro' level. It is concerned with how organizational characteristics shape HR practices and priorities (Schuler & Jackson, 1989) and how these HR practices contribute to the bottom line (Martell & Carroll, 1995). Reflecting this orientation, recent HR research has taken more of a macro or systems view, examining the impact of 'bundles' of HR practices on organizational outcomes. More recently, research attention has focused on high performance work practices (HPWPs), a term used to denote a system or bundle of management and HR practices designed to elicit employee commitment and involvement such that employees become a source of sustainable competitive advantage (Lawler, 1992; 1996; Levine, 1995; Pfeffer, 1998). Levine (1995) discusses three preconditions necessary for creating successful employee involvement. First, workers must be given the opportunity and responsibility for organizational change and improvement. Second, employees must be motivated to avail themselves of this opportunity and responsibility. Third, workers must have the knowledge and skills enabling them to contribute to workplace improvement. HPWPs represent a system of mutually reinforcing, overlapping and synergistic HR practices which help to establish these preconditions and employee involvement (MacDuffie, 1995). Based on conceptual/prescriptive (e.g., Lawler, 1992; Levine, 1995; Pfeffer, 1998) and empirical work (e.g., Arthur, 1994; Huselid, 1995), HPWPs would include practices such as rigorous selection procedures, internal merit-based promotions, grievance procedures, cross-functional teams, high levels of training, information sharing, participatory mechanisms, group-based rewards and skill-based pay. Research on HPWPs includes Huselid's (1995) landmark study of U.S. corporations, which found a positive association between the use of what he termed "high performance" HR practices and firm success. Other studies have also indicated a relationship between variations in HR system configurations and firm outcomes (e.g., Arthur, 1994; Delery & Doty, 1996; Guthrie, 2001; Koch & McGrath, 1996; MacDuffie, 1995).

Recent strategic HR literature has also discussed the importance of achieving a fit between a firm's set of HR practices and contextual features, most notably organizational strategy. The underlying premise is that organizational effectiveness is augmented to the extent that there is an appropriate fit between a firm's approach to its HR systems and its approach to its competitive markets (Youndt, Snell, Dean & Lepak, 1996). However, research to date has not fully considered other important contextual conditions which may moderate the efficacy of alternative HR practice configurations. For example, while the strategic management literature emphasizes the role of industry as a critical contextual variable (see Dess, Ireland & Hitt, 1990), the role that industry conditions play in defining the value-adding potential of human resource practices has remained unexplored.

The Value of HPWPs: A Contingency Theory Perspective

Proponents of the resource based view of the firm (e.g., Barney, 1991; Wernerfelt, 1984) have argued that certain organizational resources are more valuable because they enable firms to create and sustain competitive advantage. Human capital, a key organizational resource, can be the basis of such advantage if it enables firms to exploit opportunities emanating from its competitive or task environment. Advocates for greater use of HPWPs argue that recent changes in firms' competitive environments have increased the degree to which human capital will be a source of valuable and inimitable competitive advantage. The arguments extend to suggest that these changes also imply a greater need for HR systems which develop and sustain human capital. For example, drawing upon Pfeffer (1994), Becker, Huselid, Pickus and Spratt (1997: 39) argue that the current economic environment "demands innovation, speed, adaptability, and low costs." They maintain that these environmental demands increase the importance of the core competencies and capabilities of employees relative to more traditional sources of competitive advantage such as, patents, economies of scale, access to capital and market regulation. Thus, their perspective is that the value of HPWPs, is magnified due to the hyper-competitive markets faced by today's firms.

Guided by contingency theory, our position is that the value of HPWPs varies as a function of a firm's environment. Contingency theory is based upon the thesis that organizations whose internal features best match the demands of the environment are best adapted for optimal functioning. Often contingency theory is deterministic in the sense that organizations must adapt to avoid loss of performance. Researchers such as Burns and Stalker (1961), Kast and Rosenzweig (1985) and Youndt et al. (1996), among others, have advocated a need for a contingency perspective in studying organizational phenomena. They argue that no single organizational practice is "best"; what really matters is the fit between practice and context. In other words, a fit between the environment and one or more aspects of organizational features will positively affect performance; a misfit will negatively affect such performance. While much of contingency theory deals with structural contingency (Donaldson, 1995), a strong argument can be made that, as an important organizational sub-system or factor, HRM systems must also exhibit a fit with the environment. In a recent article exploring the issue of human resource "fit" versus "flexibility", Wright and Snell make an important point in stating that: "....today, most firms face environments characterized by increasing dynamism and competition. In such a case, sustainable fit can be achieved only by developing a flexible organization" (1998: 758). Porter (1985) also discusses the desirability of matching human resource management policies to the needs of the environment, believing that such a match can represent a significant source of competitive advantage. In other words, there are important interactions between a firm's human resource management practices and the sources of advantage found in firms' competitive markets and industries. More specific to the SHRM literature, perhaps the most widely cited and best-articulated contingency perspective is the "role behavior perspective" proposed by Jackson and Schuler (e.g., Schuler & Jackson, 1987; 1989). This approach stipulates that HR practices need to elicit employee behaviors which are aligned with the requirements imposed by contextual conditions. While the role behavior perspective focuses primarily on the need for HR practices to elicit employee behaviors consistent with firm strategy, the arguments extend fairly easily to other industry conditions. In fact, in their review article examining "Human Resource Management in the Context of Organizations and their Environments", Jackson and Schuler specifically note this in stating that employee behavioral role requirements "depend on contextual factors such as business strategies and the nature of the industry" (1995: 239). Even Lawler, a leading proponent of using high involvement work practices, concedes that these practices are "not necessarily ... right .... for all environments" (1992: xiv).

Consistent with the industrial organization economics (Bain & Qualls, 1987; Scherer, 1980), strategy (Porter, 1980), and organizational theory (Pfeffer & Salancik, 1978; Thompson, 1967) literatures, Wright and Snell (1998) highlight the importance of industry as a critical contextual variable for HRM. Wright and Snell (1998) recognize this by emphasizing that the increased dynamism and competition characterizing many industries requires a flexible organization and workforce enabling it to reconfigure resources and activities in response to environmental demands. Thus, consistent with the contingency perspective, one can argue that the relative importance of HPWPs depends on the environment and industry and that an appropriate fit between HPWPs and these conditions should contribute to superior performance.

Industry Conditions and Employee Discretion

Specific to the moderating effect of industry on the value of a firm's human capital, Lieberson and O'Conner (1972) noted that the influence of top management on organizational performance varies considerably across industries, and that managers have greater influence on performance in some industry contexts relative to others. More recently, Rajagopalan and Datta (1996) and Datta and Rajagopalan (1998) have established significant relationships between the industry context, CEO characteristics and firm performance. Studies linking industry, top management characteristics, and firm performance are consistent with the concept of "managerial discretion" advocated by Hambrick and Finkelstein (1987). Managerial discretion has been defined as latitude for action and has been proposed as a theoretical construct explaining variability in the relative influence that top managers have on organizational outcomes (Hambrick & Finkelstein, 1987; Hambrick & Abrahamson, 1995). A manager or group of managers who have multiple courses of action that lie within the zone of acceptance is said to have discretion. In essence, managerial discretion equates to the magnitude of the upper and lower bound of management's potential impact. Hambrick and Finkelstein (1987) argue that a firm's industry environment greatly affects the level of managerial discretion. In some task environments, such as in slow growth or undifferentiated industries, the potential for managers to "make a difference" is quite limited, while in other contexts, marked by greater discretion, managers can have more of an impact.

The above notion of "managerial discretion", typically applied by strategy researchers to the executive ranks, is similar to Mischel's (1977) interactionist perspective on strong versus weak situations, invoked as a general framework by management scholars in explaining organizational behavior (e.g., Weiss & Adler, 1984). According to Mischel (1977), a strong situation is one which provides strong, fairly deterministic cues as to the appropriate behavior. In strong work situations, individual differences tend to have less influence on behavior and/or performance. Weak situations, on the other hand, tend to be more uncertain and ambiguous, leading to individual differences having more of an impact on behavior and performance. Researchers have shown, for example, that autonomy in one's job moderates the impact of individual dispositions on work performance (Barrick & Mount, 1993).

These perspectives have relevance for understanding the potential impact of HR systems on organizational effectiveness and performance. While Hambrick and Finkelstein (1987) argue that organizational leaders are more important in environments providing greater discretion, the potential for enhanced employee-based competitive advantage in high discretion environments should not be limited to the executive level. A number of contextual factors should affect employee discretion – creating "weaker" situations where, in the words of Pfeffer (1994), employees will be more of a "crucial, differentiating factor." A key set of factors relate to industry conditions. We propose that high performance HR systems are more efficacious in particular industry conditions, in general those that are associated with increased dynamism, complexity and/or uncertainty.

While the SHRM literature has focused on discussing and researching the notion of the "fit" of HR practices and employees with competitive strategy, Wright and Snell (1998) point out that the notion of "fit" implies a static, stationary contextual template to which practices and people can be "fitted." Clearly, task environments faced by firms vary in the extent to which they offer a stationary versus a moving target for achieving this fit. Firms facing more (less) dynamic, competitive environments, may find greater (lesser) value investing in high performance work practices promoting the acquisition, development and motivation of individuals who are able and willing to adapt to the needs of the competitive environment. These work environments will generally be imbued with higher levels of employee latitude for action and a greater, but varying, need for contributions on the part of employees. Thus, analogous to the concept of "managerial discretion" developed to explain conditions under which leaders "matter", employees also "matter" more or less depending on the level of discretion in their operating environment. In weaker, high discretion contexts, marked by uncertainty and change, firms need HR systems that promote employee and organizational flexibility to continually re-establish fit (e.g., with changing market and production strategies) over time. Industry conditions account for "the broadest and perhaps most fundamental of the loci of discretion" (Hambrick & Abrahamson, 1995: 1428). Thus, in our view, industry conditions should have broad implications for the relative value of high performance HR systems.

RESEARCH HYPOTHESES

Our principal argument is fairly straightforward: since industries and competitive markets vary widely in the extent to which they can be characterized by the changes (e.g., dynamic, hyper-competitive, etc.) noted by authors (e.g., Becker et al., 2001; Pfeffer,1994; 1998), the relative need for HR systems which facilitate an employee-based capability for "innovation, speed, adaptability and low costs" (Becker et al. 1997) will also vary. This is an important point since the extensive use of HPWPs represents an investment of organizational resources. Basic microeconomics suggests that investments in human capital (employees) are justified to the extent that such investments yield future marginal returns (in the form of increased productivity and economic value) in excess of the marginal cost of such investments. This perspective is consistent with Lepak and Snell's (1999) argument that the appropriateness of different HR configurations (i.e., systems) depends on the value and uniqueness of a firm's human capital, with high performance HR configurations being most appropriate when employees are both very unique and very valuable. Based on their general arguments, more intensive use of HPWPs is justified as a firm's human capital increases in uniqueness and value; fewer investments in HPWPs are warranted when these human capital factors diminish.

As we specify below, industry characteristics affect the value-adding potential of firms' human capital and, by extension, the use of HPWPs. Thus, industry conditions should moderate the affect of HPWPs on firm outcomes. In assessing the influence of HR systems on such outcomes, there are a number of performance measures which might apply, including human resource outcomes (e.g., turnover, absenteeism), organizational outcomes (e.g., productivity) and financial outcomes (e.g., profits, market value) (Dyer & Reeves, 1995). While it seems logical that HPWPs will have the greatest and most direct effect on human resource outcomes (Dyer & Reeves, 1995), we believe that industry conditions will be more manifest in their affect on the relationship between HPWPs and organizational outcomes. In other words, investments in human capital via HPWPs will tend to have a positive and universal impact on human resource outcomes such as turnover and absenteeism. In contrast, we expect that the impact of HPWPs on outcomes such as productivity will be contingent on industry (and other contextual conditions) affecting employee discretion. In this paper we specifically focus on productivity as a measure of organizational effectiveness. We adopt this focus for a number of reasons. First, productivity is a crucial organizational outcome. At a general level, labor productivity is defined as "total output divided by labor inputs" (Samuelson & Nordhaus, 1989). It indicates the extent to which a firm's human capital is efficiently creating output. While labor productivity may not be the sine qua non for long-term organizational success, it is often a necessary, if not a sufficient, condition. Second, while human resource outcomes such as turnover may ultimately impact firm performance (e.g., Guthrie, 2001), many managers may not view HR outcomes such as turnover to be of great strategic importance (Dyer & Reeves, 1995). Third, because connections between human capital and productivity -- especially labor productivity -- are relatively direct, the face validity for this outcome is also relatively high (Dyer & Reeves, 1995). Fourth, in part because of the aforementioned reasons, productivity has been used as a measure of organizational effectiveness in a fairly large body of work in the SHRM literature (e.g., Arthur, 1994; Guthrie, 2001; Ichniowski, Shaw & Prennushi, 1997; Koch & McGrath, 1996; MacDuffie, 1995).

In the following paragraphs we discuss how key industry characteristics (namely, capital intensity, growth and differentiation) moderate the relationships between HPWPs and firm productivity.

Industry Capital Intensity

Capital intensity, an indicator of industry entry barriers, has important implications for industry competitors. Firms in capital-intensive industries are generally committed to a course of action; capital intensity often creates rigidity such that new products or markets cannot be accommodated as fixed costs are high and deviations tend to be expensive (Ghemawat, 1991; Hambrick & Lei, 1985). Firms in these industries tend to focus on leveraging their investments, resulting in a greater concern for cost and efficiency considerations (Hambrick & Schecter, 1983). This results in a reduced range of discretionary options, and increases the reliance upon organizational sub-systems promoting cost-reduction and rationalization (as opposed to innovation and creativity). Further, relative to more capital-intensive industries, human capital in more labor-intensive industries are more central to organizational success. That is, intangible (human) assets are likely to be more valuable relative to tangible (physical) assets. Moreover, as capital intensity increases, employee discretion will likely be more constrained by the greater levels of automation and task structure found in these industries (Terpstra & Rozell, 1993), creating a "stronger" situation for employees. Thus, firms competing in industries with lower levels of capital intensity should receive a larger "payoff" when utilizing commitment-enhancing HR systems (i.e., HPWPs) relative to control-oriented HR systems.

Industry Growth

Arguments can also be made in the context of industry market growth, an industry characteristic featured prominently in the organizational theory and strategic management literature (e.g., Anderson & Zeithaml, 1984). Demand growth has been associated with greater market opportunity and competitive variation, providing managers and employees with more discretionary opportunities. High growth industries are typically associated with significant market opportunities and competitive variation. They are characterized by decisionmaking in the entrepreneurial mode, with greater opportunities for industry initiatives and decision-making freedom. Hambrick and Finkelstein (1987) suggest that industry growth results in an expanded set of options for firms, reducing the tendency for organization inertia. These industry features are associated with enhanced discretion and weaker work environments, increasing the relative benefit of investments in human capital through high performance HR policies and practices.

Industry Product Differentiation

Industries also differ in terms of "differentiation". Product differentiability forms an important basis for industry competition. In relatively undifferentiated industries, firms tend to have relatively similar, commodity-like products and attend primarily to cost and efficiency considerations (Porter, 1980). In relatively differentiated industries, competition turns on having products that stand out from competitors on the basis of product features, quality, design, etc. In highly differentiated industries there are typically more avenues for competition and a wider range of feasible competitive actions exist, with means-end linkages being relatively poorly understood. The multitude of ways in which firms can choose to create and maintain competitive advantage leads to firms more often breaking from past practices and norms (Porter, 1980; Sutton, 1991). Thus, on average, firms shift production and organizational processes more frequently to meet changing market and customer preferences. The increased uncertainty leads to less standardization, creating a work situation that is "weaker". These contexts likely magnify the value of utilizing high performance practices such as broadly defined tasks, decentralized decision-making, greater use of teams, cross-utilization, more training, etc. Jobs are more complex and varied, requiring more capable individuals possessing the skills and potential to succeed in more challenging circumstances. In contrast, a control-oriented approach to management, which tends to emphasize narrow, well-defined jobs, centralized decision-making, lower skill demands, little training and less interdependence would be more appropriate in an environment/industry where the basis for competition and, in turn, organizational sub-systems are more stable and predictable.

Study Hypotheses

Based on the above arguments, we test a number of hypotheses. Our first hypothesis builds on previous work and suggests a direct relationship between high performance work practices and firm productivity.

Hypothesis 1: High performance work practices will be positively associated with firm productivity. Our next set of hypotheses propose that industry conditions moderate this relationship.

Hypothesis 2(a): Industry capital intensity will moderate the relationship between high performance work practices and firm productivity with the relationship being stronger in industries having lower levels of capital intensity Hypothesis 2(b): Industry growth will moderate the relationship between high performance work practices and firm productivity with the relationship being stronger in high growth industries.

Hypothesis 2(c): Industry product differentiation will moderate the relationship between high performance work practices and firm productivity with the relationship being stronger in industries having higher levels of product differentiation.

METHOD

Sample and Data Collection

The sample of firms for this study was selected based on several criteria. First, we limited the study to firms in the U.S. manufacturing sector (firms with primary 2-digit SIC code 20-39). Second, since the influence of industry characteristics can only be meaningfully assessed in non-diversified firms, the sample had to be primarily single-business firms (operationalized as deriving at least 60% of sales revenues from a single 4-digit SIC). Third, similar to previous studies (e.g., Huselid, 1995), we required that firms meet minimum size requirements, which we set at 100 employees and $50 million in sales. Fourth, only those firms where we could identify a senior HR executive were included. Names and addresses for these individuals were obtained from the Directory of Corporate Affiliations, Hunt-Hanlon Select Guide to HR Executives and the Society for Human Resource Management Membership Directory. Finally, firms had to be publicly traded so that organizational data could be obtained from published sources. The final sample of firms (which satisfied all the above criteria) consisted of 971 firms.

After pilot testing, surveys were mailed to the identified HR executives in the sample firms. The initial mailing was followed by a reminder letter, a second survey, and finally a telephone reminder. This resulted in a total of 144 responses (a 15 % response rate). However, for 12 of the 144 firms providing survey responses, relevant firm-level data proved unavailable due to de-listings because of acquisition, merger or going private. As a result, the usable sample for this study was 132 firms. Although somewhat low, our response rate is consistent with other studies of survey-based "high performance work systems" reviewed by Becker and Huselid (1998), which had response rates ranging from 6% to 28%, with an average of 17.4% (a test of non-response bias for this study is reported below). Several weeks after the initial response was received, a second respondent was identified and mailed a survey. While initial respondents were typically Senior Vice–President or Vice President, HR, the modal title of the second respondent was HR Manager. We received second responses from a total of 33 of the sample firms. As described below, multiple survey responses from organizations were used to assess the reliability of the HR system measure.

Measures

Firm Productivity

As is common in the literature (Guthrie, 2001; Huselid, 1995; Koch & McGrath, 1996) firm productivity was operationalized as the ratio of firm sales to the number of employees. Data were obtained from Compustat. Given that productivity levels vary significantly across industries (even for industries within the manufacturing sector), it was important to control for these differences. Using a full set of industry codes as controls in our multivariate analyses is problematic because it leads to an unfavorable ratio of cases to predictor variables (Brace, Kemp & Snelgar, 2000). As an alternative, we collected productivity data on every firm in each of our sample firm's 3-digit SIC industries, calculated industry means and standard deviations, and used these values to compute productivity z-scores. The z-scores for our sample firms represent their relative standing within their respective 3-digit industry and serves as a direct control for industry productivity differences.

High Performance Work Practices (HPWPs)

Drawing upon previous empirical work (Guthrie, 2001; Huselid, 1995), the extent of a firm's use of HPWPs for exempt and non-exempt employees was measured by assessing the relative use of 18 practices. These practices included: intensive/extensive recruiting, hired on the basis of testing, use of internal promotions, use of performance (versus seniority) based promotions, receive performance feedback on a routine basis, receive multi-source performance feedback, use of skill-based pay, use of groupbased (gainsharing, profit-sharing) pay, intensive/extensive training in firm-specific skills, intensive/extensive training in generic skills, use of cross-training or cross-utilization, use of employee participatory programs, provided operating performance information, provided financial performance information, provided information on strategic plans, use of attitude surveys, use of teams and access to grievance system. Instead of clustering or categorizing firms into discrete typologies of industrial relations systems (e.g., Arthur, 1994), each firm's relative use of HPWPs was measured on a continuous scale. In this measurement approach, firms may vary in both the number of practices utilized and the extensiveness of employee coverage. In theory, organizations may range from those making no use of HPWPs to those using all of the practices for all employees. A high score on the HPWP measure indicates relatively intensive use and investment in high performance human resource practices; lower scores on this measure indicate less extensive use of HPWPs. Estimates of the proportion of each employee group (exempt and non-exempt) covered by each high involvement practice (0-100%) were obtained. Using the number of employees in each group, a weighted average for each practice was computed. The Cronbach's alpha for the composite HPWP scale was .78.

Scholars in the strategic HR literature, however, have debated the merits of relying on internal indices of reliability (such as Cronbach's alpha) to support the reliability of HR system measures. In the context of a broader discussion regarding the existence and implication of error in the measurement of firm-level systems of HR practices (e.g., Gerhart, 1999; Gerhart, Wright, McMahan & Snell, 2000; Huselid & Becker, 2000), questions have been raised about the reliability of "single resource organizational survey" based measurements of HR practices and systems. Because of these concerns, researchers have been urged to collect descriptions of HR practices from multiple informed organizational respondents and to estimate measurement reliability across these responses (Gerhart et al., 2000). Following this advice, we collected multiple responses (2 or 3) from a subset of firms (n = 33) contained in our sample. As a check on the reliability of our HR data, we calculated the inter-class correlation coefficient,

ICC(1), which can be conceptualized as the proportion of variance in a measure explained by group membership (Bryk & Raudenbush, 1992). As noted by Bliese (2000: 356), "when ICC(1) is large, a single rating from an individual is likely to provide a relatively reliable rating of the group mean; when ICC(1) is small, multiple ratings are necessary to provide reliable estimates of the group mean." For the HPWP scale, the ICC(1) value is .620 which, based on available standards (e.g., Bliese, 2000; Gerhart et al., 2000), would be characterized as "large" and supportive of an acceptable degree of agreement across raters.1

Industry Characteristics

Industry Capital Intensity was defined as the 3 year (1997- 1999) average ratio of fixed assets/sales for firms in each industry (in Compustat) at the 3-digit SIC level (Chang & Singh, 1999). Industry Growth was defined as the average annual growth rate in value of shipments in the five-year period 1992-97 based on the data available in the U.S. Census of Manufactures. This measure of industry growth has been widely used in the literature (Hambrick & Abrahamson, 1995; Rajagopalan & Datta, 1996). Following Haleblein and Finkelstein (1993) and Hambrick and Finkelstein (1987), Industry Product Differentiation was computed as a composite measure of industry R&D intensity and advertising intensity. Industry R&D intensity was measured as the three year (1997-99) average at the 3-digit SIC level, with R&D intensity for a given year being defined as the average ratios of R&D expenditures to total sales for all firms belonging to the sample firms' 3-digit SIC in Compustat (Baysinger & Hoskisson, 1989; Chang & Singh, 1999). Similarly, industry advertising intensity was operationalized as the three year average (1997-99) at the 3-digit SIC level, with advertising intensity for a given year being defined as the average ratio of advertising expenditures to total sales for all firms in the Compustat database within the 3-digit defined SIC industries. These two measures (industry R&D and advertising intensity) were standardized in z-score format (mean=0; s.d.=1) and averaged to yield a composite measure of industry product differentiation.

Control variables

Multivariate analyses controlled for firm size, firm growth, relative firm capital intensity and level of employee unionization. Firm size was operationalized as the natural logarithm of the number of employees (e.g., Dalton and Kesner, 1983; Guthrie, 2001) and firm sales growth was measured as the growth in firm sales over 1997-99. Relative firm capital intensity was defined as mean of firm capital intensity (fixed assets/sales) divided by industry capital intensity. These data were obtained from Compustat. Finally, the level of unionization, was operationalized as the proportion of a firm's workforce that was unionized. These data were obtained from survey responses.

DATA ANALYSIS AND RESULTS

Table 1 presents the means, standard deviations and zero-order correlations among all study variables. Average values and standard deviations on the measures of industry characteristics display reasonably high variance in the underlying sample, indicating that the sample does not reflect idiosyncratic industry conditions. Moreover, the modest inter-correlations among the independent variables reduce problems associated with multicollinearity. Further, it confirms the assumption that the underlying industry characteristics do not co-vary significantly and their effects need to be assessed independently. Also given a 15% response rate, we checked for possible non–response bias by comparing "late" versus "early" respondents along key study variables (first suggested by Oppenheim, 1966). The assumption behind this "time trend extrapolation test" (Armstrong & Overton, 1977) for non-response bias is that "late" respondents (those responses received after the second round of mailing and follow-up telephone calls) are very similar to non-respondents, given that they would have fallen into that category had not the second set of questionnaires been mailed. T-tests conducted showed no significant differences between the two groups (i.e., "early" versus "late" respondents) along any of the key study variables, namely, firm productivity, HPWPs, industry capital intensity, growth and product differentiation, attesting to the representativeness of the sample.

Table 1: Means and Correlation Coefficients

	Variables	Means	s.d.	1	2	3	4	5	6	7	8
1.	Firm Productivity	-0.19	0.66								
2	High Performance Work Practices	49.26	15.63	0.15							
3	Industry Capital Intensity	0.41	0.57	0.10	-0.11						
4.	Industry Growth	0.40	0.30	-0.08	0.04	-0.20					
5.	Industry Differentiation	-0.02	0.75	-0.06	0.15	-0.25	0.17				
6.	Firm Size	1.14	1.47	0.05	0.12	-0.20	-0.19	0.08			
7.	Firm Sales Growth	0.20	0.56	0.26	-0.06	-0.06	0.23	0.10	-0.02		
8.	Firm Unionization	16.35	26.33	-0.07	-0.11	-0.01	-0.10	-0.19	0.23	0.01	
9.	Firm Relative Capital Intensity	1.09	0.64	-0.05	0.09	0.02	-0.03	0.07	0.05	-0.23	-0.09

[a]Correlations greater than .14 are significant at $p < .10$, greater than .18 are significant at $p < .05$ and greater than .24 significant at $p < .05$

Given a continuous dependent variable (firm productivity) ordinary least squares regressions were used to test hypotheses 1-4. The first "main effects" model (Model 1) included the control and industry characteristics variables along with the HPWP measure. Models 2, 3 and 4 involve moderated regression models with the addition of the interaction effects (industry characteristics and HPWPs). The results of the OLS regressions are presented in Table 2.

The first overall conclusion that can be drawn from Table 2 is that high performance work practices (HPWPs) explains a significant portion of the variance in firm productivity after controlling for firm and direct industry effects ($p < 0.05$) This supports Hypothesis 1 and indicates that the use of high performance work practices is positively associated with firm productivity.

Table 2: Regression Results: HPWPs, Industry Characteristics and Firm Productivity

Variable	Model 1	Model 2	Model 3	Model 4
Intercept	-0.582*	-0.803*	-.139	-.649*
	(.252)	(.274)	(.361)	(.250)
High Performance Work Practices	.008*	.013**	-.002	.009*
	(.004)	(.005)	(.007)	(.004)
Industry Capital Intensity	.115	.535*	.092	.070
	(.094)	(.245)	(.109)	(.110)
Industry Growth	-.263	-.261	-.169*	-.249
	(.210)	(.207)	(.868)	(.207)
Industry Differentiation	-.086	-.083	-.081	-.664*
	(.084)	(.083)	(.083)	(.294)
Firm Size	.026**	.033	.035	.011
	(.043)	(.043)	(.043)	(.043)
Firm Sales Growth	.375***	.387***	.439***	.407***
	(.110)	(.109)	(.116)	(.110)
Firm Unionization	-.003	-.002	-.002	-.002
	(.002)	(.002)	(.002)	(.002)
Firm Relative Capital Intensity	-.003	.003	.046	-.009
	(.094)	(.093)	(.098)	(.093)
High Performance Work Practices X Ind. Capital Intensity		-.011*		
		(.006)		
High Performance Work Practices X Ind. Growth			-.028†	
			(.017)	
High Performance Work Practices X Ind. Differentiation				.011*
				(.005)
R^2	.147*	.175*	.169*	.179*
Change in R^2		.028	.022	.032

†$p < .10$; *$p < .05$; **$p < .01$; ***$p < .001$

The results associated with models 2-4 relate to the interaction effects of industry characteristics and the use of HPWPs, illustrating the impact of HPWPs on firm productivity under different industry conditions. Hypothesis 2(a) predicts that HPWPs will be more positively associated with firm productivity when industry capital intensity is low. To test this hypothesis we added the interaction of HPWPs and industry capital intensity to the base model. As evident from Model 2 of Table 2, this interaction term was significant in the regression model ($p < .05$), suggesting that industry capital intensity moderates the relationship between use of HPWPs and firm productivity. Using the procedure outlined by Aiken and West (1991), the plot of the interaction effects indicates that the relationship between HPWPs and firm productivity is relatively stronger when industry capital intensity diminishes. We conducted supplementary analyses using subgroups (displayed in Table 3) in which the sample was divided into two subgroups using the median spit on industry capital intensity. The OLS regression results for the two groups indicate that while there is a significant relationship between HPWPs and firm productivity in the low capital intensity subgroup ($p < .05$), no such relationship exists in the high capital intensity subgroup. These results, along with the moderated regression analysis findings, support Hypothesis 2(a).

Similarly, the interaction term involving industry growth and HPWPs in Model 3 indicates modest support ($p < .10$) for Hypothesis 2(b), which predicted that the relationship between HPWPs and firm productivity is moderated by industry growth. Again, plotting the interaction effects shows that the relationship between HPWPs and firm productivity is relatively stronger under circumstances of high industry growth. Further confirmation is provided by the results of our subgroup analysis (Table 3), which indicates that the relationship between HPWPs and firm productivity is significant in the high industry growth subgroup ($p < .05$) but not in the low industry growth subgroup.

Table 3: Sub-group regression results: firm productivity

Variables	Model 1 (Industry Capital Intensity)		Model 2 (Industry Growth)		Model 3 (Industry Differentiation)	
	High	**Low**	**High**	**Low**	**High**	**Low**
Intercept	-.169 (.363)	-.499[†] (.297)	-1.256[***] (.304)	-.301 (.317)	-1.167[**] (.337)	.150 (.345)
High Performance Work Practices	-.001 (.006)	.011[*] (.004)	.012[*] (.004)	.007 (.006)	.013[*] (.005)	.001 (.005)
Firm Size	-.026 (.071)	.071 (.051)	.026 (.052)	.011 (.066)	-.030 (.054)	.073 (.066)
Firm Sales Growth	.781[**] (.286)	.312[**] (.110)	.385[***] (.097)	.473[†] (.267)	.411[***] (.113)	.461 (.279)
Firm Unionization	-.005[†] (.003)	.001 (.003)	-.002 (.002)	-.003 (.003)	-.004 (.003)	-.001 (.002)
Firm Relative Capital Intensity	.274[†] (.156)	-.286[*] (.118)	.136 (.109)	-.137 (.127)	.175 (.115)	-.300[*] (.141)
Industry Capital Intensity			.598[*] (.289)	.025 (.137)	.405 (.421)	.109 (.118)
Industry Growth	-.419 (.295)	-.399 (.291)			-.155 (.227)	.590 (.391)
Industry Differentiation	-.112 (.112)	-.024 (.128)	-.054 (.094)	-.127 (.139)		
F	2.04[*]	3.27[**]	3.47[**]	1.06	3.12[**]	2.06[*]
R²	.237	.287	.327	.110	.300	.202

[†] $p < .10$, [*] $p < .05$, [**] $p < .01$, [***] $p < .001$

Finally, the significance ($p < .05$) of the regression coefficient associated with the interaction of industry product differentiation and HPWPs in Model 4 indicates that industry differentiation moderates the relationship between HPWPs and firm productivity. Plotting the interaction effects illustrates that the relationship between HPWPs and productivity is greater when industry differentiation is higher. Additional confirmation is available from the results of the subgroup analysis which indicates that the relationship between HPWPs and firm productivity is significant and positive in the high differentiation subgroup ($p < .05$) but not in the low differentiation subgroup. Thus, Hypothesis 2(c) is also supported.

DISCUSSION AND CONCLUSIONS

This analysis supports arguments and previous findings suggesting that firm competitiveness can be enhanced by utilizing high- performance work practices; (Arthur, 1994; Huselid, 1995; Koch & McGrath, 1996; Kochan & Osterman, 1994 Lawler, 1992; 1996; Levine, 1995; MacDuffie, 1995; Pfeffer, 1998). The primary contribution of this study, however, is to illustrate the potential for contextual conditions to moderate the relationship between HR systems and organizational effectiveness. Two primary perspectives, a universal approach and a contingency approach, have been used to model the link between HRM and firm effectiveness (Youndt, et al., 1996). The universal approach posits a direct relationship between "best practice" HRM and firm performance. In contrast, the contingency approach proposes that the effect of HRM on firm performance will depend on a firm's context or environmental exigencies.

Our results support the contingency perspective in that the characteristics of a firm's industry were shown to affect the impact of a system of high performance HR practices on firm productivity. We suggest that industry conditions affect the discretion available to employees (Hambrick & Finkelstein, 1987) or, in the words of Mischel (1977), the extent to which employees work in a "strong" versus a "weak" situation.

High discretion environments (i.e., "weaker" situations) magnify the potential for a firm's human resources -- the collective human and social capital of the workforce -- to impact organizational success. Specifically, study results indicate that three prominent industry features -- capital intensity, differentiation and growth -- influence the relative efficacy of high performance work systems. The moderated regression and sub-group analyses suggest that HPWPs display a stronger association with firm productivity in industries with lower capital intensity, greater differentiation or faster growth. These results should be interpreted cautiously given the limitations inherent in this study. A legitimate concern is the question of simultaneity. While data are analyzed and discussed as if the use of HPWPs affects firm productivity, this interpretation is limited by the cross-sectional nature of the data. Respondents completed surveys and described HR systems in place during calendar year 1999. Firm productivity data are also from 1999. Thus, while it is more plausible to argue that HR systems and management practices influence labor productivity, it is certainly possible that firms experiencing higher productivity are better positioned to invest in greater levels of HPWPs. A second concern is bias introduced by non-respondents; i.e., the persons and companies which did respond to the survey may differ significantly from those which did not. Again, while this threat cannot be dismissed, the time trend extrapolation test for non-response bias lessens this concern.

Within the limitations outlined above, this study supports the argument that industry conditions influence the impact of HR systems and human capital. Arguments proffered by authors such as Pfeffer (1998), Lawler (1996), Becker et al. (2001) and others are undoubtedly true in the main: The basis for competition in many industries and markets is changing such that the relative importance of "intangible assets" -- especially human capital -- is increasing.; and, as these trends continue, the strategic importance of utilizing sophisticated HR systems will likely magnify. However, as our results indicate, industry conditions do vary, and this variance influences the relative impact of HR on firm effectiveness. Much work remains in determining the pathways by which HPWPs affect employees' attitudes, behaviors and, in turn, the manner in which these individual-level measures affect organizational-level measures of success. We hope that academics and practitioners will find this study a meaningful contribution to the literature examining HRM and firm outcomes.

REFERENCES

1. Aiken, L. S., & West, S. G. 1991. Multiple Regression: Testing and Interpreting Interactions. Newbury Park, CA.: Sage.

2. Anderson, C.R. & Zeithaml, C.P. 1984. Stage of the product life cycle, business strategy, and business performance. Academy of Management Journal, 27: 5-24.

3. Armstrong, S.J. & Overton, T.S. 1977. Estimating nonresponse bias in mail surveys. Journal of Marketing Research, 14: 396-402.

4. Arthur, J.1992. The link between business strategy and industrial relations systems in American steel minimills. Industrial and Labor Relations Review, 45: 488-506.

5. Arthur, J. 1994. Effects of human resource systems on manufacturing performance and turnover. Academy of Management Journal, 37: 670-687.

6. Bain, J.S. & Qualls, P.D. 1987. Industrial Organization: A treatise. Greenwich, CT: JAI Press.

7. Barney, J. 1991. Firm resources and sustained competitive advantage. Journal of Management, 17:99-129.

8. Barrick, M.R & Mount, M.K.. 1993. Autonomy as a moderator of the relationship between the Big Five personality dimensions and job performance. Journal of Applied Psychology, 78: 111- 118.

9. Baysinger, B., & Hoskisson, R. E. 1989. Diversification strategy and R&D intensity in multiproduct firms. Academy of Management Journal, 32: 310-332.

10. Becker, B.E. & Huselid, M.A. 1998. High performance work systems and firm performance: A synthesis of research and managerial implications. In. K.M. Rowland & G.R. Ferris (eds). Research in Personnel and Human Resource Management, Greenwich, CT: JAI Press.

11. Becker, B.E., Huselid, M.A. & Ulrich, D. 2001. HR Scorecard, Boston: HBS Press.

12. Brace, N., Kemp, R. & Snelgar, R. 2000. SPSS for psychologists, London: MacMillan.

13. Bryk, A. & Raudenbush, S. 1992. Hierarchical Linear Models. Thousand Oaks, CA: Sage.

14. Burns, T. & Stalker, G.M. 1961. The Management of Innovation, London: Tavistock.

15. Chang, S.J. & Singh, H. 1999. The impact of modes of entry and resource fit on modes of exit by multibusiness firms. Strategic Management Journal, 20:1019-1035.

16. Dalton, D.R. & Kesner, I.F. 1983. Inside/outside succession and organizational size: The pragmatics of executive replacement. Academy of Management Journal, 26: 736-742.

17. Datta D.K. & Rajagopalan, N. 1998. Industry Structure and CEO Characteristics: An Empirical Study of Succession Events, Strategic Management Journal, 19:833-852.

18. Delery, J.E. & Doty, D.H. 1996. Theoretical frameworks in strategic human resource management: Universalistic, contingency and configurational perspectives. Academy of Management Journal, 39: 802-835.

19. Dess, G.G., Ireland, R.D. & Hitt. M.A. 1990. Industry effects and strategic management research. Journal of Management, 16: 7-27.

20. Donaldson, L. 1995. Contingency theory. Vol. 9 in D.S. Pugh (ed.), History of Management Thought. Aldershot: Dartmouth Press.

21. Dyer, L. & Reeves, T. 1995. Human resource strategies and firm performance: What do we know and where do we need to go? The International Journal of Human Resource Management, 6: 656-670

22. Gerhart, B. 1999. Human resource management and firm performance:

Measurement issues and their effect on causal and policy inferences. In P.M. Wright, L.D. Dyer, J.W. Boudreau & G.T.

23. Milkovich (Eds.), Research in Personnel and Human Resources Management, Supplement4 (pp. 31-51). Greenwich, CT: JAI Press.

24. Gerhart, B., Wright, P., McMahan, G. & Snell, S., 2000. Error in research on human resources and firm performance: How much error is there and how does it influence effect size estimates? Personnel Psychology, 803-834.

25. Ghemawat, P. 1991. Commitment: The dynamic of strategy. New York: Free Press.

26. Guthrie, J. P., 2001. High involvement work practices, turnover and productivity: Evidence from New Zealand. Academy of Management Journal, 44: 180-190.

27. Haleblian, J. & Finkelstein, S. 1993. Top management team size, CEO dominance, and firm performance: The moderating roles of environmental turbulence and discretion. Academy of Management Journal, 36: 844-863.

28. Hambrick, D.C. & Abrahamson, C. 1995. Assessing the amount of managerial discretion in different industries: A multi-method approach. Academy of Management Journal, 38: 1427-1441.

29. Hambrick, D. C. & Finkelstein, S. 1987. Managerial discretion: A bridge between polar views on organizations. In L. L. Cummings & B. M. Staw (eds.), Research in Organizational Behavior, 9: 369-406. Greenwich, CT: JAI Press.

30. Hambrick, D.C. & Lei, D. 1985. Toward an empirical prioritization of contingency variables for business strategy. Academy of Management Journal, 28: 763-788.

31. Hambrick, D.C. & Schecter, S.M. 1983. Turnarounds strategies for mature industrial-product business units. Academy of Management Journal, 26: 231-248.

32. Huselid, M.A. 1995. The impact of human resource management practices on turnover, productivity, and corporate financial performance. Academy of Management Journal, 38: 635-672.

33. Huselid, M.A. & Becker, B.E. 2000. Comment on "Measurement error on research on human resources and firm performance: How much error is there and does it influence effect size estimates", Personnel Psychology, 53: 835-854.

34. Ichniowski, Shaw & Prennushi. 1997. The Effects of Human Resource Management Practices on Productivity. American Economic Review, 86: 291-313.

35. Jackson, S.E. & Schuler, R.S. 1995. Understanding Human Resource Management in the Context of Organizations and Their Environments. Annual Review of Psychology, 46: 237-64.

36. Kast, F.E. & Rosenzweig, J. 1985. Organization and Management, 4th Ed. New York: McGraw-Hill.

37. Koch, M.J. & McGrath, R.G. 1996. Improving labor productivity: Human resource management policies do matter. Strategic Management Journal, 17: 335-354.

38. Kochan, T. & Osterman, P. 1994. The mutual gains enterprise. Boston, MA: Harvard Business School Press.

39. Lawler, E. 1992. The ultimate advantage: Creating the high-involvement organization. San Francisco:Jossey-Bass.

40. Lawler, E. 1996. From the Ground Up: Six Principles for Building the New Logic Corporation. San Francisco: Jossey-Bass.

41. Lee, M.B. & Johnson, N.B. 1998. Business environment, high-involvement management, and firm performance in Korea. In D. Lewin & B. Kaufman, B. (Eds.), Advances in Industrial and Labor Relations, Greenwich, CT: JAI Press, 67-87.

42. Lepak, D.P. & Snell, S.A. 1999. The human resource architecture: Toward a theory of human capital allocation and development. Academy of Management Review, 24: 31-48.

43. Levine, D. 1995. Reinventing the workplace: How business and employers can both win. Washington, DC: Brookings Institution.

44. Lieberson, S. & O'Connor, J.F. 1972. Leadership and organizational performance: A study of large corporations. American Sociological Review, 37: 117-130.

45. MacDuffie, J. 1995. Human resource bundles and manufacturing performance: Organizational logic and flexible production systems in the world auto industry. Industrial and Labor Relations Review, 48: 197-221.

46. Martell, M. & Carroll, S.J. 1995. How strategic is HRM? Human Resource Management, 34: 253- 267.

47. Miles, R.E. & Snow, C.C. 1978. Organizational strategy, structure and process. New York: McGrawHill.

48. Mischel, W. 1997. The interaction of person and situation. In D. Magnusson & N.S. Endler (Eds.), Personality at the crossroads: Current issues in interactional psychology, Hillsdale, NJ: Erlabum, 333-352.

49. Oppenheim, A.N. 1966. Questionnaire Design and Attitude Measurement. New York: Basic Books, Inc.

50. Pfeffer, J. 1994. Competitive advantage through people, Boston: MA: Harvard Business School Press.

51. Pfeffer, J. 1998. The human equation: Building profits by putting people first, Boston, MA: Harvard Business School Press.

52. Pfeffer, J. & Salancik, G. R. 1978. The external control of organizations: A resource dependence perspective. New York: Harper and Row.

53. Porter, M. E. 1980. Competitive strategy. New York: The Free Press.

54. Porter, M.E. 1985. Competitive advantage. New York: The Free Press.

55. Rajagopalan, N. & Datta, D.K. 1996. CEO Characteristics: Does Industry Matter?, Academy of Management Journal, 39:197-215.

56. Samuelson, P.A. & Nordhaus, W.D. 1989. Economics (13th ed.). New York: McGraw-Hill.

57. Scherer, F.M. 1980. Industrial market structure and economic performance. Second Edition, Boston: Houghton Mifflin.

58. Schuler, R. 1990. Human resource management: Transformation or demise? Academy of Management Executive, 4: 49-60.

59. Schuler, R.S. & Jackson, S.E. 1987. Linking competitive strategies with human resource management practices. Academy of Management Executive, 1: 207-219.

60. Schuler, R.S. & Jackson, S.E. 1989. Determinants of human resource management priorities and implications for industrial relations. Journal of Management, 15:89-99.

61. Sutton, R. 1991. Sunk cost and industry structure. Cambridge, MA: MIT Press.

62. Terpstra, D.E. & Rozzell, E.J. 1993. The relationship of staffing practices to organizational level measures of performance. Personnel Psychology, 46: 27-48.

63. Thompson, J. A. 1967. Organizations in action. New York: McGraw-Hill.

64. Weiss, H.M. & Adler, S. 1984. Personality and organizational behavior. In B.M. Staw & L.L. Cummings (Eds.), Research in organizational behavior (Vol. 6). Greenwich, CT: JAI Press, 1-50.

65. Wernerfelt, B. 1984. A resource-based view of the firm. Strategic Management Journal, 5:171-180.

66. Wright, P.M. & McMahan, G.C. 1992. Theoretical perspectives for strategic human resource management. Journal of Management, 18: 295-320.

67. Wright, P.M. & Snell, S.A. 1998. Toward a unifying framework for exploring fit and flexibility in strategic human resource management. Academy of Management Review, 23: 756-772.

68. Youndt, M. A., S. A. Snell, J. W. Dean, and D. P. Lepak. 1996. Human Resource Management, Manufacturing Strategy, and Firm Performance. Academy of Management Journal, 39: 836- 65.

HRM AND PERFORMANCE: WHAT'S NEXT?

Jaap Paauwe and Jean Paul Boselie

Erasmus University Rotterdam

ABSTRACT

The last decade of empirical research on the added value of human resource management (HRM), also known as the HRM and Performance debate, demonstrates evidence that 'HRM does matter' (Huselid, 1995; Guest, Michie, Conway and Sheehan, 2003; Wright, Gardner and Moynihan, 2003). Unfortunately, the relationships are often (statistically) weak and the results ambiguous. This paper reviews and attempts to extend the theoretical and methodological issues in the HRM and performance debate. Our aim is to build an agenda for future research in this area. After a brief overview of achievements to date, we proceed with the theoretical and methodological issues related to what constitutes HRM, what is meant by the concept of performance and what is the nature of the link between these two. In the final section, we make a plea for research designs starting from a multidimensional concept of performance, including the perceptions of employees, and building on the premise of HRM systems as an enabling device for a whole range of strategic options. This implies a reversal of the Strategy-HRM linkage.

Citation: Paauwe, J. & Boselie, J.P. (2004). HRM and Performance: What's Next? http://digital-commons.ilr.cornell.edu/intlvf/13/

INTRODUCTION

Empirical results on HRM and performance have been presented in a range of special issues of international academic journals like the Academy of Management Journal, the International Journal of Human Resource Management and the Human Resource Management Journal. The empirical results suggest the added value of HR interventions. However, there are still a number of unresolved issues. In 1997 Guest argued that there was a need for (1) theory on HRM, (2) theory on performance, and (3) theory on how the two are linked (Guest, 1997). Seven years later we observe only modest progress on those three fundamental issues. Boselie, Dietz and Boon (2005) conducted an exploratory analysis and overview of the linkages between human resource management and performance in 104 empirical articles published in prominent international refereed journals between 1994 and 2003. Their findings demonstrated a deficiency in the literature regarding alternative theories on the concept of HRM, the concept of performance, and on how the two are linked. Strategic contingency theory, AMO theoryii and the resource-based view appear to be the most popular theories applied in the 104 articles, but in most cases it is not clear how these theories link HRM and performance. Hence, we need to turn back to Guest's (1997) plea for theoretical foundation of HRM, performance and the link between the two and ask ourselves three questions:

- What is HRM?
- What is performance?
- What is the nature of the link between HRM and performance?

Based on these three headings/questions we will be able to categorize the still unresolved issues and explore possible avenues for research in the future.

WHAT IS HRM?

Under the heading of this clear - but apparently difficult to answer - question we deal with the following issues: the lack of consensus with respect to the constituent parts of HRM; the best practice versus the best fit approach; the different fits; coverage of different employee groups; and the need to consider how HR practices are perceived.

Lack of Consensus

There appears to be no consensus on the nature of HRM. Some studies focus on the effectiveness of the HR department (Teo, 2002), others focus on the value of human resources in terms of knowledge, skills and competencies (Hitt, Bierman, Shimizu and Kochhar, 2001), several studies define HRM in terms of individual practices (Batt, 2002) or systems/bundles of practices (Capelli and Neumark, 2001), and yet others acknowledge the impact of these practices or systems on both the human capital value – in terms of knowledge, skills and abilities – and on employee behaviour directly in terms of higher motivation, increased satisfaction, less absence and increases in productivity (Wright, McMahan and McWilliams, 1994). We observe that the majority of the studies define HRM in terms of HR practices or systems/bundles of practices.

Boselie et al. (2005) show the enormous variety of different practices being used in the 104 analysed articles. There is not one fixed list of generally applicable HR practices or systems of practices that define or construct human resource management. In total they are able to list 26 (!) different practices, of which the top four- in order- are training and development, contingent pay and reward schemes, performance management (including appraisal) and careful recruitment and selection. These four practices can be seen to reflect the main objectives of the majority of 'strategic' HRM programmes (e.g., Batt, 2002): namely, to identify and recruit strong performers, provide them with the abilities and confidence to work effectively, monitor their progress toward the required performance targets, and reward staff well for meeting or exceeding them. Another issue is that even if we use the same concepts, the underlying meaning of the practice can be totally different. This begs the question, how can a field of academic inquiry ever manage to make progress if it is not able to come to terms with one if its central concepts? Using content analysis Boselie et al. (2005) found that among the three most often used theoretical frameworks, the AMO-framework is the only one used in more than half of all articles published after 2000. In contrast, for the papers using strategic contingency theory and RBV, more than half of them were published before 2000. So we may be witnessing the birth of at least a certain commonality around how HRM might be constituted in exploring the relationship between HRM and Performance.

Best practice vs. best fit

One of the key discussions within HRM is the distinction between the so-called best practice and the best-fit approaches. Some say there are universalistic best practices in HRM (Pfeffer, 1994), others argue that there are only best-fit practices (Wood, 1999), stating that the effect of HR practices depends on the specific (internal and external) context. It seems logical to believe in a best-fit approach in contrast to a somewhat simplistic best practice approach, but the empirical evidence still supports the best practice approach (Delery and Doty, 1996). Gerhart (2004) demonstrates a critical analysis of those who claim that some form of internal fit – the alignment of practices with each other – outperforms the lack of this type of fit. Gerhart's (2004) evaluation is very convincing in showing that the systems approaches that build on the notion of internal fit do not outperform the other approaches in which individual HR practices are not aligned.

Boxall and Purcell (2003) argue that both streams – best practice and best-fit– might be right each in their own way. Some basic principles like employee development, employee involvement and high rewards are universally successful, but the actual design of the HR practice depends to some degree on unique organizational contexts. The internal context - for example, the nature of the production system (e.g., assembly line) - might create restrictions with respect to the successful design of some HR practices (e.g., teamwork, performance related pay), but also the external context - for example, the legislation and trade union influence - might have a direct impact on the optimal HRM design. So the whole debate about universalistic best practices versus best-fit practices actually represents two sides of the same coin and both are relevant in exploring the linkage between HRM and Performance.

Different fits Wood (1999) makes a distinction between four different 'fits': internal fit, organizational fit, strategic fit and environmental fit. Although this is in line with what many other researchers consider to be the possible range of fits in HRM research, one of the most important seems to be missing. That is, the fit between how the employee perceives HR practices and whether that perception aligns with the values and goals of the organization. That kind of fit is well known under the heading of Person-Organiza- tion fit (P-O fit), which Kristof (1996) defines as the compatibility between people and organizations that occurs when: (a) at least one entity provides what the other needs, or (b) they share similar fundamental characteristics, or (c) both. A number of authors in the field of HRM and Performance emphasize the importance of including workers' perceptions. As Van den Berg and colleagues note (1999: 302), 'an organisation may have an abundance of written policies concerning [HRM], and top management may even believe it is practised, but these policies and beliefs are meaningless until the individual perceives them as something important to her or his organisational 'well- being'. Wright and Boswell, (2002: 263) also note that in measuring HRM, it is vital to distinguish between policies and practices. The former is the organisation's stated intentions regarding its various 'employee management activities', whereas the latter are the actual, functioning, observable activities, as experienced by employees. This is yet another plea to pay more attention to workers' perceptions and the importance of person-organisation fit. This theme will recur in our final section when we discuss the importance of the strength of the HRM system (Bowen and Ostroff, 2004).

Coverage of different employee groups

If we look more closely at the conceptualization and operationalization of HR practices or systems of practices we observe little or no attention to the degree of coverage of HRM –differentiation between employee groups and the percentage of employees covered by the practices – and the intensity of HRM in terms of, for example, daily, weekly, monthly or yearly interventions. Most prior research either uses simplistic scales focusing on the application (or lack thereof) of a specific practice (Guest et al., 2003) or some kind of scale that is supposed to capture the 'degree to which the target group has to do with' a specific practice (Huselid, 1995).

The early empirical studies on HRM mainly used the input of single respondents, in most cases the input from HR managers (Huselid, 1995). Gerhart et al. (2000) demonstrate the low inter-rater reliability between employees, line managers and HR managers. This is an interesting and highly relevant notion, but at the same time difficult to solve since these empirical results demonstrate fundamental differences between employee groups within an organization. These results suggest that different employee groups have fundamentally different priorities and needs, something that should be taken into account in future research. Lepak and Snell (2002) argue that HR differentiation towards specific employee groups is necessary for overall effectiveness. The classification of employee groups within an organization depends on factors like the nature of their jobs (e.g., production, technical support, administration, management), their professional backgrounds (e.g., level of education, degree of professionalization of the occupation) and needs and wants of individuals (e.g., degree of employment security, need for challenging tasks).

To make life even more complicated Wright and Nishii (2004) build a strong argument to make a clear distinction between intended HR practices (those designed on a strategic level), actual – or implemented – HR practices (those implemented by for example the direct supervisor), and perceived HR practices (those perceived by the employees). The majority of prior research on HRM and performance appears to focus on intended HR practices, mainly designed at the strategic level of the organization. Little is known about the actual enactment or implementation of HR practices and employees' perception of them.

WHAT IS PERFORMANCE?

In this section we pay attention to the variety of performance indicators used in empirical research, the distinction between shareholder and stakeholder approaches, and the kind of implication it has for our understanding of the concept of performance.

Measuring Performance

The performance outcomes of HRM can be captured in a variety of ways. We draw a distinction, adapted from Dyer and Reeves (1995), between:

1. Financial outcomes (e.g., profits; sales; market share; Tobin's q; GRATE)
2. Organisational outcomes (e.g., output measures such as productivity; quality; efficiencies)
3. HR-related outcomes (e.g., attitudinal and behavioural impacts among employees, such as satisfaction, commitment, and intention to quit)

Based on the overview by Boselie et al. (2005) we can conclude that financial measures are represented in half of all articles (104) included in their analysis. Profit is the most common followed by various measures for sales. Actually, this is quite problematic as financial indicators are being influenced by a whole range of factors (both internal and external), which have nothing to do with employees and their related skills or human capital. As already noted by Kanfer (1994) and Guest (1997) the distance between some of the performance indicators (e.g., profits, market value) and HR interventions is simply too large and potentially subject to other business interventions (e.g., research and development activities, marketing strategies). For example, having smart policies for managing working capital can increase earnings substantially, but have nothing to do with the proclaimed effect of HR practices (apart from apparently having selected the right treasury manager). The use of these kind of indicators becomes even more serious if we take a closer look at an analysis carried out by Wright et al. (in press) as summarized by Wright and Haggerty (2005). Their literature review identified 67 empirical studies, which analyzed the relationship between HR practices and performance. By far the majority of studies used a design labelled post-predictive because "……. it measures HR practices after the performance period, resulting in those practices actually predicting past performance" (Wright and Haggerty, 2005:8). Only a few studies explored the effect of HR practices on performance in the correct way by assessing HR practices at one point in time and relating them to subsequent performance. This simply means that the majority of studies have ignored a very basic rule for demonstrating causal relationships (Wright and Haggerty, 2005).

Shareholder vs. stakeholder approach to performance

The use of financial indicators emphasizes a shareholders' approach to the concept of performance, emphasizing that HR practices and systems contribute a sustained competitive advantage through enhancing skills and human capital. This assumes that organizations can maintain or create sustained competitive advantage through unique/rare, scarce, inimitable, and valuable internal resources (Barney, 1991). Human resources are a powerful potential internal resource that fits this general resource based view idea (Paauwe, 1994; Wright et al., 1994; Boxall and Purcell, 2003). The next step in the theory is that employees or human resources are manageable (manoeuvrable) and developmental. In other words, HR practices can (a) increase the value of the human capital pool through development (e.g., skills training, general training, job rotation, coaching) and (b) influence employee behaviour in the desired direction. The search for the Holy Grail in HRM is the search for those 'best practices' or 'best-fit practices' that ultimately result in sustained competitive advantage of the organization. This can only take place if employees are willing to stay within the organization. Thus, employee commitment in terms of willingness to stay with the firm and willingness to put in extra effort are very important in this context. This is probably why research in the area of HRM and performance is becoming more interested in creating high commitment work environments through HR practices or high involvement – high performance work practices (HIWP's and HPWP's). The high involvement – high performance work practices perspective (See also AMO-model) can thus be seen as an extension of the resource based view.

The aforementioned also implies that we have to look for more proximal instead of distal indicators of performance. Both organisational outcomes and HR related outcomes can be considered more proximal and thus more suited towards measuring performance. However, in this shareholders' approach the organisational and HR related outcomes are still considered to be a means to an end, i.e., contributing to bottom-line performance of the firm. Such a financial meaning can be criticized for being "too limited" (Truss, 2001: 1123).

The stakeholders' approach offers a different perspective by emphasizing the objectives of other constituencies with an interest in HRM practices and subsequent performance of an organization. This approach can be traced back to the seminal writings of Beer et al. (1984). More recently we encounter full support for this approach by, amongst others, Boxall and Purcell, (2003: 13), who define three important goals of HRM, among which social legitimacy aimed at bringing about employment citizenship, and Paauwe (2004). The latter argues that the survival of an organization not only depends on financial competitiveness, but also on its ability to legitimize its existence towards society and relevant stakeholders of the organization (e.g., employees, customers, trade unions, local government). Legitimacy is an important concept for sustainability on an organizational level, but also the organization's role towards the individual employee and his or her moral values are important: the concept of fairness. If the relationship between the employer and the individual employee is out of balance - for example, in the case of increased performance pressures without fair pay - employees might feel they are being exploited, resulting in low commitment levels towards the organization (Paauwe, 2004).

Performance as a multidimensional concept Using a stakeholders' perspective implies that authors (Truss, 2001; Guest and Peccei, 1994) are in favour of using multiple measures of performance in order to do justice to the multiple goals of HRM and to the different parties involved, both inside and outside the firm. So, on the one hand we have the more strategic aspect of performance (based on economic rationality), which emphasizes outcomes such as labour productivity, innovation, quality, efficiency gains and flexibility (Boselie et al., 2005) and on the other hand the more societal aspect of performance (based on relational or normative rationality) emphasizing legitimacy and fairness (Paauwe, 2004). The latter two can be operationalized through indicators like OCB, commitment, trust, perceived security, and perceived fairness.

What is the nature of the relationship between HRM and performance? The most crucial part in our overview of issues relating to the HRM and performance debate is of course the linkage between the two, here we concentrate on the following topics: the nature of the linkage, the relevance and non-relevance of strategy, the importance of the institutional context and arising conflicting demands, the need for multi-level analysis, and how to cope with reverse causality

The nature of the linkage

Wright and Gardner (2003) question how many boxes should be taken into account when studying the HRM - performance linkage. Becker, Huselid, Pickus and Spratt's (1997) 13 model incorporates 7 boxes, starting with 'business and strategic initiatives' and finishing with 'market value'. In their model the design of the HRM system is derived from the overall business strategy (See Figure 1).

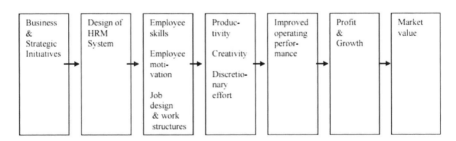

Figure 1: Conceptual model of Becker, Huselid, Pickus and Spratt

Guest's (1997) model has 6 boxes, starting with a Porter-like strategy typology – distinguishing differentiation/innovation, focus/quality and cost reduction oriented HRM strategies – and ending with the financial outcomes return on investment (ROI) and profits. Again, the HR practices are derived from the overall strategy (See Figure 2).

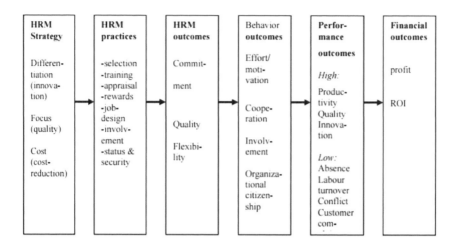

Figure 2: Conceptual model of Guest.

Appelbaum et al.'s (2000) AMO-model links 3 boxes. The first box covers high performance work systems and comprises: (1) ability/skills (e.g., formal and informal training, education), (2) motivation/incentives (e.g., employment security, information sharing, internal promotion opportunities, fair payment, PRP) and (3) opportunity to participate (e.g., autonomy, team membership, communication). The second box consists of effective discretionary effort and the final box reflects the plant performance (e.g., quality and throughput time, labour cost per unit of output, operating profit). See Figure 3 for a visual representation of their model.

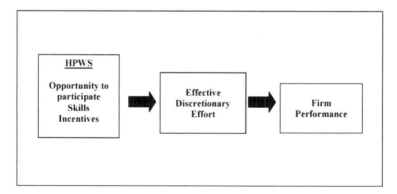

Figure 3: Conceptual model of Appelbaum, Bailey, Berg and Kalleberg

To study the effects of HR interventions, either multiple individual HR practices or systems/bundles of practices, it is preferable to use outcome variables that are closely linked to these interventions, for example: attitudinal outcomes (e.g., employee satisfaction, motivation, commitment, trust), behavioural outcome (e.g., employee turnover, absence), productivity (output per unit effort), and quality of services or products. As stated before, there is little or no convincing empirical evidence that coherent and consistent systems or bundles automatically lead to higher performance (Gerhart, 2004). This theoretical claim is built on the notion of internal or horizontal 'fit'. But there is another proposition that affects the HRM - performance relationship, at least in theory: the notion of external or vertical/strategic 'fit'. The underlying idea is that matching the overall company strategy with the HR strategy or system will result in increased performance. In this respect it is striking that the framework by Appelbaum et al. (2000), being the most commonly used and depicted above, does not take strategy as a starting point, whereas the other two do so. So it is worthwhile to take a closer look at the (non)relevance of including strategy in the chain of linkages.

The (Non) Relevance Of Strategy

Many authors and popular textbooks in HRM mention the importance of the link between corporate strategy and HRM. Unfortunately, there is no convincing empirical evidence for this proposition (Purcell, 2004). Huselid (1995), for example, does not find any empirical evidence for increased performance when aligning the overall company strategy with the HR system of a specific organization. There are several plausible explanations for this lack of evidence of the presumed necessary strategic fit.

First, strategy is often defined in a rather old-fashioned and relatively simplistic Porterlike manner, such as differentiation/innovation, focus/quality and cost reduction. Organizational reality is much more complicated and not easy to capture in a simple 'three-piece suit'. The Porter-like definitions of the 1980s are rather static and do not take into account the possibility of hybrid strategies or combinations of strategies that companies might use, serving different markets at the same time. For this reason Purcell (2004) argues that instead of trying to define a firm's strategy in terms of differentiation, focus or cost reduction it is much more interesting to try and determine "...how the firm will deploy its resources within its environment and so satisfy its long-term goals, and how to organise itself to implement that strategy (Grant, 2002: 13)". Incidentally, this is a more up to date definition of what strategic management nowadays entails/ encompasses (see Grant, 2005:19). Second, both Gerhart (2004) and Purcell (2004) underline the complexity of management research in large companies, in particular multinational companies (MNC's). Often, these large companies are conglomerations of strategic business units, each serving its own markets, customers and products/ services. Therefore, Gerhart (2004) states that there are fewer reliability problems with analysis at the plant or unit level.

Third, there is no convincing theory or strong empirical evidence on the possible time-lag between a change in strategy, any subsequent HR intervention and performance. The few studies on HRM and performance that take a longitudinal perspective (Paauwe, 1989; d'Arcimoles, 1997; Guest et al., 2003), suggest that the majority of HR interventions have a long term effect on performance, sometimes taking up to two or three years before generating effects. Some HRM practices (e.g., individual performance related pay) might have a direct, short-term effect on performance (e.g., productivity), but most other practices (e.g., training and development, participation, teamwork, decentralization) probably have little effect in the short-run or (worst case scenario) fail to have any effect. Wright, Dyer and Takla (1999) asked 70 HR managers to assume that a major strategic change necessitated a significant overhaul of their firm's HRM systems and were asked to estimate the time it would take to design HR systems for delivery and implementation (Wright and Haggerty, 2005). Their answers were in the range of nine to ten months for the design and an additional ten to twelve months for the delivery, and then we still need to add further months before the changed HR systems start to affect subsequent performance.

Fourth, a whole range of factors other than strategy influence subsequent HRM strategy. Based on an overview of the strategic management literature and its relevance for the HRM/Performance relationship, Paauwe (2004) refers to the following: the role of the entrepreneur, often also the founder and owner with his or her preferences for HRM policies and practices; difference in cognitive processes of the participants involved in the strategy making process, which can give rise to different mental maps and different choices (see also Purcell, 2004); power relationships and the kind of resources being controlled by the actors involved, which can give rise to non-strategic choices in HRM policies and practices; culture and ideologies of the actors involved, which will also affect the kind of choices in HRM; and, finally environmental and institutional forces, stemming from trade unions and tripartite or bipartite consultative bodies (government, trade unions, employers' federations), which can have a large impact upon an organization's HRM strategy (see below).

Because of this, questions arise about the supposedly dominant role of corporate strategy in defining subsequent HRM strategy. We cannot define strategy with a specific meaning, the field of strategic management itself has shifted to more internal organisational and implementation issues, empirical evidence is lacking and other factors also play a significant role. So, in the final section of this paper, we downplay the influence of corporate or business strategy on HRM strategy, and instead make a strong plea for regarding HRM policies and practices as an enabler for a whole range of strategic options (Paauwe, 2004: 99).

Institutional embeddedness and conflicting demands

Paauwe and Boselie (2003) argue that as organizations are embedded in a wider institutional context this plays a role in shaping HRM practices and policies. Institutional mechanisms (e.g., legislation with respect to conditions of employment, collective bargaining agreements, employment security, trade union influence, employee representation) shape employment relationships and HR decision making in

organizations. Paauwe (2004), for example, argues that most of Pfeffer's (1994) best practices (e.g., high wages, employment security, employee participation) are institutionalized in a country like the Netherlands. Most of these best practices are formalized and institutionalized through collective bargaining agreements. Some industries, for example, prescribe a minimum amount to be spent on training by every organization each year, defined in terms of a fixed percentage of the total labour costs. This formalization might also have an effect on employees' perception of these institutionalized practices. Pension schemes, for example, are collectively arranged in the Netherlands, mainly on industry level. Pension schemes are probably not considered to be employee benefits and best practices in the Dutch context, as this would be in a country like the USA. Another example is the best practice labelled wage compression. The typical Dutch egalitarian culture (e.g., relatively low power distance, aim for marginal differences between population groups in terms of prosperity) is reflected in collective wage compression through a strong progressive tax system in which employees with high incomes pay relatively more tax than those with lower incomes.

Paauwe (2004) acknowledges institutional differences at both a country level, for example the US versus the Netherlands, and at an industry level, for example traditional branches of industry such as the metal industry and the construction building industry versus emerging branches of industry such as the ICT industry. Institutional mechanisms (mimetic, normative and/or coercive) affect the relationship between HRM and performance and should therefore be taken into account in future research (Paauwe and Boselie, 2003). Moreover, they also draw our attention to the possibility of conflicting demands. HRM theorisation is dominated by a unitarist perspective, but starting from a more institutional perspective our eyes are opened to conflicting demands between professionals, managers, and different occupational groupings that are represented by their interest groups outside the organisation (e.g., professional associations, trade unions, etc). Also the practices themselves might give rise to conflicting outcomes in terms of increased productivity, which managers will appreciate, and increased levels of stress, which workers will probably dislike. Labour intensification through increased employee participation, decentralization, and emphasis on performance management (practices that can be seen as high performance work practices) might create competitive advantage in terms of financial performance, but the individual worker might experience increased levels of stress and anxiety (Legge, 1995). We have to take into account conflicting HRoutcomes in future research on HRM and performance.

Multi-level analysis

Prior research on HRM and performance has been mainly focused on organizational level analysis. Wright and Boswell (2002) stress the importance of blending research on the individual employee level (typical OB studies) with research at the organizational level (typical SHRM studies). Multi-level theories seek to explain simultaneous variance at multiple levels of analysis (Bowen and Ostroff, 2004). Multilevel analysis is simply inevitable when looking at the sequence of boxes that reflect the HRM and performance linkage (Guest, 1997; Becker et al, 1997; Appelbaum et al, 2000). The boxes in the existing conceptual models implicitly reflect analyses at different levels of the organization. If we want to know more about, for example, intended HR practices we have to look at the job or employee group level, according to Wright and Nishii (2004), while if we want to know more about how these practices are perceived by employees we are in need of data at the individual employee level. Employee behaviour (e.g., employee turnover, absence) and organizational performance (e.g., productivity, quality) can be determined at employee group level in some cases and at plant unit level, while financial performance indicators are probably exclusively available at plant or company level.

Reverse causality

Paauwe and Richardson (1997) observe the risk of overlooking the possibility of reverse causality in linking HRM and performance. The most obvious form of reverse causality can be illustrated by the following examples. First, organizations with high profits might reveal a higher willingness to invest in HRM (e.g., profit sharing schemes, training and development) than those that are less successful financially. Second, in times of national or regional economic crisis organizations might have a tendency to recruit less - or in some cases no - new employees and restrict, for example, training and development expenditures. The cross-sectional nature of the majority of research on HRM and performance makes it impossible to rule out these types of reverse causality. But there are other potential forms of reverse causality (Den Hartog, Boselie and Paauwe, 2004). High firm performance outcomes (e.g., high profits, market growth) might have a positive effect on employee satisfaction and commitment. Most people enjoy being part of 'a winning team' and high firm performance also signals organizational health and thus employment security. In a longitudinal study Schneider, Hanges, Smith and Salvaggio (2003), for example, find that profitability is more likely to cause job satisfaction than job satisfaction is to cause profitability. Longitudinal research is important for determining the real effects of HRM interventions on performance.

Challenges for future research

A number of conclusions can be drawn from this overview of research issues. Related to the concept of HRM we see convergence arising around AMO theory and the associated set of HR practices. The discussion on best practice versus best fit is an artificial one and is highly dependent on our own perspective at the 'surface (context specific)' or at the 'underpinning (generic)' level (Boxall and Purcell, 2003:69). The range of fits analysed in HRM-research needs to be supplemented by the Person-Organization fit in order to include perceptions of workers and to be able to differentiate between employee groups. In measuring performance there should be a clearer focus on more proximal outcomes and research design should allow for the analysis of HR-practices and outcomes in the right temporal order (causes should precede effects). Just defining performance in its contribution to bottom-line financial performance does not do justice to the various actors (both inside and outside the organization) involved in either the shaping of HRM practices or affected by it. It is better to opt for a stakeholders' approach, which also implies opting for a multi-dimensional concept of performance. Along with corporate or business strategy, a whole range of other factors play a role in shaping the relationship between HRM and performance, among which the institutional context is critical. Finally, we have emphasized the need for multi-level analysis and that more attention should be paid to the possibility of reverse causality.

So, in the process of discussing a whole range of issues we have made a number of choices, which we think are highly relevant. However, is that enough? Does that justify the title 'HRM: What's next'? Will it take the field forward or is more needed? Below, we point out two (highly interrelated) topics that need further exploration.

1. HRM as an enabling device for a whole range of strategic options (critical goals):

The Balanced HR perspective Boxall and Purcell (2003: 7) build a framework for goal-setting and evaluation in HRM and start by "positing two broad goals for business firms": (1) viability with adequate returns to shareholders and (2) sustained competitive advantage or consistent and superior profitability, the latter representing an ultimate goal beyond the (first) survival goal. In their model these ultimate business goals can be achieved by meeting critical HR goals (increased labour productivity, organisational flexibility, and social legitimacy) and critical non-HR goals (e.g. sales, market share). In previous analysis of HRM and performance most attention has been paid to the cost-effectiveness element as the ultimate HR goal, specifically 'financial performance outcomes' (Boselie et al., 2005). We are in need for a more balanced perspective (e.g. Deephouse, 1999), taking into account both the cost-effectiveness HR goal (represented by labour productivity and product/service quality), the organisational flexibility urgency, and the social legitimacy dimension. In a longitudinal study of commercial banks Deephouse (1999) finds empirical support for strategic balance theory, which states that moderately differentiated firms – with a balance between an institutional/legitimate focus and a market focus have higher performance than either highly conforming (emphasis on the institutional/legitimate dimension) or highly differentiated firms (emphasis on the market/economic dimension). Strategic balance theory acknowledges the relevance of both market competition, represented by labour productivity and flexibility in the framework of Boxall and Purcell (2003), and social legitimacy for firms seeking competitive advantage. Until now little attention has been paid to the two critical HR goals of flexibility and legitimacy. These two might turn out to be important for a more realist perspective in future HR research.

First, based on the increased dynamics of the market place and the occurrence of organizational change within companies as the new status quo, the goals of strategic HRM systems (should) also encompass flexibility (Boxall and Purcell, 2003) and agility (Dyer and Shafer, 1999). Dominated by both resource based and knowledge based views of the firm, researchers in the field of strategic management increasingly emphasize topics like absorptive capacity, knowledge management and the need for organisations being able at the same time to respond to issues of exploitation and exploration. In fact, the latest trend in the range of popular work systems (after 'lean and mean', and 'high performance - high involvement') seems to be the creation of the 'agile' organization. Agility is described as focussing on customer rather than market needs, mass customization rather than mass or lean production (Sharp et al., 1999). Agility entails more than just the production system. It is a holistic approach incorporating technical (the operational system as emphasized by Boxall, 2004) information and human resource considerations. In essence, an agile organisation (see Dyer and Shafer, 1999) implies a very fast and efficient adaptive learning organisation, encouraging multi-skilling, empowerment and reconfigurable teams and work designs. Under such a system, HRM practices focus particularly on employee development, the encouragement of learning and knowledge management. So, if we have managed to create a workforce which is eager to learn, displays a willingness to change, is adaptive, flexible, etc., then we have developed through our HRM systems the kind of knowledge, skills and abilities upon which we can realize a whole range of strategic options (Paauwe, 2004). Cost effectiveness (or labour productivity) and organisational flexibility (or agility) mainly represent the employer's perspective and do not fully take into account the employee's perspective and the societal dimension. Therefore, the third critical HR goal in Boxall and Purcell's (2003) basic framework is equally important for this proposed 'balanced HR perspective': social legitimacy. This brings us to the second issue.

Second, creating a cost-effective and agile organisation is possible once we recognise that employees should be treated fairly. The overall HRM system should be based upon added value (cost effectiveness and flexibility) and moral values (social legitimacy and fairness towards individuals), both economic and relational rationality (Deephouse, 1999). The latter refers to establishing sustainable and trustworthy relationships with both internal and external stakeholders, based on criteria of fairness and legitimacy (Paauwe, 2004). Failing to meet objectives of legitimacy and fairness can lead to perceived injustice by those involved (e.g. employees, managers, works council representatives, trade union officers) and affect both employee behaviour and social relations within an organisation. "People care deeply about being treated fairly... the evidence suggests that people can and do distinguish their own absolute outcomes for two key dimensions of justice: distributive, or how they did relative to others; and procedural, the process by which the outcome was achieved (Baron and Kreps, 1999: 106)." The meta-analytical review of organizational justice by Colquitt, Conlon, Wesson, Porter and Ng (2001) shows unique positive effects of perceived justice (both procedural and distributive) on job satisfaction, organizational commitment, employee trust and OCB underlining the relevance of fairness and legitimacy in organizations. Meeting the criteria of relational rationality in essence implies that managers need to 'treat their people well'.

So, the signals communicated through HR practices by line managers must be clear /distinct, consistent, and uniformly applied. Employees must not discern a lack of clarity, a lack of consistency and a lack of consensus. This brings us to the importance of the strength of the HRM system (Bowen and Ostroff, 2004).

2. The strength of the HRM system

Bowen and Ostroff (2004) are extremely interested in the relationship between HRM and performance, and while accepting the evidence that HRM can indeed make a difference they still wonder through which process this occurs. In order to answer that question they develop 'a framework for understanding how HRM practices as a system can contribute to firm performance by motivating employees to adopt desired attitudes and behaviours that, in the collective, help achieve the organization's strategic goals' (Bowen and Ostroff, 2004: 204). A crucial linkage in the relationship between HRM and performance is their focus on organisational climate, which they define as 'a shared perception of what the organization is like in terms of practices, policies and procedures, routines and rewards, what is important and what behaviours are expected and rewarded (Bowen and Ostroff, 2004: 205; referring to Jones and James, 1979 and Schneider, 2000). The concept helps them to develop a higher order social structure perspective on the HRM – firm performance relationship, which Ferris et al. (1998) call social context theory views of the relationship between HRM and Performance. They apply this kind of theorizing to HRM by emphasizing the importance of processes as well as content of HRM.

By process, Bowen and Ostroff refer to 'how the HRM system can be designed and administered effectively by defining metafeatures of an overall HRM system that can create strong situations in the form of shared meaning about the content that might ultimately lead to organisational performance' (2004:206). These metafeatures ensure that unambiguous messages are sent to employees that result in a shared construction of the meaning of the situation. So they concentrate on understanding what features of the HRM process can lead employees to appropriately interpret and respond to the information conveyed in HRM practices. In this way they apply the concept of strong situations to the so-called strength of the HRM system, which is a linking mechanism that builds shared, collective perceptions, attitudes and behaviours among employees. Characteristics like distinctiveness, consistency and consensus are key process features. Distinctiveness is built by HR practices, messages, signals that display a large degree of visibility, understandability, legitimacy and relevance. Here we see the connection with the importance of values alignment and Person-Organisation fit. Individual employees must perceive the situation as relevant to their own goals, which should be fostered in such a way that they can be aligned to those of the organization. Of course, a strong climate or strong HRM system might run the risk of being rigid. However, as Bowen and Ostroff (2004:215) correctly remark, if the process of HRM emphasises a strong climate including elements that focus on flexibility, innovation and willingness to change, then employees will sense and share the idea that adaptability and agility is expected of them.

Final remarks

We are convinced that progress in understanding the relationship between HRM and performance can be achieved by taking into account all the points made so far. However, that kind of progress will be piece-meal. Consequently, real progress can only be made by looking at the broader picture of developments in the field of strategic management, the speed of change within companies and what this implies for managing people and stakeholders. How can we achieve flexibility, agility and what is needed in terms of value alignment at the various levels of analysis? We need to look beyond practices such as staffing and the management of human resource flows. These are the kinds of hygiene factors, which if not delivered cost-effectively will lead to underperformance of the organisation. A real contribution to performance (in its multidimensional meaning) will only happen once we approach HRM from a more holistic and balanced perspective, including part of the organizational climate and culture, aimed at bringing about the alignment between individual values, corporate values and societal values. This will be a unique blending for each organization, which is difficult to grasp by outsiders (including competitors) and thus contributes to sustained competitive advantage[iii].

REFERENCES

1.   Appelbaum, E., Bailey, T., Berg, P. and Kalleberg, A. 2000. Manufacturing advantage: why high-performance work systems pay off. Ithaca: Cornell

University Press.

2. d'Arcimoles, C.H. 1997. Human resource policies and company performance: a quantitative approach using longitudinal data, Organization Studies, 18(5): 857-74.

3. Barney, J.B. 1991. Firm resources and sustainable competitive advantage. Journal of Management, 17: 99-120.

4. Baron, J.N. and Kreps, D.M. (1999) Strategic human resources: Frameworks for general manager. New York: John Wiley.

5. Batt, R. 2002. Managing customer services: Human resource practices, quit rates, and sales growth. Academy of Management Journal, 45(3): 587-97.

6. Becker, B.E., Huselid, M.A., Pickus, P.S. and Spratt, M.F. 1997. HR as a source of shareholder value: research and recommendations. Human Resource Management, 36: 39-47

7. Beer, M., Spector, B., Lawrence, P.R., Mills, D.Q. and Walton, R.E. 1984. Managing human assets. New York: Free Press

8. Boselie, P., Dietz, G. and Boon, C. 2005. Commonalities and contradictions in research on Human Resource Management and Performance. Human Resource Management Journal (forthcoming)

9. Bowen, D.E. and Ostroff, C. 2004. Understanding HRM-Firm Performance linkages: The role of the "strength" of the HRM system, Academy of Management Review, 29(2): 203-221

10. Boxall, P. and Purcell, J. 2003. Strategy and human resource management, London: Palgrave Macmillan.

11. Cappelli, P and Neumark, D. 2001. Do 'high-performance work practices improve establishment-level outcomes? Industrial and Labor Relations Review. 54(4): 737-775.

12. Colquitt, J.A., Conlon, D.E., Wesson, M.J., Porter, C.O.L.H. and Ng, K.Y. 2001. Justice at the millennium: A meta-analytic review of 25 years of organizational justice research, Journal of Applied Psychology, 86(3): 425-445.

13. Deephouse, D.L. 1999. To be different, or be the same? It's a question (and Theory) of strategic balance, Strategic Management Journal, 20: 147-166.

14. Delery, J.E. and Doty, D.H. 1996. Modes of theorizing in strategic human resource management: tests of universalistic, contingency, and configurational performance predictions. Academy of Management Journal, 39: 802-835.

15. Dyer, L. and Reeves, T. 1995. Human resource strategies and firm performance: what do we know, where do we need to go? The International Journal of Human Resource Management, 6: 656-670.

16. Dyer, L and Shafer, R.A. 1999. From human resource strategy to organizational effectiveness: lessons from research on organizational agility. Research in Personnel and Human Resource Management, 4: 145-174.

17. Ferris, G.R., Arthur, M.M., Berkson, H.M., Kaplan, D.M., Harrel-Cook, G.,

and Frink, D.D. 1998. Toward a social context theory of the human resource management-organization effectiveness relationship. Human Resource Management Review, 8 235-264.

18. Gerhart, B., Wright, P.M. and McMahan, G. 2000. Measurement error in research on the human resource and firm performance relationship: further evidence and analysis. Personnel Psychology, 53: 855-872.

19. Gerhart, B. 2004. Research on human resources and effectiveness: selected methodological challenges. Working paper presented at the International seminar on HRM:What's Next? Organized by the Erasmus University Rotterdam, June 2004.

20. Grant, R. 2002. Contemporary strategic analysis: Concepts, techniques, applications. 4th edition, Malden, MA, Blackwell Publishers.

21. Grant, R. 2005. Contemporary strategy analysis. 5th edition, Malden, MA, Blackwell Publishers.

22. Guest, D.E. and Peccei, R. 1994. The nature and causes of effective human resource Management. British Journal of Industrial Relations, 32: 219-241.

23. Guest, D.E. 1997. Human resource management and performance: a review and research agenda. The International Journal of Human Resource Management, 8: 263-276.

24. Guest, D.E., Michie, J., Conway, N. and Sheehan, M. 2003. Human resource management and corporate performance in the UK. British Journal of Industrial Relations. 41(2): 291-314.

25. Guthrie, J.P. 2001. High-involvement work practices, turnover, and productivity: evidence from New Zealand. Academy of Management Journal, 44: 180-190.

26. Hartog, D.N. den, Boselie, P., and Paauwe, J. 2004. Future directions in performance management, Applied Psychology: an International Review, 53(4): 556-569.

27. Hitt, M.A., Bierman, L., Shimizu, K., and Kochhar, R. 2001. Direct and moderating effects of human capital on strategy and performance in professional service firms: A resource-based perspective. Academy of Management Journal, 44(1): 13- 28.

28. Huselid, M.A. 1995. The impact of human resource management practices on turnover, productivity, and corporate financial Performance. Academy of Management Journal, 38: 635-672.

29. Jones, A.P. and James, L.R. 1979. Psychological climate: Dimensions and relationships of individual and aggregated work environment perceptions. Organizational Behavior and Human Decision Processes, 23: 201-250

30. Kanfer, R. 1994. Work motivation: new directions in theory and research, p.158-188, in: C.L. Cooper and I.T. Robertson (eds.) (1994) Key reviews in managerial psychology. New York: Wiley.

31. Kristof, A.L. 1996. Person-organization fit: An integrative review of its

conceptualizations, measurement, and implications. Personnel Psychology, 49: 1- 49.

32.   Legge, K. (1995). Human resource management, rhetorics and realities. London: MacMillan Business.

33.   Lepak, D.P. and Snell, S.A. 2002. Examining the human resource architecture: The relationship among human capital, employment, and human resource configurations. Journal of Management. 28:4, 517-43.

34.   Paauwe, J. 1989. Sociaal ondernemingsbeleid: tussen dwang en ambities. Dissertatie, Alphen aan den Rijn: Samson Bedrijfsinformatie.

35.   Paauwe, J. 1994. Organiseren: een grensoverschrijdende passie. Oratie, Alphen aan den Rijn: Samson Bedrijfsinformatie. Paauwe, J. and Richardson, R. 1997. Introduction special issue on HRM and Performance. The International Journal of Human Resource Management, 8: 257-262.

36.   Paauwe, J. and Boselie, P. 2003. Challenging 'strategic HRM' and the relevance of the institutional setting. Human Resource Management Journal, 13(3): 56-70. Paauwe, J. 2004. HRM and Performance: unique approaches for achieving long term viability. Oxford: Oxford University Press.

37.   Pfeffer, J. 1994. Competitive advantage through people. Boston: Harvard Business School Press.

38.   Purcell, J. 2004. Business strategies and human resource management: Uneasy bedfellows or strategic partners? Working paper presented at the International seminar on HRM: What's Next? Organized by the Erasmus University Rotterdam, June 2004

39.   Schneider, B. 2000. The psychological life of organizations. In: N.M. Ashkanasy, C.P.M. Wilderom and M.F. Peterson (Eds.). Handbook of organizational culture and climate: xvii-xxii. Thousand Oaks, CA: Sage.

40.   Schneider, B., Hanges, P.J., Smith, B. and Salvaggio, A.N. 2003. Which comes first: employee attitudes or organizational financial and market performance. Journal of Applied Psychology, 88: 836-851.

41.   Sharp, J.M., Irani, Z. and Desai, S. 1999. Working towards agile manufacturing in the UK industry. International Journal of Production Economics, 62 (1/2), 155-169.

42.   Teo, S.T.T. 2002. Effectiveness of a corporate HR department in an Australian public sector entity during commercialization and corporatization. The International Journal of Human Resource Management, 13(1): 89-105.

43.   Truss, C. 2001. Complexities and controversies in linking HRM with organizational outcomes. Journal of Management Studies, 38(8): 1121-1149.

44.   Van den Berg, R.J., Richardson, H.A. and Eastman, L.J. (1999). 'The impact of high involvement work processes on organizational effectiveness'. Group and Organisation Management, 24:3, 300-339.

45.   Wood, S. 1999. Human resource management and performance. International Journal of Management Reviews, 1: 367-413.

46. Wright, P.M., McMahan, G.C. and McWilliams, A. 1994. Human resources and sustained competitive advantage: a resource-based perspective. The International Journal of Human Resource Management, 5: 301-326.

47. Wright, P.M., Dyer, L.D. and Takla, M.G. 1999. What's next? Key findings from the 1999 State of the art & practice study. Human Resource Planning, 22(4), 12-20.

48. Wright, P.M. and Boswell, W.R. 2002. Desegregating HRM: a review and synthesis of micro and macro human resource management research. Journal of Management, 28(3): 247-276.

49. Wright, P.M., Gardner, T.M. and Moynihan, L.M. 2003. The impact of HR practices on the performance of business units. Human Resource Management Journal, 13(3): 21-36.

50. Wright, P.M. and Gardner, T.M. 2003. Theoretical and empirical challenges in 34 studying the HR practice – firm performance relationship. In: D. Holman, T.D. Wall, C. Clegg, P. Sparrow and H. Howard (eds.), The new workplace: people technology, and organisation. Sussex, UK, John Wiley and Sons.

51. Wright, P.M. and Nishii, L.H. 2004. Strategic HRM and organizational behaviour: integrating multiple levels of analysis. Working paper presented at the International seminar on HRM: What's Next? Organized by the Erasmus University Rotterdam, June 2004.

52. Wright, P., Gardner, T., Moynihan, L. and Allan, M. (2005, in press). The HR – Performance relationship: examining causal direction. Personnel Psychology.

53. Wright, P.M. and Haggerty, J.J. 2005. Missing variables in theories of strategic human resource management: time, cause and individuals. Working Paper Series 05-03. CAHRS, Cornell University.

HUMAN RESOURCE PRACTICES AND ORGANIZATIONAL COMMITMENT: A DEEPER EXAMINATION

Patrick M. Wright and Rebecca R. Kehoe

Department of Human Resource Studies Center for Advanced Human Resource Studies (CAHRS) School of ILR Cornell University

In a world increasingly characterized by globalization of product markets, the importance of human capital as a resource that can potentially provide competitive advantage has become more important. Because a firm's people are integral to its success, researchers interested in managing human capital have increasingly focused on HR practices as the levers through which firms might build the human capital that makes up resources and capabilities. The fact that HR practices are related to firm performance has been well documented. Substantial research on the HR Practices performance relationship has demonstrated that HR practices are related to a number of firm performance measures such as Market Value (i.e., Tobin's Q) (Huselid, 1995), Return on Equity (Delery and Doty, 1996), and operational measures of performance (MacDuffie, 1995). While the literature establishing an HR – performance relationship is substantial, what is lacking is empirical research examining the mechanisms through which this relationship works (Wright & Gardner, 2003). Authors have referred to this as the "black box" problem, and many have called for more theory and research on the mediating mechanisms through which HR practices influence organizational performance (Becker and Gerhart, 1996). A recent stream of thinking in this area has focused on the ways in which HR practices can elicit organizational commitment from employees, a construct which is argued to impact their motivation and desire to stay with the firm. However, recent advances have been made in the conceptualizations of both HR practices and organizational

Citation: Wright, P. M. & Kehoe, R. R. (2007). Human resource practices and organizational commitment: A deeper examination, http://digitalcommons.ilr.cornell.edu/cahrswp/

commitment. The purpose of this chapter is to provide a more detailed analysis of the link between HR practices and organizational commitment.

HR PRACTICES AND ORGANIZATIONAL COMMITMENT

A plethora of research exists examining the relationship between HR practices and performance. Such research has been conducted at the corporate (e.g., Huselid), business unit (e.g., Wright, Gardner, and Moynihan, 2003) and department level (e.g.,). Studies have examined multiple industries (e.g, Guthrie, 2001), within a single industry (e.g., MacDuffie, 1995) or even within a single corporation (Wright et al., 2003). While the observed effect sizes may differ across studies, qualitative reviews of this literature conclude that in almost all cases HR practices are found to be at least weakly related to performance (Boselie, Dietz, & Boon, 2005; Wright, Gardner, Moynihan, & Allen, 2005). This conclusion is supported by a recent meta-analysis concluding that the mean effect size for the HR – performance relationship is approximately .14 (Combs, Ketchen, Hall, & Liu, 2006) implying that a one standard deviation increase in the use of high-performance work systems is associated with a 4.6% increase in return on assets. However, these empirical results tie HR practices to distal performance measures, without measuring more proximal outcomes.

In an early review of the HRM – performance literature, Dyer and Reeves (1995) posited 4 levels of outcomes of HRM practices—employee, organizational, financial, and market— suggesting that the impact of HRM is likely to work outward through these levels. Employee outcomes consist of affective reactions such as satisfaction and commitment as well as behavioral reactions such as absenteeism and turnover. Organizational outcomes focus primarily on operational performance measures such as quality, productivity, and customer satisfaction. Financial outcomes, such as accounting profits, represent the next step in their causal chain. Finally, market outcomes consist of measures of the market value of firms based on stock price.

Becker et al. (1997) similarly argued that HRM practices operate most directly through employee skills, motivation, and work design, resulting in behavioral outcomes such as creativity, productivity, and discretionary effort, which are expected to work through operational and eventually through financial market outcomes. Hence, in order to assess the most immediate consequences of an HRM system, Becker et al. (1997) and Dyer and Reeves (1995) would suggest examining employee outcomes as they are predicted to be affected most directly.

More recently, Wright and Nishii (2006) offered further justification for examining outcomes of HRM below the organizational level. Specifically, these authors argued that, while most of the research to date has focused on the links between business level HRM practices and performance, the theoretical explanations offered for these relationships cross multiple levels of analysis, including individuals and job groups. For instance, the authors argued that HRM practices are largely implemented at the job group level (i.e., different jobs have different practices within a business unit). In addition, individuals within jobs may perceive and react (both affectively and behaviorally) differently to the same practices. These individual level reactions are both influenced by others in the job group and aggregated back to job group level outcomes. Finally, the performance of different job groups aggregates to affect business unit performance. Most importantly, however, Wright and Nishii noted that empirical research has focused only on the business unit linkages between practices and performance, and has virtually ignored the lower level mechanisms through which these linkages are purported to occur. Usually in discussions of the most proximal employee outcomes researchers mention or focus on the construct of organizational commitment.

Several researchers have examined the relationships between HRM practices and organizational commitment. For example, in an individual-level analysis, Paul and Anantharaman's (2004) study of software professionals showed that HRM practices had a significant positive relationship with organizational commitment. HRM systems have also been found to relate to commitment in samples of frontline employees from car rental, retail, and hospitality organizations in South America (Browning, 2006). Payne and Huffman (2005) found in a longitudinal study that organizational commitment mediated the relationship between mentoring, an HRM practice in the organization studied, and employee turnover over time. In a unit-level study, Wright, Gardner, & Moynihan (2003) found a positive relationship between HRM practices and organizational commitment in a study of 50 business units from a large food service corporation.

Three basic themes emerge from much of the work tying HR practices to organizational commitment. First, these empirical and conceptual analyses focus on the concept of commitment, most often organizational commitment. Different conceptualizations of organizational commitment have been used in the literature. However, perhaps most important with regard to HRM practices is the concept of affective organizational commitment. This type of commitment refers to a positive affection toward the organization, reflected in a desire to see the organization succeed in its goals and a feeling of pride at being part of the organization (Cohen, 2003). While affective commitment to the firm may be one interesting conceptualization of commitment, it may also be a limited one. However, recent advances in examining the concept of commitment may lead to a more complex treatment of the construct (Klein, Morrow, and Brinsfield, in press).

Second, these attempts to examine the impact of HR practices on organizational commitment as a precursor to their impact on firm performance assume a simple, unidimensional, view of the HR practices. Normally the HR practices are measured with a multiitem scale (e.g., Wright et al., 2005). However, support for a more complex treatment of HR practices (relative to a unidimensional scale of "high commitment" practices) has been emerging in the SHRM literature (Gardner, Moynihan, & Wright, 2007).

Finally, these treatments seem to assume and look for a universally positive set of relationships (HR practices positively impact commitment, and commitment positively impacts performance.) However, given the increasing complexity of conceptualizations of HR practices and commitment, such an assumption may be misleading. Juxtaposing these more complete and complex views of these constructs may lead us to a better understanding of how HR practices can positively (or negatively) impact firm performance. In order to do so, we will first examine the more recent conceptualizations of commitment, then the more recent conceptualizations of HR practices. These examinations will enable us to explore more complex ways in which these constructs might interact to impact firm performance.

CURRENT CONCEPTUALIZATIONS OF ORGANIZATIONAL COMMITMENT

While the concept of commitment has a long history within the organizational literature (Becker, 1960) as frequently noted (e.g., Meyer & Allen, 1991; Mowday, Porter, & Steers, 1982; Reichers, 1985; Stebbins, 1970), commitment is inconsistently defined both within and across the various workplace commitments. This can be traced to several factors such as the different perspectives (e.g., economic, behavioral, psychological) from which researchers have studied commitment and the fact that several early writers defined commitment in multiple ways, as having multiple bases, or as being characterized by multiple indicators.

For instance, Porter, Steers, Mowday and Boulian (1974) defined organizational commitment as the strength of an individual's identification with and involvement in a particular organization but then further stated that commitment is characterized by three factors (a) a belief in and acceptance of goals and values, (b) a willingness to exert effort, and (c) a strong desire to maintain membership. In their review of the workplace commitment literature, Klein, Morrow and Brinsfield (in press) defined commitment as an individual's perception that they are bound to a given target. This definition depicts commitment as attachment rather than a force. They note that defining commitment as a perceived bond rather than a force more clearly (a) distinguishes commitment from its antecedents, (b) places commitment within the individual, and (c) recognizes the considerable variance in how individuals make sense of their environment (James & Mazerolle, 2002; Weick, 1995). Their examination of commitment posits three aspects that are relevant to this paper: the elements of commitment, the outcomes of commitment, and competing commitments.

Elements of Commitment

They pose three distinct elements of commitment that need to be distinguished. First, the commitment target refers to the foci or object to which one is committed. An individual can be simultaneously committed to a wide variety of different targets but the commitment construct is essentially the same regardless of the target. In addition, we assert that different workplace targets are not facets or dimensions that underlie a global commitment construct in a hierarchical structure (e.g., Bagozzi & Edwards, 1998). Research has demonstrated that employees can be highly committed to some workplace targets and not others (e.g., Becker & Billings, 1993).

Commitments to different workplace targets need not be highly related (e.g., one could be committed to their job, but not the organization), although spillover between different targets is possible (e.g., commitment to a supervisor can impact commitment to the organization).

Second, commitment strength reflects the intensity or degree to which someone is committed to a target. According to Klein et al's (in press) conceptualization, commitment is (a) dynamic but can be relatively stable, (b) not necessarily consciously perceived or intentional, and (c) socially constructed within the individual. Unlike a multidimensional view, commitment strength is singular: one can be committed to multiple targets but commitment strength has the same singular meaning regardless of the target.

Third, commitment rationales are the multiple possible self-explanations a person can hold for their commitment to a given target, i.e., how one makes sense of or rationalizes their commitment. According to Klein et al. (in press), an individual can have multiple rationales for a particular commitment, those rationales can change over time, and may be conscious or unconscious. Commitment rationales are in some ways analogous to attributions. Attributions are not the performance itself but are the individual's self-explanation for why they performed the way they did (Weiner, 1985). Similar to attributions, commitment rationales may not reflect the "objective" antecedents of commitment, yet those rationales still determine the individual's reactions and responses.

It is clear that there can be multiple rationales, but the exact number and structure of distinct rationales is indeterminate from the literature. Although research has generally supported Allen and Meyer's (1990) framework there have been numerous exceptions supporting alternative models (Meyer & Herscovitch, 2001). Furthermore, the various bases of commitment underlying most frameworks are rooted in research conducted nearly fifty years ago. Just as Brief (1998) questioned whether the facets of job satisfaction might have changed in relevance over time, the types and importance of rationales for workplace commitments have likely changed given the considerable changes in the nature of work and the employment relationship. Determining the precise configuration of distinct commitment rationales is both a conceptual and an empirical question that cannot be resolved here.

Commitment Outcomes

The first category of commitment outcomes identified by Klein et al. concerned affect, or the emotions, positive or negative, that one feels towards a target. They argue that the nature of the affective response depends upon the commitment rationale. The second general outcome category they identified was continuance, or the unwillingness to withdraw from the target. Both intentions and behaviors are included in this category. Continuance is not necessarily indefinite but instead implies the expected duration of the association. For instance, with the organization as the target, commitment has been shown to relate to turnover, absenteeism, and tardiness (e.g., Mathieu & Zajac, 1990). Finally, motivation outcomes include both the willingness to exert effort in support of the target and persistence in maintaining that effort over time. Commitment to an organization involves a willingness to exert effort in support of that organization, group, or person. The specific nature of the effort (e.g., in-role vs. extra-role, minimal vs. optimal) depends on both commitment rationales and strength.

Competing Commitments

A final contribution that Klein et al make is specifically recognizing multiple commitments. They note that individuals have multiple commitments within the workplace (e.g., Simon, Smithburg, & Thompson, 1950) as well as to other institutions outside of work (e.g., family, professional and social organizations, political parties, religious organizations) (Morrow, 1983; Reichers, 1985). While the capacity for an individual to form commitments across targets may be boundless, there are limits on an individual's resources (e.g., time, emotion, attention) (Kanfer & Ackerman, 1989; Naylor, Pritchard, & Ilgen, 1980). Multiple commitments need not be in conflict (Randall, 1988) particularly when the different targets have compatible demands (Angle & Perry, 1986). However, competing commitments can both inhibit commitment strength or impede a commitment leading to the expected consequences.

Implications

These elements, outcomes, and competing commitments ideas have implications for how HR practices might impact commitment. First, while most of the research has focused on the organization as the target of commitment, one could conceive of other targets both that might be impacted by HR practices and that might subsequently impact performance. For instance, commitment to goals, to the job, to the supervisor, or to the workgroup might play as significant a role as commitment to the organization. This suggests a broader view of the potential commitments that could be impacted by HR practices and that might be related to firm performance. Second, the concept of rationales recognizes that people make sense of the HR practices they experience, and this sensemaking may influence their response in terms of commitment. For instance, Wright and Nishii (2006) developed a multilevel model of the impact of HR practices on performance and noted that individuals must perceive, interpret, and react to those practices, and that information processing will be largely influenced by their past experiences. For instance, individuals who have worked for employers that attempted to exploit them might interpret a new employer's gain sharing or profit sharing program as simply one more way to exploit the workforce. On the other hand, an employee who came from a positive previous work experience might interpret the same programs as an altruistic way in which the firm wants to share its success with employees. Similarly, with regard to commitment, one highly paid employee may attribute his/her desire to remain as a function of a lack of alternatives where they could make as much money. Thus, the outcomes may be affective resentment, high continuance, and low motivation. On the other hand, another might feel obligated to stay because the firm has chosen to pay them so well. His/her outcomes might be affective appreciation, high continuance, and high motivation. Clearly the attribution for commitment can vary within the same HR practice experience.

Finally, multiple commitments implies that even when HR practices elicit the organizational commitment desired, the outcomes may not be observed if they conflict with other commitments. An individual can be highly committed to an organization, but a commitment to a family may supersede the commitment to the firm. For instance, an EVPHR at a brand name firm recently resigned his position. When asked about it, he said that it was hard because he had finally found the company with the right values and a CEO who had the right personality to create a job he loved. However, due to a family tragedy, he needed to move his family away; in essence he described a family commitment that got in the way of his organizational commitment.

Having examined commitment, we will now turn our attention to conceptualizations of HR practices.

HRM PRACTICE BUNDLES AND PERFORMANCE

Most SHRM scholars agree that systems or bundles of HRM practices are required for organizations to achieve sustained performance results (Delery & Shaw, 2001; MacDuffie, 1995). HRM practice bundles include generally complete sets of mutually reinforcing or synergistic practices (Dyer & Reeves, 1995). SHRM scholars have argued that systems of HRM practices are more likely to drive sustainable performance outcomes than are individual practices. For example, Dyer and Reeves (1995) argued that employee performance is likely to be greatest when its two components, ability and motivation, are influenced in multiple, redundant ways. Specifically, the authors suggested that performance is likely to be maximized when several reinforcing practices—such as rigorous selection mechanisms and ample training opportunities—elicit required employee skills, and many incentives—such as peer pressure to perform and monetary and non-monetary rewards—increase employee motivation. Additionally, Delery and Shaw (2001) noted that, while certain individual HRM practices are viewed as superior to others, a single superior HRM practice without other supporting practices in the system is inadequate as a driver of sustainable performance outcomes. Rather, the authors argue, individual "best practices" must be part of a larger, universally superior HRM system to support sustainable success.

Researchers have consistently demonstrated an association between what have been variously called High Performance Work Systems, High Commitment HRM models, and High Involvement HRM systems and firm financial performance. While the specific HR practices included in these commitment-based systems have varied across studies, these "best practice" models share certain defining characteristics. In particular, these models typically include performance-based compensation schemes which reward group and organization-level performance outcomes and provide opportunities for employees to participate in organizational decision making (Arthur, 1992). Employee development, reward, and retention plans encourage long-term employment relationships and often promote strong internal labor markets, regular team-focused assignments, and an emphasis on firm-specific knowledge (Arthur, 1992; Tsui, Pearce, Porter, & Tripoli, 1997). Past research in HR practices has often operationalized the HR system as a single scale of HR practices (Guthrie, 2001, Datta Guthrie & Wright, 2001) or sometimes an empirically derived multidimensional scale (e.g., Huselid, 1995). However, a number of SHRM researchers have noted that human resource systems can be described along three common dimensions {Appelbaum et al. 2000; Delery 1998; Dyer & Holder 1988; Lepak et al., 2005}. First is the degree of investment in HR practices intended to improve the knowledge, skills and abilities of the companies' employees. These include recruiting, training, selection, socialization, and any other practice functioning to enhance the workplace competencies of the employees. Such practices seek to build specific relevant skills, or increase the level of those skills among the focal human capital group. With regard to capabilities, this category of practices can aim to ensure that the organization has the skills and skill levels required by those employee key to the execution of business processes.

The second dimension is the degree of investment in HR practices functioning to motivate employee behavior. In general, HR practices can seek to elicit task related behavior (that necessary to perform the basic job), encourage employees to exhibit discretionary behavior (i.e., go outside the expected job behaviors to positively impact organizational effectiveness), or to discourage counterproductive behavior (actions that negatively impact the firm such as theft, sabotage, etc.) Practices such as incentive pay plans, performance bonuses, gainsharing, and performance management systems primarily aim at managing employee behavior. Because business processes require certain behaviors of key employee groups, one focus of the HR system has to be on eliciting the positive behaviors and inhibiting the negative ones.

Finally, HR practices function to provide opportunities to participate in substantive decision-making regarding work and organizational outcomes. These include such practices as quality circles, suggestion systems, granting discretion and authority on the job, information sharing about the service or production process, and opportunities to communicate with employees and managers in other workgroups. This is one area where differentiation may be seen across a variety of business processes. For instance, Starbucks, the outstanding coffee retailer, seeks operational excellence in the processes used to make a cup of coffee. A number of training programs teach specific procedures for exactly how much of each ingredient should be used, in what order, etc. In these processes there is little opportunity for employees to deviate from the prescribed behavior. However, in terms of serving customers, Starbucks employees have great latitude to deviate from prescribed behavior, or share ideas and suggestions for certain aspects of the operation.

While the practice can be subcategorized within the AMO framework, Lepak et al., (2005) note that the framework does not preclude overlap among the practices. For instance, training programs primarily may aim at building the requisite skill base, but may also communicate a commitment to the employee that elicits motivation as well. Similarly, participation programs provide opportunity, but may also help build the knowledge and motivation of employees.

This more complex treatment of HR practices seems both theoretically justified and empirically more fruitful. For instance, Gardner, Moynihan, and Wright (2007) found that the motivation and opportunity focused bundles of HR practices positively related to affective commitment and negatively related to turnover. However, skill oriented practices were unrelated to affective commitment and positively related to turnover. Adding complexity to the HR practice measures provides a deeper understanding of their impact.

Each of the three dimensions of HR practices can be expected to have unique effects on commitment. Motivation enhancing practices should positively influence commitment, and result in motivational outcomes. Consistent with the perceived organizational support arguments, incentives and other rewards-for-performance practices signal a positive valuation of employee efforts thus increasing reciprocal commitment (Meyer and Allen, 1997; Rhoades et al., 2001). Additionally, Klein's (1987) extrinsic satisfaction model suggests that financial rewards designed to increase commitment to work outcomes align employee interests with the organizations resulting in greater commitment to the organization. However, these practices may not impact continuance outcomes unless the pay is at a level that would require employees to take a pay cut if they left.

Secondly, empowerment enhancing practices are expected to have a positive impact on organizational commitment, and probably impact the affect, motivation, and continuance outcomes. Organizations that allow employee input into decisions, share information, and treat employees with respect strengthen shared perceptions of congruence between employee and organizational values, integrate employees into the life of the firm, and increases employees' identification with the firm thus enhancing commitment (Arthur, 1994; Long, 1980; Meyer and Herscovitch, 2001). Additionally, the teamwork and social interactions inherent in empowering HR practices function to accelerate the A-S-A process while simultaneously creating a sense of community, thus strengthening the forces of social cohesion among group members and thus the commitment to the organization (Morrison, 2002; Osterman, 1995).

Finally, skill enhancing practices may have no, or even a negative impact on commitment, particularly on the continuance outcomes. While training investments may increase employees' perceptions that the organization values their current and future contributions and thus their level of commitment (Meyer and Allen, 1997; Tannenbaum et al., 1991), they also may increase the marketability of those employees. Human capital theory and the March and Simon (1958) ease-of-movement framework suggest that HR practices that improve the knowledge, skills, and abilities of the employees flowing into and within the organization would result in increased aggregate voluntary turnover (Benson, et al. 2004; Oatey 1970; Williamson, et al. 1975). Trevor (2001) defined the set of individual attributes that enhance employees' ability to secure employment outside of their employing organizations as 'movement capital.' These attributes include task specific abilities, productivity, education, cognitive abilities, and general skills. Trevor's (2001) research complements March and Simon's (1958) work on ease of movement by demonstrating that employees with greater movement capital are more likely to leave their employing organization for another employer.

However, even the AMO framework may be deficient, mainly in that it largely ignores certain practices, particularly those that do not fit well within the framework. For instance, stock options, a compensation scheme that has increased in popularity over the past few decades (particularly in the U.S.) may encourage recipients to stay in the short term as departure results in forfeiting the options. However, after the options have vested, and particularly if they have resulted in substantial wealth accrual, they may enable the recipient the ability to leave the firm. In fact, during the 1990's Microsoft found a disproportionate level of turnover among employees who had been with the company between 7 and 10 years, the time at which they were able to exercise a large number (and value) of options.

In addition, while many of the HR practice scales contain items such as "promotion from within" policies, such policies can vary substantially. For instance, unionized, seniority based pay and promotion systems would qualify as a "promote from within" policy, but such policies may have very different effects on commitment and commitment outcomes. One need look no further that the U.S. Airline industry, where seniority based systems virtually preclude movement from one airline to another. Having engaged in cutbacks in salaries and benefits, these airlines have created workforces with commitment outcomes of low affect, low motivation, but unfortunately, high continuance.

IMPLICATIONS AND CONCLUSIONS

As noted previously, researchers on the HR and firm performance relationship have increasingly called for research on the "black box," or more proximal mediators of this relationship. Much attention within this realm has focused on organizational commitment as one such potential mediator. However, recent conceptualizations of HR practices and commitment call for a more nuanced approach to studying this relationship.

Klein et al.'s (in press) conceptualization of commitment as an individual's perception that they are bound to a given target certainly focuses on the psychological process through which employees form such perceptions. Bowen and Ostroff (2004) argued that HR practices serve as communications mechanisms to employees, and these communications must be interpreted through each individual's personal lens (Wright & Nishii, 2006). Again, the concept of rationales, or attributions focuses attention on individual differences in reactions to the same sets of HR practices.

Separating the commitment construct from the outcomes of affect, continuance, and motivation outcomes may seem to be theoretical nitpicking. However, it focuses research attention on the variety of outcomes that can be observed, and considering these outcomes with different HR practice sub-bundles leads to better understanding of the impact that each subbundle can have. Rather than focus on laundry lists of "high commitment" or "high performance" HR practices, the AMO approach enables a more theoretically specific understanding of the relationships between HR practices and organizational commitment.

In addition, as noted before, much of the previous research focused only on the affective commitment measure, which tended to include items that might reflect continuance commitment (e.g., "I would turn down a job with more money to stay with this organization.") This newer conceptualization of commitment might suggest developing more specific and more comprehensive measures of commitment outcomes to ensure that each category is adequately covered.

Finally, this analysis suggests that in order to truly understand how HR practices impact firm performance, we must measure all the practices, not just those we think are "high commitment" or "high performance" ones. While the AMO framework provides more specificity than the unidimensional scale (Delery, 1998; Delery and Shaw, 2001; Lepak et al., 2005) it still seems to only assess practices that are deemed to have strong positive outcomes. However, many practices exist that might not meet this criteria but may still impact performance. It would behoove the field to broaden our measures to include such practices.

REFERENCES

1. Appelbaum, E., Bailey, T., Berg, P. and Kallenberg, A.L. 2000. Manufacturing advantage. Why high-performance work systems pay off. New York. Cornell University Press.

2. Allen, N. J., & Meyer, J. P. 1990. The measurement and antecedents of affective, continuance and normative commitment to the organization. Journal of Occupational Psychology, 63, 1-18.

3. Angle, H. L., & Perry, J. L. 1986. Dual commitment and labor-management relationship climates. Academy of Management Journal, 29, 31-50.

4. Arthur, J. B. 1992. The link between business strategy and industrial relations systems in American steel minimills. Industrial and Labor Relations Review, 45, 488-506.

5. Arthur, J. B. 1994. Effects of human resource systems on manufacturing performance and turnover. Academy of Management Journal, 37, 670-687.

6. Bagozzi, R. P., & Edwards, J. R. 1998. A general approach for representing constructs in organizational research. Organizational Research Methods, 1, 45-87.

7. Becker, H. S. 1960. Notes on the concept of commitment. American Journal of Sociology, 66, 32-40.

8. Becker, T. E., & Billings, R. S. 1993. Profiles of commitment: An empirical test. Journal of Organizational Behavior, 14, 177-190.

9. Becker, B., & Gerhart, B. 1996. The impact of human resource management on organizational performance: Progress and prospects. Academy of Management Journal, 39, 779-801.

10. Becker, B., Huselid, M., Pinckus, P. & Spratt, M. 1997. HR as a source of shareholder value: Research and recommendations. Human Resource Management, 36, 39-48.

11. Benson, G. S., Finegold, D., & Mohrman, S. A. You paid for the skills, now keep them: tuition reimbursement and voluntary turnover. Academy of Management Journal, 47, 315-331.

12. Boselie, P., Dietz, G. and Boon, C. 2005. Commonalities and contradictions in HRM and performance research. Human Resource Management Journal, 15, 67-94

13. Bowen, D. E., & Ostroff, C. 2004. Understanding HRM-firm performance linkages: The role of "strength" of the HRM system. Academy of Management Journal, 29, 203-221.

14. Brief, A. P. 1998. Attitudes in and around organizations. Thousand Oaks: CA. Sage.

15. Browning, V. 2006. The relationship between HRM practices and service behaviour in South African service organizations. International Journal of Human Resource Management, 17, 1321-1338.

16. Cohen, A. 2003. Multiple commitments in the workplace. Mahwah, NJ: Lawrence Erlbaum Associates.

17. Combs, J., Liu, Y., Hall, A., & Ketchen, D. 2006. How much do high performance work practices matter? A meta-analysis of their effects on organizational performance. Personnel Psychology, 59, 501-528

18. Datta, D. K., Guthrie, J. P., & Wright, P. M. 2005. HRM and labor productivity: Does industry matter? Academy of Management Journal, 48, 135-145.

19. Delery, J. E. 1998. Issues of fit in strategic human resource management: Implications for research. Human Resource Management Review, 8, 289-309.

20. Delery, J.E. and Doty, D.H. 1996. Modes of theorizing in strategic human resource management: tests of universalistic, contingency, and configurational performance predictions. Academy of Management Journal, 39, 802-835.

21. Delery, J. E., & Shaw, J. D. 2001. The strategic management of people in work organizations: Review, synthesis, and extension. Research in Personnel and Human Resource Management, 20, 165-197.

22. Dyer, L., & Holder, G. W. 1988. A strategic perspective of human resource management. In L. Dyer (Ed.), Human Resource Management: Evolving Roles and Responsibilities: 1.1-1.46. Washington, D.C.: The Bureau of National Affairs.

IMPACT OF HUMAN RESOURCES MANAGEMENT PRACTICES ON TURNOVER, PRODUCTIVITY AND CORPORATE FINANCIAL PERFORMANCE

Dr. Danial Saeed Pirzada[1], Farah Hayat[2], Amjad Ali Ikram[3], Muhammad Ayub[4] and Kamran Waheed[5]

[1]Associate Professor, Center for Advanced Studies in Engineering,19-Ataturk Avenue, G-5/1, Islamabad, Pakistan

[2]Ph.DScholar, Center for Advanced Studies in Engineering, 19-Ataturk Avenue, G-5/1, Islamabad, Pakistan

[3]M.Sc Engineering Management, Center for Advanced Studies in Engineering, 19-Ataturk Avenue, G-5/1, Islamabad, Pakistan

[4]M.Sc Engineering Management, Center for Advanced Studies in Engineering, 19-Ataturk Avenue, G-5/1, Islamabad, Pakistan

[5]M.Sc Engineering Management, Center for Advanced Studies in Engineering, 19-Ataturk Avenue, G-5/1, Islamabad, Pakistan

ABSTRACT

In developing countries, the human resource availability is quite easy but the most unfortunate part is its effective and efficient management. It is a well established fact that it is human beings behind the machines which can drive or drown the organizations. Human behavior and psychology is driven and motivated by varying degree of factors. The researchers across the globe have evolved and successfully practiced certain HRM techniques in order to achieve best performance and productivity from human capital. Unfortunately this area remained neglected and human resource could not be exploited to its full potential in Pakistan despite the fact that the country possesses one of the

Citation: Danial Saeed Pirzada, Farah Hayat, Amjad Ali Ikram, Muhammad Ayub and Kamran Waheed,2013,Impact of Human Resources Management Practices on Turnover, Productivity and Corporate Financial Performance, ISSN 2222-2839

best human capital in the world. This paper is an Endeavour to identify the best Human Resource Management practices applicable to Pakistani environments and analyze their positive effects on labor turnover, productivity and corporate financial performance. In order to achieve this objective, a survey questionnaire was designed and disseminated among respondents. A total of 200 questionnaires were distributed, out of which 145 completed questionnaires were received. The authors analyzed the data by using statpro software. the major conclusions and findings were; Need for articulation of vision, mission and values for organization, lack of performance management system, lack of benefit and compensation program, issue of corporate loyalty, poor workforce alignment, absence of HR development and training programs, lack of Human Resource Information System(HRIS),and non adoption of TQM.

INTRODUCTION

Human Resources is the most important asset for any organization, and it is a major source of achieving competitive advantage. Managing Human Resources is an extremely challenging task as compared to managing capital or managing technology. Human Resource Management should be backed up served HRM practices. HRM practices refer to organizational activities directed at managing the poor of human Resources and ensuring that resources are employees towards the fulfillment of organizational goods. In the contemporary era it is not uncommon to see the poor turnover as well as productivity of labor intensive organizations and companies. Before proceeding further it is necessary to elucidate what does turnover mean. Employees turnover is the difference between the rate of employees leaving a company and new employees filling up their positions. As the world progress towards globalization, this has become a serious issue which has laid serious effects on productivity as well as corporate financial outlay.

The tendency is much higher in those companies who offer low paying jobs. It is an established act that numerous factors and actors significantly contribute towards employees turnover. Such factors can stem from companies as well as the employees. Being an expensive aspect of business, the employees give more importance to turnover rate. This is so because, when an employee leaves the company the employer has to incur a considerable amount of direct and indirect expenses. These costs normally include, advertising expenses, headhunting fees, resources management expenses, loss of time and productivity, work imbalance, employee training and development expenses for new joiners. The second aspect related to turnover is productivity. The productivity is a measure of quantity and quality of work done, in relation to the resources expended. Synonymous to poor turnover, productivity is also affected by various factors such as, job stress, boredom, lack of challenge, poor work conditions and life balance, confined spaces, lack of health and safety program, lack of professional development program and training. In order to address these issues, worldwide researchers and modern organizations and companies have evolved certain good practices relating to Human Resources Management. Although such practices are not standardized however, these can be modified and tailored according local Pakistani Industry environments.

RESEARCH OBJECTIVES

The objective and scope of this research is spanned over the following areas:-

a.   To identify the most common and proven HRM practices in the construction industry.

b.   To identify the impacts of these practices over turnover, productivity and corporate performance.

c.   To recommend suitable options in order to address these three factors.

LITERATURE REVIEW

Human Resource is a very essential component for an organization in terms of labor turnover, productivity as well as financial growth of an organization. Similarly good Human Resource management practices play a pivotal role in employees retention and their productivity. (Peer-Olaf Siebers,et al-2008).

There are numerous factors and actors which influence this aspect, like inadequate incentives, inadequate wages, salaries or allied benefits, poor reward system and lack of health and safety facilities.(Esra NEMLI-2010–Choi Sang Long et al, 2012).

Employees get frustrated due to imbalance in the work and their personal life and fail to render optimum performance (Mourad , 2011-Ayesha et al, 2012). Occasionally it has also been observed that job stress and unfair testament by the HR department or manager demotivates the even talented employees. Those organizations which do not evolve and implement human recourse plan (HRP) often expedience HR related issues (Patrick M. Wright et al,2012). Consequently people cannot acquire professional development through training, mentoring or coaching. Thus the work force faces issues like; boredom or lack of challenge in the work environment (Rosemond Boohene et al, 2011-Shri Chimanbhai Patel et al, 2012). As a result of globalization new corporate companies or organization can not absolve themselves from corporate social response (CSR). In the past traditional corporate culture, least attention was paid towards health, safety, compensation and benefits, diversity and good working environments. Perhaps the sole reason was to save the money by any menus possible may it be at the cost of human capital. Unlike this trend, now organization have to discharge their corporate special responsibilities by taking care of their human resource (WWAN Sujeeva, 2011-Shikha N. Khara, 2011).

Productivity in defined, as "a measure of quantity and quality of work done, considering the cost of resources used". Mathematically it can be stated as, productivity (P) = Ability (A) x Effort (E) x Support (S).(MehdadArshpur et al,2011-Dave Ulrich,2012-Tahir Masood et al, 2010) That means, productivity is directly linked with turnover. Absenteeism on large proportions will result into low productivity. It can be inferred that turnover and productivity must be addressed simultaneously (NakhonKokkaow et al,2011- Andreas de Grip,2012).

Various researches and past literature has highlighted the causes of poor productivity the mostly occurring causes of low productivity are, dilution of supervision, increase in staffing level without increase in supervision, alternating, staggering or rotating work schedules, mismatch of skill sets and delay in site mobilization(Andrew Daninty,2012-Stuart D. Green,2012). Moreover issues like over manning, constructability issues, learning curve, sources of materials and leads, barriers to authority and tools and equipment shortages drastically retard the performance and progress of work. Majority of these issues can be resolved by imparting on-job training (OJT), improvement in technical know how and evolving a sound human resource management information (HRIS). To add this aspect, judicial utilization of available resources and improved working conditions can augment the productivity levels(Andrew Daninty,2012-Stuart D. Green,2012). As far as improvement of corporate financial stature is concerned, it can be the direct product of good turnover and best productivity of work force. Companies investment for ensuing profits which can only be achieved if the companies possess high performing teams who believe in system thinking rather than focusing on individual performances. High performing teams or work force will always be quality focused and quality conscious. These will Endeavour to eliminate wastes, scraps and reworks; eventually saving huge amount of money(Mehdad Arshpur et al,2011-Dave Ulrich,2012-Tahir Masood et al, 2010). Developments in the field of human resource management are now well documented in the literature. As firms and companies are entering into more robust world of international business due to globalization, HRM issues appear be gaining momentum. Both practitioners and academics in the field of HRM are increasingly aware of the need to examine and understand the HRM system suitable to different parts of the world. They are also finding best HRM practices for resolving the issues related to turnover, performance(Esra NEMLI-2010–Choi Sang Long et al, 2012). Organizations will have to manage their human resorts effectively and efficiently, if they are to get the minimum contribution of their employees. HRM practices have not developed in an isolation rather these have been evolved basing of data and results obtained from sister departments within firms and companies(WWAN Sujeeva,2011-Shikha N. Khara,2011).

RESEARCH METHODOLOGY

A critical review of contemporary literature including various studies conducted in Pakistan as well as abroad related directly or indirectly to the topic under study, has facilitated the identification and selection of human resource practices contributing to the organization's turnover, productivity and financial performance. Various HRM practices, which are perceived to affect the organizational performance in the three areas as described earlier, have been identified and selected for this research. For data collection the survey instrument used for this research study was meticulously designed structured questionnaire. Validity of the questionnaire used as survey instrument for the research study needs to be established it has been considered necessary to pretest validity of all the questions with a pilot study. For this purpose, the first draft of questions was administered to HRM practitioners and professionals. The results indicated good consistency and correlations. On the basis of its findings, the main questionnaire was refined and modified. At total of 200 questionnaires were disseminated to the industry related professionals. Out of 200 questionnaires, 150 questionnaires were received which comes out to be 75perent of response rate.

RESULTS AND DISCUSSIONS

This research effort was comprised of following domains:

- What are the contemporary HRM practices available in the world.
- How these practices influence the labor turnover.
- What are the effects of HRM practices on Productivity of a company.
- How HRM practices affect corporate financial performance.
- What are the likely courses of actions or options available to address these problems.

Contemporary Best HRM Practices

Human Resource Management is very complicated subject in which standardized practices cannot be implemented and followed. This is so because human beings possess varying degree of psychological behaviors, skills, expertise, emotions, motivation levels, loyalty and desire for professional growth. In order to get maximum productivity of human resource operating in any field, company or organization, there is need to adopt those practices which held increase the performance levels of the employees. It is not always to adopt lucrative benefits and compensation scheme rather sometimes professional growth and development of employees may serve as the best solution. The top management must consistently and periodically review the results of HR practices in their companies so that these should serve the company's mission statement and quality policy. The authors have identified 27 best HRM practices after carrying out pilot survey and structured interviews with pertinent respondents as enlisted in Table-1. The respondents were asked to rank these practices on the scale of 1 (the highest value) to 27 (the lowest value). The results indicate that Articulation of vision, mission and values within an organization lay foundation for employees turnover, productivity and financial performance. The other HRM practices which received well attention by respondents are; Performance Management System for employees. That means employees expect recognition of their efforts by their managers as well as the top management. When it is not done properly, the workforce gets frustrated and turns towards bad performance or leaving the organization. The other practice is Benefits and compensation scheme that is in vogue in the companies. World has witnessed and subjected to the worst economics recession in the contemporary era which has inflicted severe economic effects till grass root level. Under such conditions there becomes a necessity to evolve and implement a well recognized and company wide acceptable program for benefits and compensation for workforce. The detailed results are appended in Fig 1(a&b) below:

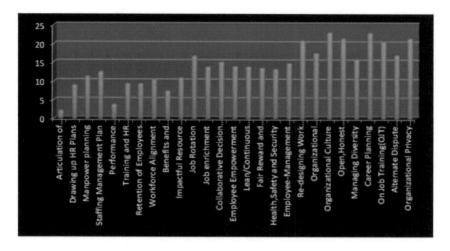

Figure 1(a): Contemporary Best HRM practices.

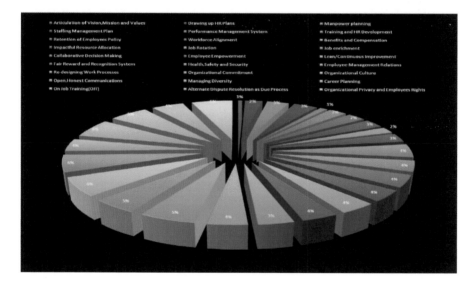

Figure 1(b): Contemporary Best HRM practices.

HRM Practices and their Effects on Turnover

After having indentified the best HRM practices, the respondents were asked to furnish the positive effects over employees turnover. After analysis of data, the anthers indentified the top three positive impacts and there are, corporate loyalty, minimum absenteeism, elimination of job stress and unfair treatment. The remaining results are graphically represented in Fig-2(a&b) below:-

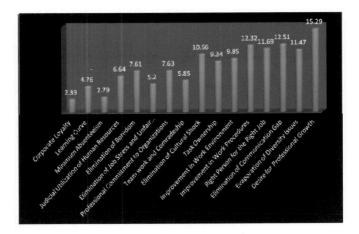

Figure 2(a): HRM Practices and their Effects on Turnover.

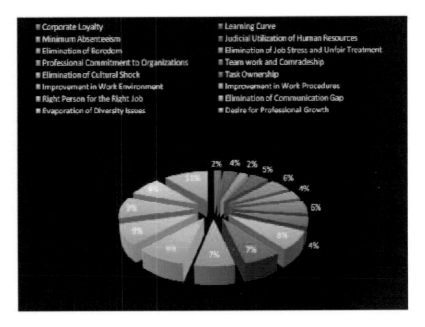

Figure 2(b): HRM Practices and their Effects on Turnover.

HRM practices and their effects on productivity. Human resource is vital component in any industry, despite the fact that the world has received state –of- art level of modernization after globalization. If the basic data is not correctly fed into the machines by workforce, there are likely chances of poor productivity. The authors identified 12 indicators which can help improve the productivity levels. The results have been tabulated in Table-1 and fig 3(a&b).

Table 1: HRM practices and their effects on productivity

	1	2	3	4	5	6	7	8	9	10	11	12	Rating Average	Rating Count
Clarity of goals	74.7 % (74)	7.1 % (7)	9.1 % (9)	6.1 % (6)	1.0 % (1)	0.0 % (0)	1.0 % (1)	1.0 % (1)	0.0 % (0)	0.0 % (0)	0.0 % (0)	0.0 % (0)	1.61	99
Maturity of Processes	1.0 % (1)	37.4 % (37)	6.1 % (6)	18.2 % (18)	15.2 % (15)	5.1 % (5)	2.0 % (2)	3.0 % (3)	6.1 % (6)	6.1 % (6)	0.0 % (0)	0.0 % (0)	4.26	99
Minimum Rework and Scrap	2.0 % (2)	3.0 % (3)	32.3 % (32)	7.1 % (7)	16.2 % (16)	19.2 % (19)	13.1 % (13)	4.0 % (4)	1.0 % (1)	2.0 % (2)	0.0 % (0)	0.0 % (0)	4.83	99
Elimination of Scope Creep	0.0 % (0)	0.0 % (0)	2.0 % (2)	31.3 % (31)	2.0 % (2)	26.3 % (26)	21.2 % (21)	8.1 % (8)	5.1 % (5)	3.0 % (3)	1.0 % (1)	0.0 % (0)	5.99	99
Better use of Skillset	0.0 % (0)	2.0 % (2)	2.0 % (2)	1.0 % (1)	32.3 % (32)	4.0 % (4)	20.2 % (20)	23.2 % (23)	11.1 % (11)	1.0 % (1)	3.0 % (3)	0.0 % (0)	6.71	99
Employees Confidence over Processes	0.0 % (0)	1.0 % (1)	0.0 % (0)	2.0 % (2)	3.0 % (3)	30.3 % (30)	3.0 % (3)	21.2 % (21)	17.2 % (17)	14.1 % (14)	6.1 % (6)	2.0 % (2)	7.85	99
Productivity Oriented	1.0 % (1)	10.1 % (10)	14.1 % (14)	7.1 % (7)	5.1 % (5)	0.0 % (0)	33.3 % (33)	3.0 % (3)	18.2 % (18)	7.1 % (7)	1.0 % (1)	0.0 % (0)	6.2	99

Culture														
Competitive Advantage	1.0 % (1)	0.0 % (0)	5.1 % (5)	13.1 % (13)	2.0 % (2)	4.0 % (4)	0.0 % (0)	32.3 % (32)	5.1 % (5)	31.3 % (31)	6.1 % (6)	0.0 % (0)	7.87	99
High Performance and Innovative Employees	15.2 % (15)	15.2 % (15)	11.1 % (11)	5.1 % (5)	12.1 % (12)	2.0 % (2)	1.0 % (1)	2.0 % (2)	31.3 % (31)	4.0 % (4)	1.0 % (1)	0.0 % (0)	5.28	99
Group Think Culture	0.0 % (0)	2.0 % (2)	2.0 % (2)	3.0 % (3)	4.0 % (4)	3.0 % (3)	5.1 % (5)	1.0 % (1)	4.0 % (4)	31.3 % (31)	44.4 % (44)	0.0 % (0)	9.42	99
System Thinking Culture	5.1 % (5)	22.2 % (22)	16.2 % (16)	6.1 % (6)	7.1 % (7)	6.1 % (6)	0.0 % (0)	1.0 % (1)	1.0 % (1)	0.0 % (0)	35.4 % (35)	0.0 % (0)	6	99
Inter Department Harmony	0.0 % (0)	0.0 % (0)	0.0 % (0)	0.0 % (0)	0.0 % (0)	0.0 % (0)	0.0 % (0)	0.0 % (0)	0.0 % (0)	0.0 % (0)	2.0 % (2)	98.0 % (97)	11.98	99

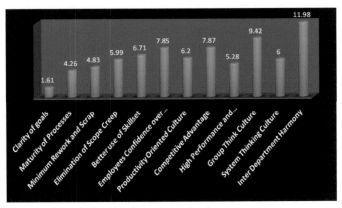

Figure 3(a): HRM practices and their effects on productivity.

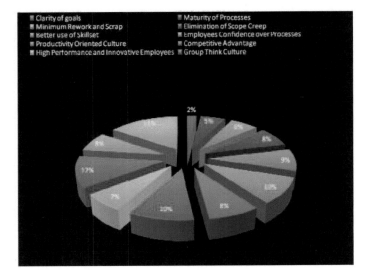

Figure 3(b): HRM practices and their effects on productivity.

HRM practices and their effects on corporate financial performance. In this domain, a total of 9 possible positive indicators were identified and respondents were asked to rank these indicators according to their experience and knowledge.

These were as under:

a.   TQM

b.   Human Resources information system (HRIS)

c.   Minimum Wastage

d.   Minimum Scrap and Re-work

e.   Empowerment to handle processes

f.   Flatter organization structure

g. Participation of employees in financial decision making

h. Efficient HR Department

i. Certified SPHR/GPHR professionals

Out of above stated indicators, the top three ranked indicators are, HRIS, TQM and minimum wastage. Human Resources information system gives guidance about manpower employment versus their productivity. It also lays foundation for preparation of staffing management plan at operational level. As for as Total Quality Management (TQM) is concerned, it is a companywide philosophy of continual improvement, involving every one and everywhere. Though effective implementation of TQM, huge scraps, wastage and frequent reworks can permanently be eliminated. The results have been plotted on Fig Table 2 and fig 4(a&b) below.

Table 2: HRM practices and their effects on corporate financial performance

	1	2	3	4	5	6	7	8	9	Rating Average	Rating Count
TQM	42.0% (42)	24.0% (24)	8.0% (8)	12.0% (12)	4.0% (4)	2.0% (2)	1.0% (1)	1.0% (1)	6.0% (6)	2.63	100
Human Resource Management Information System	46.0% (46)	41.0% (41)	8.0% (8)	4.0% (4)	1.0% (1)	0.0% (0)	0.0% (0)	0.0% (0)	0.0% (0)	1.73	100
Minimum Wastage	2.0% (2)	2.0% (2)	61.0% (61)	11.0% (11)	15.0% (15)	6.0% (6)	3.0% (3)	0.0% (0)	0.0% (0)	3.65	100
Minimum Scrap and Rework	0.0% (0)	0.0% (0)	4.0% (4)	62.0% (62)	9.0% (9)	15.0% (15)	5.0% (5)	5.0% (5)	0.0% (0)	4.7	100
Empowerment to Handle processes	1.0% (1)	2.0% (2)	1.0% (1)	1.0% (1)	57.0% (57)	18.0% (18)	16.0% (16)	3.0% (3)	1.0% (1)	5.5	100
Flatter Organizational Structu	0.0% (0)	3.0% (3)	1.0% (1)	2.0% (2)	1.0% (1)	57.0% (57)	17.0% (17)	17.0% (17)	2.0% (2)	6.37	100

re											
Particip ation of Employ ees in Financi al Decisio n Making	0.0% (0)	11.0% (11)	4.0% (4)	4.0% (4)	1.0% (1)	1.0% (1)	55.0% (55)	13.0% (13)	11.0% (11)	6.49	100
Efficie nt HR Depart ment	0.0% (0)	3.0% (3)	8.0% (8)	0.0% (0)	2.0% (2)	0.0% (0)	1.0% (1)	61.0% (61)	25.0% (25)	7.6	100
Certfie d SPHR/ GPHR professi onal	9.0% (9)	14.0% (14)	5.0% (5)	4.0% (4)	10.0% (10)	1.0% (1)	2.0% (2)	0.0% (0)	55.0% (55)	6.33	100

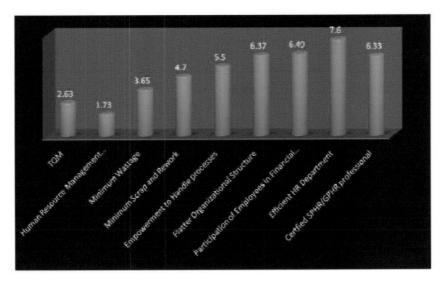

Figure 4(a): HRM practices and their effects on corporate financial performance.

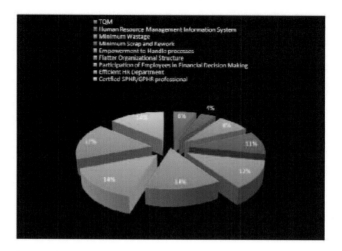

Figure 4(b): HRM practices and their effects on corporate financial performance.

CONCLUSIONS AND FINDINGS

From the results and discussions, following findings and conclusions have been drawn:-

a. Organization and companies can not achieve good productivity and financial performance without implementing well recognized vision, mission and values for the organization as a whole.

b. An effective appraisal and performance management system helps curtailing turnover issues, and low productivity. c. A well recognized benefits and compensation program helps in motivating employees.

d. Corporate loyalty is one of the prime departure factors through which productivity oriented culture can be created in companies.

e. Through effective implementation of HRM practices, high rate of absenteeism can be controlled and minimized.

f. Work force and work alignment are complimentary to each other. Works or tasks should be allocated according to abilities and capabilities of employees. Over allocation of works leads to jib stress and unfair treatment in an organization.

g. For better productivity and high performance, goods must be clear to every employees of the company.

h. Articulation of vision, mission and values helps improve maturity and refinement of process.

i. Through training and HR department, companies can eliminate remarks and scraps, thus saving huge expenditure. j. In the modern area, companies can not solely rely on traditional way of management of employees. Now a day, implementation of HRIS is mandatory for multinational companies, companies and organizations.

k.   Total quality management (TQM) is a companywide quality management philosophy which fosters training, workforce empowerment, good employees – management relatives and formation of high performing teams. By implementing TQM, companies can response work process, working environment and productivity levels very effectively and efficiently.

l.   Remedy to control over wastages, remarks and scraps lies in adopting TQM for organizations.

RECOMMENDATIONS

From the finding and conclusions, following workable options are recommended:

a. Articulation of vision, mission and values statements

The edifice strategic as well as the operational framework rests over sound vision, mission and values of the companies or organizations vague and ambiguous policies do not transcend good results rather originations suffer chaos, uncertainly and continuous volatile state within employees and the rater department relationship. Hence it is very much mandatory to skill fully and diligently craft companies' mission, vision and values in order to achieve competitive advantage over the companies.

b. Effective performance management system

The employees leave the organizations and companies when they see, a poor or based performance and appraisal system. Alone effective performance management system can eradicate the necessity of even employees retention program. In the work of fair appraised and performance management system, employees will be more involved in achieving good results contributing to good financial performance as a whole. Therefore it is recommended that companies must adopt companywide recognized performance managing system for its employees.

c. Benefits and Compensation Scheme

This is very important due to fragile economic environments of these days. The domain of benefits courses variety of options like, rewarding monetarily, bonuses, pay raise for certified employees and accommodation and transport. Similarly the old aged retires must be compensated for their services to the companies in a dignified manner. This will boost motivation of other employees who are awaiting retirement.

d. Culture of Corporate

When employees enjoy good relations with management and they have been granted fair empowerment in controlling process and the tasks, coupled with good served and recognition system, they become loyal to the organizations and companies. Thus employees do not think a switch over to other organizations and performance exceptionally well in their parent companies.

e. Benefits and Compensation Scheme

This is very important due to fragile economic environments of these days. The domain of benefits courses variety of options like, rewarding monetarily, bonuses, pay raise for certified employees and accommodation and transport. Similarly the old aged retires must be compensated for their services to the companies in a dignified manner. This will boost motivation of other employees who are awaiting retirement.

f. Culture of Corporate

When employees enjoy good relations with management and they have been granted fair degree empowerment in controlling process and the tasks, coupled with good served and recognition system, they become loyal to the organizations and companies. Thus employees do not think a switch over to other organizations and performance exceptionally well in their parent companies.

g. Employees Retention Policies

Employees always leave the company when they do not see positive future prospects. Such uncertainty drastically affects their behavior and performance. In order to avoid people fleeing out of companies, the top management must evolve and supplement employees retention policy. This policy should address areas like, re-designing work process for elimination of boredom and fatigue, job rotation, job enrichment by adding more responsibilities and judicious employment across all departments. Those individuals who performance well, must be retained in the companies.

h. Training and HR Department

On the job training (OJT) or academic course training helps in professional development of employees which enlaces their potential for achieving high productivity and performance levels. Training should focus on learn or continuous improvement, TQM and professional certifications like management professional (PMP), Global professional for HR (GPHR) and six sigma belts courses.

i. Human Resources Information System. (HRIS) An HRIS saves two purposes in organizations. One relates to administrative and operational efficiency and other to effectiveness. The first purpose of an HRIS is to deprave the efficiency with which data on employees and HR activities in gathered. The other purpose is related to HR planning. Having accessible data enables HR planning and managerial decision making on quantities basis rather than intuitions or perceptional basis.

The uses of HRIS are:-

- HR Planning and Analysis
- Equal employment
- Staffing
- HR Development
- Compensation and severity

- Health, safety and Security
- Employee – management relationships

Keeping in view, its wide applications, it is recommended that companies should implement HRIS.

j. HR Goals

Companies must establish HR goals covering productivity, quality, service financial goals, like net profit and return on investment and marketing goals like market share and sales growth. This will keep the whole company under one umbrella of corporate goals.

k. TQM

Total Quality Management (TQM) in the contemporary management philosophy which helps building quality oriented culture in an entire organizations. It has been very successfully in USA, Europe and Japan in service, manufacturing and construction and engineering see tens. There in fair degree of reluctance in developing countries due to misconceptions like higher costs enormous paper work, rigid bye-laws and contacting procedures. This in all wrong because money invested in TQM, in promptly recovered through waste control and remark. It helps grow a company continually.

l. Certified SPHRs/GPHRs

Human Resources management has now become a specialized field. There are prestigious institutions like Human Resource Institute (HRI), USA who offer global credentials in HRM. It is recommended that HR managers be trained and certified in the HRM so that they are equipped with state of the art tools and techniques to manage human capital in a productive manner.

REFERENCES

1. Peer Olaf Siebers et al(2008), "Enhancing Productivity: The Role of Management Practices" . A/M Working Paper Series – 062- February 2008 – ISSN 1744-0009.

2. Esra NEMLI CALISKAN(2010), The Impact of Strategic Human Resource Management on Organization Reference, Journal o Naval Science and Engineering 2010, Vol 6. No. 2, PP. 100-116.

3. Choc Sang Long et all (2012), "The Impact of Human Resource Management Practices on Employees Turnover Intention: A Conceptual Model," Interdisciplinary Journal of Contemporary Research in Business, Vol 4, No. 2, Jun 2012.

4. MouradMansour(2011), " HR Practices Impact on Firm Performance: An Empirical Study". King Fahd University of Petroleum and Minerals, management and Marketing Department.

5. Ayesha Jahanian et al (2012), "human Resource Management and Productivity:

A Comparative Study Among Banks in Bahawalpur Division". European Journal of Business and Management, Vol 4.No. 8, 2012.

6.   Patrick M. Wright et al (2003), " The Impact of HR Practices on the performance of business units". Human Resource Management Journal, Vol 13, No. 3, 2003, Page 21-36.

7.   RosemondBoohene, et al (2011), "The Effect of Human Resource management Practices on Corporate Performance: A Study of Graphic Communication Group Limited", International Business Research, Vol 4, No. 1, January 2011.

8.   Sri chimanbhai Patel et al (2012), " human Resource Management Practices" A Comprehensive Review," Pakistan Business Review, January 2012.

9.   WWAN Sujeeva, (2011), " Relation Ship between Human Resource Management Practices Non Managerial Employee Intention to Turnover in Garment Industry in Sri Lanka, " International Conference on management, Economies and Social Sciences (IC MESS 2011), Bangkok Dec 2011.

10.   Shikha N. Khera (2011), "Human Resource Parties and their Impact on Employee Productivity. A Perceptual Analysis of Private, Public and Foreign Review, in India," DSM Business Review, Vol. 2, No. 1, June 2011.

11.   MehrdadArashpour et al (2011), " Gaining the Best Value of HR in Construction Companies".

12.   Dave Ulrich, (2012), " Measuring Human Resources: An overview of Practice and a Prescription far Results," Human Resource Management, Vol 36, No. 3, PP. 303-320.

13.   TahirMasood Qureshi et al (2010), " Do Human Resource Management Practices have an Impact on Financial Performance of Bank", African Journal of Business management Vol.4 (7), PP. 1281-1288, 4 July 2010.

14.   NakhonKokkaew et al (2011), "Current Practices of Human Resource Management in thei Construction Industry: A Risk and Opportunity Perspective", Review Integrative Business and Economies, Research, Vol (I).

15.   Andries de Grip, IngeSieben, (2012), " The Effects of Human Resource Management on Workers, Wages and Firms productivity". ISBN 90-5321383-X Sec 03, 193. doc.

16.   Andrew Dainty, martin Loose more (2012), " Human Resource Management in Construction", ISBN 978-0-415-59307-6, Publisher, Rout ledge Taylor and Francis Group.

17.   Stuart D. Green (2012), " The Human Resource Management Implications of Lean Construction, Critical Perspectives and Conceptual Chasms". Wher reading ac. Uk/ on kesgrest / Lean – hrm. Htm

MOSTLY DISCUSSED RESEARCH AREAS IN HUMAN RESOURCE MANAGEMENT (HRM)–A LITERATURE REVIEW

Mansoor Hussain[1] and Mushtaq Ahmad[2]

[1]Corresponding Author - M.phil scholar, Army Public College of Management and Sciences (APCOMS),Rawalpindi,Pakistan, University of engineering and technology (UET) Taxila, Pakistan Corresponding Address: CB-194, Lane-3 Sherzaman Colony Tulsa Road Lalazar, Rawalpindi, Cantt ,Pakistan

[2]Army Public College of management and sciences (APCOMS) Rawalpindi,Pakistan University of Engineering and Technology(UET), Taxila Pakistan

ABSTRACT

This field of HRM is still in its evolutionary phase and it is difficult to identify any crystal clear framework to retrofit the existing strewn perspectives. Available literature shows that HRM is a system that strives to achieve a dynamic balance between the personal interests and concerns of people and their economic added value. In this study all those papers which are published in prominent HR journals were scanned and those published during last five year period were kept under sharp focus. Papers pertaining to the field of HRM and organizational performance were categorized and examined in detail. Categorization of the literature according to various dimensions enabled the researcher to explore new areas that are not adequately covered in the literature; hence this study is a structured overview covering significant aspects. It was found that HRM is an area that continues to evoke a lot of debate and body of work in HRM is relatively small, and most of the questions are sorely in need of further attention.

Citation: Mansoor Hussain and Mushtaq Ahmad, 2012, Mostly Discussed Research areas in Human Resource Management (HRM) ? A Literature Review, http://www.managementjournals.org/ijems/23/IJEMSi2n3i2i1222209.pdf

INTRODUCTION

Human resource management (HRM) is making the best possible use of individuals for achieving the organizational objectives. The definition was developed in late twentieth century; thereafter employee motivation and job satisfaction came under focus instead of mere rational administration (Hartel, Fujimoto, Strybosh and Fitzpatrick 2007). In present day world organizations all over the world are facing critical challenges and survival has been linked with the development of new capabilities. There is a need to find opportunities through these emerging challenges like globalization, change management, investment in human capital, growth etc. Human resource strategies can be used as a vibrant tool vital towards success. Strategic alignment of human capital can best be achieved through effective HR practices. Management of the human capital has assumed added significance after realization of the fact that people are assets of strategic importance. The concept of personnel management is no more relevant in the context after evolution of strategic concept of human resource management. After this paradigm shift of the emphasis human resource policies are being aligned with business strategies. According to resource-based view organizations can attain competitive advantage with the help of value created by them which is exceptional and perfectly inimitable (Baker, 1999). Sources like economies of scale, technology, natural resources etc are often considered vital towards achieving competitive advantage but resource based view states that these can be easily imitated. In this backdrop HR practices may prove to be a major cause of sustainable competitive advantage (Lado & Wilson, 1994). Analyses of available literature on the subject provides critical insights and shows that HR practices if employed appropriately can prove to be a vibrant tool towards enhancing the level of organizational performance.

Most organizations operate on a piecemeal basis, responding to sudden emergent pressures, and are subject to a variety of powerful internal political pressures which contribute to inconsistencies among their policy choices. Most of the literature in the area of human resource strategies ignores the actual process by which the strategies are formed and concentrates instead on the chosen policies and practices. This is an important gap. In fact, most researchers in this field measure the firm's plan of action purely by its choice of HR practices; indeed, that is typically how they represent the HR strategy itself (ie different HR objectives are very often ignored). In other words, researchers tend to focus exclusively on the combination of individual HR practices that a firm does or does not adopt; it is a particular combination of practices which assigns the firm to one strategy category or another; the specification of strategic objectives, the problems of policy implementation, and the nature of the arguments that might link policies to objectives are usually not explored in any depth. In this study researcher will focus on available literature in various journals pertaining various HR practices and organizational performance with a view to facilitate future research by identifying significant areas and gaps in the body of knowledge. Available literature reveals that, HRM is entire system of values, policies and practices which focuses on maximizing the performance of people in organizations, with a view to achieving a dynamic balance between the personal interests and concerns of people and their economic added value.

LITERATURE REVIEW

This part of study literature review includes available research relating to the dimensions identified in introduction. The material incorporated in this chapter is taken from different resources. Significant dig outs from research already done related to above mentioned issues are reproduced below:

Author	Year	Source/journal	Findings and conclusion
Tharenou And others	2007	Human resource management review	Study concluded that research on training and organizational-level outcomes differs as a function of the outcome variables which are categorized as:- 1. HR outcomes 2. Organizational performance outcomes 3. Financial or accounting outcomes 4. In case of publicly listed companies stock market outcomes
Katou and Budhwar	2010	European Management Journal	Business strategies, managerial style and organizational culture moderate HRM policies. Moreover, it was found that HRM policies do not have a direct impact on organizational performance, but their impact is fully mediated by employee skills, attitudes, and behaviour.
Steinmetz	2011	Human Resource Management Review	There is a need to standardize the process of research particularly in the field of HR .Researchers need to develop a process in which development of questionnaire, administration of questionnaire and structuring of comparable measures should follow the same way. Results of such a research cannot be generalized without a process which is close to uniformity.
Minbaeva	2008	International Business Review	Study concluded that if HRM practices are used to develop competencies that are firm specific and creation of organizational knowledge than these can also contribute to sustained competitive advantage.
Turner, Huemann and Keegan	2008	International Journal of Project Management	For optimum performance project assignments should be linked with career development so that employees may feel that specific project assignments are likely to create opportunities for development. HRM practices in contemporary organizations most of the times overlook needs of stake holders in favour of the organization. Fairness and justice assume added significance towards HRM practices.(Greenwood,2002)
Gooderham and Nordhaug	2010	Human Resource Management Review	Institutional context is highly relevant in Practices of HRM. HRM framework is essentially required which should be able to incorporate contextual factors in question. Few suggested are:- 1. Culture 2. Legislation 3. Role Of The State 4. Trade Union Representation institutional context
Werbel,and DeMarie	2005	Human Resource Management Review	HRM practices including performance appraisal, compensation, selection practices, and training and development practices can be clustered as a means to communicate to the employees regarding various skills and behaviours required to create and sustain a competitive advantage

Author	Year	Source/journal	Findings and conclusion
Lengnick-Hall and Others	2009	Human Resource Management Review	With the growth of strategic HRM role that HRM has towards organizational effectiveness is becoming more significant. Collins and Smith (2006) concluded that HR practices have a great impact towards organization's social climate, which leads to knowledge exchange resulting into improved organization performance.
Mc gunnigle	2000	Employee Relations journal	Organizations embarking upon the correct HRM approach shall tend to recruit individuals with most desirable behavior to fit with cultures. Consistent recruitment and selection procedures get relevant in the context. Training and developmental programs can further supplement the commitment.
Maxwell and Farquharson	2007	Employee Relations journal	Bowen and Ostroff's (2004) concluded that "the strength of the HRM system affect organisational effectiveness." HRM is said to have a central role in business performance as per the theory (Richard and Brown Johnson, 2001). Thus HRM strategies are deep rooted in business needs with a firm integration with business strategy.
Harris	2007	Employee Relations journal	Developing HR practices meant to make the most of individual performance have never been accorded significance in public service. There are ill-defined boundaries about HR responsibilities of managers at various levels and specializations each with different perspectives.
Othman and Poon	2007	Employee Relations journal	Relationship of HRM practices is comparatively stronger with management orientation than competitive strategy. Strategy can be manipulated or changed with more ease than orientation of the management. Therefore HRM practices can contribute to a great extent towards organizational performance orientation remains in the right direction.
Tissen and others	2010	The International Journal of Human Resource Management	In the recent past a wide range of studies suggested a positive relationship between HRM and the performance of organizations (including Guest 1989; Clark 1993; Paauwe and Richardson 1997; Guest 1997; Gelade and Ivery 2003). The majority of this literature is increasingly regarded as being outdated. It is viewed as 'first generation' research in which the importance of HRM is recognized, yet little or no attention is placed on what is known as the causal process between HRM and the functioning of the organization.

Author	Year	Source/journal	Findings/conclusion
Keegan, Huemann and Turner	2011	The International Journal of Human Resource Management	Various HRM responsibilities of managers especially in project oriented companies is a concern that is not given the attention by HRM literature. More clear and specific elaboration of responsibilities in contemporary organizations can increase performance at each level manifolds.
Shen and Zhu	2011	The International Journal of Human Resource Management	More and more organizations seek to improve their performance by using appropriate HRM policies and practices. Due to the importance of CSR to business, it is important for HRM policies and practices to address both the firm's strategic needs and the interests of internal and external stakeholders
Gellatly and others	2009	The International Journal of Human Resource Management	Employee commitment should be considered as a resource by the organizations which can be used to uphold the workforce capabilities providing sustained advantage over competitors. HRM practices can be used as a tool to inculcate the desired commitment among the employees limiting their desire to leave the organization and demonstrate higher citizenship behaviour
Teo,Clerc and Galang	2011	The International Journal of Human Resource Management	Investment in human resources (HRs) through embracing human capital enhancing (HCE) human resource management (HRM) system is positively linked to organizational performance. Moreover, Front line employees are strategically significant and important source of competitive advantage.
Zanko	2008	The International Journal of Human Resource Management	Legge's (1978) argued that HRM requires power and influence to be effective and implement its agenda. Its true role, perceptions and problem solving abilities will then be understood by line management.
McKenna and others	2010	The International Journal of Human Resource Management	Modern HRM practices afford an opportunity to gain increasing control over line managers, other employees and their behaviour.Critical approaches to management imply the need for scepticism about the purposes of the global transferability of HR ideas and practices. Moreover, rather than focusing on whether practices can be transferred, the barriers to transfer, or how they are transferred, a key theme in a critical approach is how work is designed and people are managed to achieve the control necessary within organisational, economic and societal contexts (Delbridge 2009).
Dany,Guedri and Hatt	2008	The International Journal of Human Resource Management	In order to strengthen the link between HRM and performance, decision making should rely upon HRM specialists in consultation with line managers. In addition to this there should be judicious distribution of roles and responsibilities between both.
Azmi	2011	The International Journal of Human Resource Management	Effectiveness of HRM function is invaluable to achieve organizational performance through HR practices. Author found four dimensions of SHRM fit 1. Fit between HRM and corporate strategy 2. Fit between HR roles and position 3. Fit within HRM function 4. Fit between HRM and other functional Areas
Martins	2007	Management Decisions	It is not possible to achieve high levels of performance with out communicating the roles with clarity. If belief of staff runs contrary to actual expectations of senior managers than desired performance level can not be met.
Luoma	2008	Management Decisions	Simply matching the HR practices with product/market strategies is no more relevant after advocates of resource based theory lay emphasis on competencies and behavior as

			vital towards creating competitiveness. Those HR practices need more attention which can develop and maintain the requisite competencies and behavior.
Appelbaum	2011	Management Decisions	After globalization and ever expanding organizations there is a need to adopt strategy and structures with cross cultural operability to optimize the efficiency. This will warrant the need to redefine HR strategies to increase or maintain organizational performance.
Gbadamosi	2007	Management Decisions	Committed employees are taken invariably as heart of the organization. Commitment towards organization is a predominant tool towards organizational performance and effectiveness.
Moideenkutty, Al-Lamki and Murthy	2009	Management Decisions	High-involvement HRM practices have positive relation ship with subjective and quantitative measure of organizational performance. This means that organizations that implement highly selective staffing, realistic training, performance management practices and employee empowerment are likely to have higher performance.

Review enabled the researcher in developing the following understanding

- This field is still in its evolutionary phase and it is difficult to identify any crystal clear framework to retrofit the existing scattered perspectives.

- Business performance will be improved only when the right fit between business strategy and HR practices is achieved

- Specific combinations of HR practices can be identified which generate higher business performance but these combinations will vary by organizational context.

- Claims that a universal best practice HR strategy has been identified are premature. It is unlikely that adopting a specified set of HR policies is the high road to organizational success. Even the large amount of empirical work that has been done has not identified all the general components such a set of policies would contain

- How something is done is often more important than what is done, and we need to pay much more attention to how clusters of HR polices are adopted and implemented as well as to the specific contexts in which policy innovation is attempted

- The way in which organizations treat their employees is at the heart of their success

- HR function is no more being taken as administrative activity rather it has assumed a central role in overall organizational activities. It is one of the main pillars which supports entire organization

- True essence of context needs to be understood for firm implementation of HR policies. Contextual factors are being given more importance by researchers all over

- It is imperative to have a strategy for any organization but at the same time even the best crafted strategy cannot ensure success. Chances of success increase manifolds when there exists a vibrant and realistic implementation mechanism. Success comes through interplay of numerous factors with dominant role of HR.

- A growing number of studies have complex measures of HR practices. These are often used in multivariate analyses, which also incorporate background variables like capital/labour ratios, firm size, industrial sector, and so on. But they only rarely include other direct measures of managerial effectiveness. This omission might mean that all aspects of managerial effectiveness are being represented just by the HR variables

- There is an upward trend towards alignment of human resource initiatives with goals of organization with a view to achieve business success.

- In essence the research on effectiveness of HRM can be captured by a number of questions:

  ➤ What is effectiveness in the HRM perspective?

  ➤ What are its indicators?

  ➤ What are its predictors?

  ➤ Can it be specified or measured?

  ➤ Can it be related to particular perspectives, environments, behaviors or structures?

  ➤ Is it a constant, or an ideal?

  ➤ Does it change with time and organizational maturity?

  ➤ Can it be sought, gained, enhanced, or lost?

  ➤ Why is one organization effective at one time with particular set of HR practices and not at another with same practices

DESIGN/METHODOLOGY

In this research all those papers which are published in prominent HR journals were scanned and those published during last five year period were kept under sharp focus. Papers pertaining to the field of HRM and organizational performance were categorized and examined in detail. Papers were qualitatively classified in accordance with selected dimensions. Process enabled the researcher to carry out a systematic review and explore new dimensions and those not adequately covered in the existing literature. It is a structured overview adequately reflecting upon salient and most pertinent aspects.

FINDINGS/RESULTS

A deep analysis of available literature enabled the researcher to explore new dimensions which are real contribution to the body of knowledge. It has been found that there is an increasing trend towards integrating traditional HR functions into wholesome strategic approach to human capital management.

Some integration opportunities include:

- Aligning employee goals with corporate goals
- Linking reward and recognition programs to performance
- Targeting learning and development toward performance gaps
- Identifying skills and competencies of top performers for retention and succession planning

OTHER SIGNIFICANT FINDINGS ARE AS UNDER

- Past research amply reflects that impact on performance will be far greater when HR practices are used in conjunction with each other instead of employing these in isolation. In other words, bundles of practices will result into more dramatic changes.

- The strongest impact of HR practices can be observed in those organizations that have strong leadership able to differentiate between performances and give performance messages

- It is imperative to carryout an ongoing goal review and get feedback from managers. The goals can be manipulated keeping in view various organizational and contextual factors.

- Organizations usually operate on a piecemeal basis, by resorting to inconsistent choices of policies as a result of various pressures. Most of the literature in the area of human resource strategies ignores the actual process by which the strategies are formed and concentrates instead on the chosen policies and practices. This is an important gap.

- Concept of fit is central to literature; several HR policies can only form an HR strategy provided it has an internal and external fit. Internal fit refers to consistency among set of HR policies in question and external fit is their congruence with firm's policy apart from HR.

- It is important to engage the employees with motivation and ability in discretionary behavior through consistent HR policies.

- Effectiveness of HRM policies largely depend on organizational culture, that requires a managerial style which is decentralized and expertise oriented.

- HRM policies cannot affect organizational performance directly. Their impact is mediated by certain other factors including employee skills, attitudes, and behaviour.

- Resource-based view of the firm became a central theme HR function in HRM literature during the 1990s. HR was considered as an asset adding value to firm thereby providing competitive advantage. Knowledge is considered as a source of competitive advantage that organizations can use SHRM to exploit.

- Talent management is considered as core competency in the domain of HR expertise. Management of people with unique and valuable capabilities taken as strategic human resources has been established as a key role for the corporate HR function

CONCLUSION

The clear point made by management scholars who are deeply involved in organizational study is that good should not be considered as good enough as that line of thinking leads the organizations towards a state of decline and blocks the road to greatness. The challenge for today's managers is to move from "effectiveness" to "greatness" to increase the potential of the modern organization. HRM is an area that continues to evoke a lot of debate body of work in HRM is relatively small, and most of the questions are sorely in need of further attention. It is fashionable to raise questions about the viability of HRM because the research stream had mixed results. Criterion measures of HRM have not fully evolved fully therefore these cannot be utilized to compare organizations and evaluate the effects of HR practices.

RECOMMENDATIONS

An effort has been made in this research to close gap in research by examining the effects of HR practices. The results assist managers in finding appropriate HR practices.

Few pertinent recommendations are:

- Significance of SHRM as an important tool of successful organizations when suitably aligned with organizational goals stands affirmed. Bundling of HR practices should facilitate the attainment of strategic objectives which are in larger organizational interest. In other words employees may be used as source of strategic competitive advantage.

- It is imperative to build supportive organizational culture for HR practices, focusing on enhancing performance.

- There is a need to narrow down the scope of ongoing research to those components of HR practices identified as feasible for organizational functioning and further refine the mechanics of their application.

- Test of leadership lies in resorting to those HR practices that are likely to raise the performance to a new height. Therefore leadership should have clear vision and communicate these visions to the employees.

- Concept of fit as perceived by researchers as highly pertinent, but how to achieve that particular fit needs further exploration .Synergetic effects of internal and external fit will equal the desirable level of organizational effectiveness. 7.6 In order to further the frontiers of knowledge it is recommended that some standardized framework accepted allover be evolved while making an effort to strike a kind of uniformity among key contextual factors. This will further expand the generalizability of results.

    ➢ It is recommended that there is a need for research methods which offer remedies to the two major problems of the past:

> ➤ Practitioners' access to and use of relevant research findings,

> ➤ Researchers' access to and experimentation with "real world" situations.

• More realistic relationships between researchers and practitioners would create a larger, more interactive community of interest among the producers and consumers of organizational research in the field of HRM. This could be achieved through researcher/practitioner partnerships based on mutual understanding of the benefits to be derived from research with engineering of effectiveness as its focal point.

REFERENCES

1. Baker, D. (1999). Strategic human resource management: performance, alignment, management. Library Career Development, 7(5),51–63.

2. Franc, Danya, o., Guedrib, Z., and Hatta, F. (2008). New insights into the link between HRM integration and organizational performance: the moderating role of influence distribution between HRM specialists and line managers. The International Journal of Human Resource Management, 19(11), 2095–2112.

3. Gellatly,I.R.,Hunter,K.H., Currie,L.G., and Irving,P.G. (2009).HRM practices and organizational commitment profiles. The International Journal of Human Resource Management, 20(4), 869–884.

4. Gillian Maxwell,G., and Farquharson,L.(2007). Senior managers' perceptions of the practice of human resource management. Employee Relations Journal, 30(3), 304-322.

5. Gooderham,P.,and Nordhaug,O.(2010).One European model of HRM? Cranet empirical contributions. Human Resource Management Review ,21 ,27–36.

6. Hartel, C.E.J., Fujimoto, Y., Strybosch, V.E., and Fitzpatrick, K. (2007), Human Resource Management: Transforming Theory into Innovative Practice, Frenchs Forest, NSW:Pearson Education Australia.

7. Hall,M.L.,Hall,C.L.,and Andrade,L.,and Drake,B.(2009).Strategic human resource management: The evolution of the field.Human Resource Management Journal,19 ,64–85.

8. Harris,L.(2007). The changing nature of the HR function in UK local government and its role as "employee champion" .Employee Relations Journal,30(1) , 34-47.

9. Katou,A.,and Budhwar.P.(2010). Causal relationship between HRM policies and organisational performance: Evidence from the Greek manufacturing sector European Management Journal, 28, 25– 39.

10. Keegan,A.,Huemann,M.,andTurner,J.R.,(2011) Beyond the line: exploring the HRM responsibilities of line managers,project managers and the HRM department in four project-oriented companies in the Netherlands, Austria,the UK and the USA. The International Journal of Human Resource Management, 1, 1-20.

11. Lado, A. A., and Wilson, M. C. (1994). Human resource systems and sustained

competitive advantage: A competency-based perspective. Academy of Management Review, 19(4), 699−727.

12. Mcginnicle,J.P.,Jameson,S.M.,(2000). HRM in Hotels: focus on commitment. Employee relations journal,22(4),403-422.

13. McKenna,S.,Richardson,J., Singha., P., and Xu.J.J(2010). Negotiating, accepting and resisting HRM: a Chinese case study. The International Journal of Human Resource Management, 21(6), 851–872.

14. Minbaeva,D.,(2008). HRM practices affecting extrinsic and intrinsic motivation of knowledge receivers and their effect on intra-MNC knowledge transfer. International Business Review ,17, 703–713.

15. Othman,R.B.,and Poon,J.M.(2000).What shapes HRM ?A multivariate Examination. Employee Relations Journal ,22(7),467-484.

16. Shen,J.,and Zhub,C.Z.(2011). Effects of socially responsible human resource management on employee organizational commitment. The International Journal of Human Resource Management, 22(15), 3020–3035.

17. Steinmetz,H., Schwens,C., Wehner,M.,and Kabst, R.(2011). Conceptual and methodological issues in comparative HRM research: The Cranet project as an example. Human Resource Management Review, 21, 16–26

18. Tharenou,P., Saks,A.,and Moore,C.(2007). A review and critique of research on training and organizationallevel outcomes. Human Resource Management Review, 17, 251–273.

19. Tissen,R.J.,Deprez,.F.R.E.,Burgers,.R.G.B.M.,and K.Montfort,V. (2010).'Change or hold: reexamining HRM to meet new challenges and demands':the future of people at work: a reflection on diverging human resource management policies and practices in Dutch organizations.The International Journal of Human Resource Management, 21(5), 637–652.

20. Turner,R., Huemann,M.,and Keegan.(2008).A Human resource management in the project-oriented organization: Employee well-being and ethical treatment. International Journal of Project Management, 26 , 577–585.

21. Teo,S.T.T.,Clerc,M.L.,and Carmen Galang,M.G.(2011). Human capital enhancing HRM systems and frontline employees in Australian manufacturing SMEs. The International Journal of Human Resource Management, 22(12), 2522–2538.

22. Werbel,J.D., and Demarie,S.M. (2005).Aligning strategic human resource management and person–environment fit. Human Resource Management Review, 15, 247–262.

23. Zanko,M.,Badham,R.,Couchman,P.,and Schubert,M.(2008). Innovation and HRM: Absences and politics. The International Journal of Human Resource Management, 19(4), 562–581.

8

CHAPTER

HISTORY OF HUMAN RESOURCE MANAGEMENT: IT'S IMPORTANCE IN ADDING VALUE TO ORGANIZATIONAL SUCCESS IN GAINING COMPETITIVE ADVANTAGE

Mubeen Mujahid, Syeda Nudrat Sameen, Hina Naz, Farkhanda Nazir and Sobia Manzoor

MS & Research Scholar, Department of Management Sciences, The Islamia University of Bahawalpur, Pakistan

ABSTRACT

Human Resources are the most important factor in attaining highest levels of organizational success by gaining competitive advantage in today's diverse business world. In order to understand the concept of Human Recourse Management entirely, researchers enlightened different phases/Origins of HRM. Researchers attempt to find out the importance of human resource management in Organizational culture by discussing the roles of Human Recourse Management and its diversity by elaborating the different types of HRM practices implemented in the organizations and their particular impact on the organizational performance. Researchers conclude authentically after discussing deeply about the HRM concept that the proper n effective application of HRM in Organizations results in organizational success by attaining competitive advantage.

INTRODUCTION

Human Resource Management is now often seen as the major factor which differentiates between successful and unsuccessful organizations, more important than technology or finance in achieving competitive advantage. This is particularly important in the service sector where workers are the primary source of contact with customers, either face-to-

Citation: Mubeen Mujahid,Syeda Nudrat Sameen, Hina Naz, et al,2014, History of Human Resource Management: It's Importance in Adding Value to Organizational Success in Gaining Competitive Advantage, ISSN 2222-2839

face in a service encounter or over the telephone or the Internet. Even in manufacturing firms the way in which human resources are managed is seen as an increasingly serious element in the production process, primarily in terms of quality and reliability. Much of this revolves around the extent to which workers are prepared to use their tact to improve products and services. In this argument a particular style of HRM is envisaged: one that can be broadly termed the 'high commitment' model. Human Resource Management is not a technology; it's an art of managing people on work to enhance their skills and motivation. Drucker (1997) suggest that "it is not technology, but the art of human and humane-management" that is the growing challenge for executives in the 21st century. Similarly, Smith and Kelly (1997) believe that "future economic and strategic advantage will be with the organizations that can most effectively attract, develop and retain a diverse group of the best and the talented people in the market place".

In general, to maintain a competitive advantage in the market place, firms need to manage its available resources to achieve the desired results of profitability and survival. The resources that are available to the firm can be categorized into three categories: physical, organizational, and human. In discussing how to gain a competitive advantage in the global market, Porter (1990) stated that management of the human resources is the most critical of the three. The idea of treating human resources as a means of gaining a competitive advantage in both the domestic and the global marketplace has been criticized by other authors. As Greer (1995) states, in a growing number of organizations human resources are now considered as a source of gaining competitive advantage. There is greater perception that distinctive competencies can only be obtained through highly developed employee skills, distinctive organizational cultures, management processes, and systems. This is in contrast to the traditional emphasis on transferable resources such as equipment. Moreover, it is being recognized that competitive advantage can be obtained with a high quality work force that enables organizations to compete on the basis of market responsiveness, product and service quality, differentiated products, and technological innovation.

LITERATURE REVIEW

With the changing trends of industry in the competitive environment of open market, human resource management becomes a significant variable for the efficient growth of any organization. Manpower planning was the very first concept used in ancient eras with the passage of the trends changes and the concept of manpower planning changed and become personal management. Today personal management is known as Human resource management. Some of the factors or significant variables mentioned by the American writers Terrey and Franklin (1996) 6 "M" of management, viz. Men and women, material, money, market and method. Among these, men and women the only living being do the effective coordination and utilization of these human and non-human resources. Managing human resource is a complex process. As Harzing and Ruysseveldt said "A better way to understand the philosophy of human resource management demands a thorough understanding about the evolution of the concept itself from the ancestral concept personnel management". Becker and Huselid (1998) indicate the most significant value that is generated in the result of Human Recourse function by focusing primarily on delivery of HR practices like staffing, development, compensation, labor relations, etc. which is based on professional and often research-based principles. These practices are important, and research indicates that when they are done well they add tangible value to the organization.

The Gilded Age

Historian Page Smith examines the industrial revolution "The War between Capital and Labor." the two sides were indeed at war, with armies of armed men fighting on both sides. The level of human violence and destruction of property did in fact often create warlike conditions, a situation exacerbated by the fact that many workers were Civil War veterans. They declared themselves just as prepared to shoot a corporate hireling as they had been ready to kill a Yankee or a rebel. America's captains of industry, who themselves often rose from very modest circumstances, saw workers as commodities to be dealt with like any raw material. Cold, ruthless, calculating and impervious to the negative effects of what they were doing, they hired their own armies to deal with recalcitrant laborers.

Posts–World War II (1945–1960)

During the war the mobilization and utilization of labor had a great impact on the enlargement of the personnel function. Managers recognize the importance of employee productivity and inspiration had a considerable impact on the effectiveness of the firm. After the war the human relations associations put emphasis on that employee were also motivated by social and psychological factors, such as receiving gratitude for work accomplished or for the achievement of work standard, not just by money. During the war, due to the categorization of large numbers of individuals in military service organized efforts began to classify workers around occupational groups in order to get better recruitment and selection measures. The innermost part of these classification systems was the job description, which scheduled the tasks, duties, and responsibilities of any individual who seized the job in question. These job description classification systems could also be used to plan suitable compensation programs, appraise individual employee performance, and provide a basis for execution.

Social Issues Era (1963–1980)

This period witnessed an extraordinary increase in the amount of labor legislation in the United States, legislation that preside over various parts of the employment association, such as the exclusion of prejudiced practices, provision of retirement settlement, the encouragement of work-related health and safety, and tax regulation. As an end result, the human resources department was loaded with the extra accountability of legislative fulfillment that required collection, analysis, and reporting of huge data to legislative authorities. For example, to make obvious that there was no favoritism in employment practices, a human resources department had to attentively collect, evaluate, and store data containing to all employment functions, such as recruitment, compensation, training, and benefits. It was about this time that personnel departments were beginning to be called human resources departments and the field of human resource management was born. The increasing need to be in agreement with several employee protection laws or experience major economic consequence that made senior managers responsive to the meaning of the HRM function.

Another factor was the economic boom in nearly all industrialized countries. As a result, employee trade unions were successfully negotiated for superior employment conditions, such as health care and departure settlement. As a result, labor costs greater than before, which force human resources managers to validate cost increases against productivity development. With the increased importance of employee involvement and empowerment, the human resources function changed into a protector relatively than a caretaker function, changing the focal point away from maintenance to advance of employees. As a result, the width and deepness of HRM functions extended and bring the need for planned thinking and superior delivery of HR services.

Cost-Effectiveness Era (1980 to the Early 1990s) U.S. and other international firms has increased their focus on cost reduction through automation and other efficiency enhancement procedures, as competition increased from rising European and Asian economies. As consider HRM, the improved managerial burden strengthens the need to execute the legislative necessities, generally the entire functional focus transfer from employee supervision to employee progress and participation. To progress the effectiveness and efficiency through cost reduction and value-added services in service deliverance, the HR area came under stress to connect technology that was becoming more powerful and cheaper. Moreover, there was an increasing insight within administration because their costs were a very important part of a company's budget. Some companies have estimated that their human resources costs were as high as 80% of their operating costs. As an effect, there was an increasing command on the HRM function to cost defend their employee agenda and services.

Technological Advancement Era and the Emergence of Strategic HRM (1990 to Present) Throughout the 1990s, economic background undergoes various drastic changes like increase globalization, technological advance especially Internet, Web services, and hectic rivalry. Business reengineering has workout and become more general and regular, follow-on in several ideas, such as the rightsizing of employee numbers, creating independent work teams, reducing the layers of management, reducing the rigidity and outsourcing. Firms today have realized that pioneering and resourceful employees offer a sustainable viable benefit because, like other assets, intellectual capital is complex for competitors to reproduce. For that reason, the human resource management function has turned into strategic in its importance and viewpoint emphasized on to attract, preserve, and hold talented employees. "These developments have direct to the formation of the HR balanced scorecard (Becker, Huselid, & Ulrich, 2001; Huselid, Becker, & Beatty, 2005), in additional to stress on the return on investment of the HR function and its plan" (Cascio, 2000; Fitzenz, 2000, 2002). The greater utilization of technology has altered the focus of the HRM meaning, and shift to add the value to the organization's product or service, that led to the appearance of the HR department as a strategic partner. As growing the magnitude and gratitude of people and human resource management in modern organizations has become significantly important in management thoughts and practices. "Strategic HRM originate its theoretical impact from the resources-based analysis of the firm that delights human resources as a strategic asset and a competitive advantage in improving organizational performance"(Becker & Huselid, 2006).

Origin of HRM

Decade	Business Realities	HR Name Changes	Issues
Pre-1900	Small Business & Guilds	Did not yet even Exist	Owners Owned the HR issues
1900	Industrial Revolution	Labor Relations	People as interchangeable parts
1920	Civil Service & WW1	Industrial Relations	Worker rights and more formalized Processes
1940	Scientific Management & WW2	Personnel Administration	Efficiency experts and more highly evolved HR processes
1960	Civil Rights & Compliance	Personnel	Legal Compliance and Reporting; "Policy Police"
1980	Human Relations, the Knowledge/Service Economy, and Mergers & Acquisitions	Human Resources People	Relevance in a fast-changing world; Motivation and "Human Relations" theories abound
2000	Modern Organizations	Organization Effectiveness? Human Capital? Organizational Capability?	No new official names, but lots of "Morphing" as the transactional parts get outsourced and the transformational parts get defined

Role of Human Resource Management in the Organization Human resource management plays a vital role in the organizational development and its progress. It is very important for the organization to get more powerful and develop its self to be the standard and success one. HRM plays an important role in promising employee satisfaction, improving performance and productivity. Moreover an organization's competitive advantage, and directly contribute to the organization's success. When any organization start to vision their business, their first priority is to hire competent work force means right person on the right job after that this man power decide about other tangible and intangible resources, where to get? How to get? How to manage efficiently? What modification required? Essentially, other resources depend on human resource without which they are worthless because if there would be no human then who will plan, organize, or monitor the other resources. The manager is recognized as a holder of organization by his knowledge and art. According to Therith (2009), HRM is important for the organization to make it competitive and helps in to gain competitive advantage. Therith (2009) elaborated the three competitive challenges:

Challenge of sustainability

There are many different type of companies or organization to operate in the world and also competed each other to gain competitive advantage and also sustainable so they try to implement many strategic for develop their HR. Among them sustainability is the main part that can be influence and encourage to reach organizational goal. There are many ways that helps organizations to reach their goals:

- Learning organization
- Balanced score card
- Total quality management

Global Challenge

For the survival organizations have to cooperate with each other. They have to struggle to defend in the local market and to reach the global goal they have to communicate with each other, and they have to compete with the foreign organizations.

The Technology Challenge

This challenge is also very important that organizations/companies should be consider and prepare strategic plan to up-date it on time and saving the cost also. New technology cause change in basic skill requirements and work roles and often results in combining job. HRM plays vital role in the organization, it includes different activities. Farndale and Truss (2005), listed some of the major role of the HRM in the organization as under:

- Managing employees and their compensation.
- Creates positive environment.
- Helps in generating applicant's pool and recruitment process.
- Helps in measuring employees' performance and preparing employees for future work.
- Helps in creating pay systems and rewards for the employees.

According to Therith (2009), the new role of the HRM in the organization is as under:

- *Change Leader*: The role associated with facilitating, driving and leading change for organization creativities, productivity and quality to reach the goal and competitive advantages over competitor.
- *Human Resources Strategist*: The role associated with integrating HR activities and result in achieving the strategic objectives of the organization. Human resources strategist thing of the pattern of planning human resources development and activities intended to enable organization to achieve the goals.
- *Business Strategist*: The role associated with participating in strategy formulation and developing possible solution to challenges facing the organization to lead business to competitive success. Good business strategy formulation leads the organization success in all aspect of business regarding customers' satisfaction, providing quality products and customer services.
- *Human Resources Function Alignment*: HR function must be integrally involved in the organization's strategic process. HR managers should have input into the strategic plan, both inter of people-related issues and in term of the ability of the human resource pool to implement particular strategic alternative; have specific of the organization goal; know what type of employee skill, behaviors, and attitudes; and develop programs to ensure that employees have those skills, behaviors and attitudes.
- *Partner to General Manager*: HR plays an important role for organization to survive, overcome competitor challenge and to pave the way for organization to get success in business. HR also closely related to line manager to set up strategy

plan and strategy implement and work design. Line managers help HRM to manage and control employees' performance whether they should be promoted, increments and need of more training, etc.

HRM Practices and their Various Types

In order to develop a sound HRM system, the organization should have effective Human Resource Management practices. As Schuler & Jackson, (1987) ; Schuler & MacMillan, (1984) ; Wright & Snell, (1991) advocate that HRM practices refer to organizational activities which generate a pool of human resource and ensuring that the resources are employed towards the fulfillment of organizational goals. Usually HRM practices may vary organization to organization or country to country.

HR practice is an old concept followed by number of years many researches on HRM practices have been conducted from time to time and researchers have identified different practices by different names. As PankajTiwari (2012) cited in "(Kok Jan de et al.,2003), researchers variously refer to certain sets of HRM practices influenced by the HRM profession as "best practice,"or "high-performance" (Huselid, 1995), "formal" (Aldrich and Langton, 1997; de Kok and Uhlaner, 2001; Heneman and Berkley,1999), "sophisticated" (Golhar and Deshpande, 1997; Hornsby and Kuratko, 1990; Goss et al., 1994; Wagner, 1998) or as "professional" (Gnan and Songini, 2003; Matlay, 1999). Pfeffer(1994; 1998), argued the most appropriate term is "Best HRM Practices"".

According to Chandler and McEvoy (2000), there is no single set of practices that represents a 'universally superior approach' to managing people. Some certain HRM practices are universally in practice of different organizations which are used separately or may be in a combination that is associated with improved organizational performance. As Boxall, (1996); Lowe and Oliver, (1991); Pfeffer, (1994) concluded in their researches that those well-paid, well-motivated workers, working in an atmosphere of mutuality and trust, generate higher productivity gains and lower unit costs.

Several attempts have been made from time to time by different researchers to identify the type of HRM practices in different sectors. Initially Pfeffer (1994) identified 16 practices which denote best practice. This was later refined to the following seven practices:

- Employment security
- Selective hiring
- Self-managed teams/team working
- High compensation contingent on organizational performance
- Extensive training
- Reduction in status difference
- Sharing information

Some key practices are identified by Redman and Matthews (1998) an 'HRM bundle' of practices which support service organizations quality strategies, these being:

- Careful recruitment and selection, for example, 'total quality recruitment', 'zero defects recruitment', 'right first time recruitment'.

- Extensive remuneration systems, for example, bonuses available for staff willing to be multi-skilled.

- Team working and flexible job design, for example, encouraging a sense of cohesiveness and designing empowered jobs.

- Training and learning, for example, front line staff having enhanced interpersonal and social skills.

- Employee involvement, for example, keeping employees informed of key changes in the organization.

- Performance appraisals with links to contingent reward systems, for example, gathering customer feedback to recognize the work by employees over and above their expected duties, which in turn is likely to lead to a bonus for staff.

Traditional Shortfall of HRM

Most of the business managers are disturbed with the establishment of HR activities if still these activities are implemented in fine and sound manner but managers are not sure how these practices are helpful in order to developing their employees in effective manner . One of the leader said that "I can realize the importance of HR activities that are relates to training, management and development but I am also concerned about that which abilities and capabilities are most essential and rather than tactical actions. Boudreau and Ramstad (2004) stated that HR managers can devote their more time on HR measurements techniques e.g., HR financial reports, HR scorecards and more focus on how can attitudes, skills, abilities and knowledge of employees can be increased and effective through HR programs like training and development. However all these HR actions can influence some important decisions of business e.g. enter and exit into a new market. These actions can give some ways that how organizations can achieve competitive advantage through effective and more skilled labor. So here the question is that Is business investments and decisions are really measure by talent?

Human resource management is very useful figure in all sectors of the organization in order to achieve competitive advantage but many firms established the Humana Resource training programs above the employees. Human resource training is competent and effective if it produces desire result and profit. When the organization is implemented the Human resource training programmers, there should be a model facility on which the measurement strategy can be increased and improved, the classification of strength of HR training and usage activities.

Marchington and Wilkinson (1997) suggested that many line managers experience that they are already suffered from the overload of the work that are given from the top management of the organization, so that's why they give no proper attention or priority on HR activities. They suggest that if the mission statement of the firm is focus on the training, development and management of their staff, then line managers may choose up different signals from top management about the order of priorities, and thus will focus on the achievement of targets which are more assessable and valued than HRM related activities. The other important issues which are measured in the traditional shortfalls of HRM are the progress of the skills required by line managers.

Boyle stated that, 'if devolution of tasks are to take place and operate effectively, line managers must be prepared to take on the people management part of their job' (1995, p.43). Although many researches indicates that the training, development, management of people and developing them in proper manner is a critical success factor for any organization (McGovern et al, 1997), According to Boyle (1995) he suggests that the development of such skills represents a particular challenge in the public sector, where managers may see themselves as specialists, rather than as managers of people. In addition to that managers also need practical and professional support from the top management and skills if they are to get on responsibility for HRM activities (Merchant and Wilson, 1994).

New origin

HRM is a modern source and through human resource activities organizations can achieve competitive advantage and different views or concepts are coming from different people or authors about HRM some says that it is personnel management and some says that it is traditional personnel management.

Lack of top management support

Top management must identify the training and development needs of their employees in order to fulfill competent task related to their jobs. HRM must have the support of top level management that can modify the attitude of the top and can bring fine result while implementing Human resource process. Because of inactive attitude at the top management level, this work is handled by personnel management people.

Improper implementation

Human resource management process should be implemented by identified the training and development needs of the employees. The needs and aspirations of people should be taken into account while farming human resource policies. Because proper training is required that are related to their job and interest is more important in order to perform and fulfill their job related tasks. Organization cannot achieve desire result without proper implementation of human resource activities and programs.

Insufficient development programs

Human resource management requires implementations of programs such as career planning like provide them career guidance that how employees make their career choices, on the job training that how employees perform their current job more efficient, development programs that are useful in their future job tasks, counseling etc. Top management must take into account that which development programs are offered to employees that are helpful in their future assignments.

Insufficient information

Some organizations have not proper information about their employees. So because of lack of information the data base system is not properly implemented. Before implementing the process of human resource management essential data about training and development needs of the employees should be collected and stored. Whenever sufficient information about employees training and development is not gathered, top management cannot give competent tasks to employees.

CONCLUSION

In this paper researchers studied about the importance of handling human recourse management of the organizations effectively in order identify its impact on attaining organizational success by getting competitive advantage. Researchers studied different origins of human resource management and its particular role in the organizations. Various type of HRM practices employed in organizations have been discussed by the researchers in order to draw the results. Researchers conclude that effectively handling of human resource management by the organizations results in attaining higher levels of organizational success by having competitive advantage over other organizations.

REFERENCES

1. Kaizenlog, (2006). The historical background of human resource management.

2. Salvatore, P., Weitzman, A., & Halem, D. (2005). How the Law Changed HR. HR Magazine, 13, 50, 47-56.

3. Senyucel, Ventus. (2009). Managing the Human resource in 21st century. ApS ISBN (978-87-7681-468-7).

4. Smith, A People's History of the Post-Reconstruction Era: The Rise of Industrial America, New York, 1984, p. xiii.

5. Vosburgh, R. M. and Resorts, M. Developing HR as an internal consulting organization. Human resource planning, 30.0.

6. Becker, B. E., Huselid, M. A., & Ulrich, D. (2001). The HR scorecard: Linking people, strategy, and performance. Boston: Harvard Business School Press.

7. Beatty, R. W., Huselid, M. A., &Schneier, C. E. (2005). New HR metrics: Scoring on the business scorecard.

8. Organizational Dynamics, 32(2), 107–121.

9. Becker, B. E., &Huselid, M. A. (2006). Strategic human resource management: Where do we go from here?

10. Journal of Management, 32(6), 898–925.

11. Cascio, W. F. (2000). Costing human resources: The financial impact of behavior in organizations (4th Ed.).

12. Cincinnati, OH: South-Western College.

13. Fitz-enz, J. (2000). The ROI of human capital: Measuring the economic value of

employee.

14. Performance. New York: AMACOM/American Management Association.

15. Fitz-enz, J. (2002). How to measure human resource management (3rd ed.). New York: McGraw-Hill.

16. Boudreau, J.W. & Ramstad, P.M. (2004). Talentship and the Evolution of Human Resource Management From "Professional Practices" To "Strategic Talent Decision Science."

IMPACT OF THE HUMAN RESOURCES ON THE RISK MANAGEMENT AND THE COMPANY PERFORMANCE

Is'haq Ibrahim Bani Melhem

Department of Economics and Muamalat, Universiti Sains Islam Malaysia, Nilai, 71800, Malaysia

ABSTRACT

According to the recent studies the human resource is the most important source and head the company on the right trail to achieve the aims, this paper led to study some factors which its impacting on the human resource existence in the company and their impact on the risk management and the total performance as well, these factors are education, skilled, and the expert human. By using the sample from USIM University and using the regression analysis, have found that there is a huge impact for these factors on the risk management and the company final performance. And that's reflecting the positive relationship between the study hypothesis and the results.

INTRODUCTION

This topic has two of parties, and both of them are so important matter in any company. If we noted recently most of CEO for the huge operation they talked about the risk. How we can do with the risk around? And they tried to avoid it, especially after the last crisis which many corporations in the worldwide they closed defiantly. And they focused to know what the risk sources exactly are? How to control, be ready and in the

Citation: Melhem IIB (2016) Impact of the Human Resources on the Risk Management and the Company Performance. Int J Econ Manag Sci 5: 320. doi:10.4172/2162-6359.1000320

suitable position? While the weak company they left the market to find new industry or for bankruptcy, the other part is the human resource which is the power of this entire world so it's the engine for the operations, manufacturing, managing, and improving the company performance. The human mind is always the gold worth for the company because, any business in this world based on notions and the notions source is the human mind and the human skills, also its having golden touch on the processing. Which it gives high performance and add value on the outcome by different characteristics in the different minds. The education level and the experience years also its have big turn to help in this processing. In addition the human resource flexible so we can guide and control it as we like and improve it also by training. As narrated by Lengnick-Hall, et al. [1], the impact of the human component in organizations is described to understand the importance and the critical role of the human resource in organizational success studies from the 1970s show the need to overhaul the traditional human resource management (HRM) which has led to the significant changes and the concentration on the strategic value of human resources. The risk management and human resource, how they support each other so this research will mention for issues of how we can prepare the risk management by using the human resource and if that have any relationship to reflect on the risk management, what is the technique for the protection mechanism from the risks, this is the issue what this study going to find the clear answer for it, which it is the value of the human resource for the risk management? When this study talk about human resources and risk management in one field so we need to investigate if we have effect first or those are separated topics after that exploring at out the affection size and mechanism as well as that is aspects which the human resources effect on the risk management, actually to know all these points we have to ask, whom are familiar with our topic about:

Q1: What is the impact of educated, skilled, and experts' human resource on the risk management?

Q2: How the human resources affect on the risk management?

Q3: Why the companies need these characteristics which we must find it in the human character?

This researcher has chosen this topic to study it as an important point and aspect, it will save the business, money, and support the aims, mission, and the vision, so the human resource management can has impact on the general performance, the conditions are what do need to know about this fact so the objective is touch the importance of human resource, and the size of the effects on the risk managing.

Recently the risks rate it grows so much, it's become big facing for all corporations which if it's can defend about its business it will survive in the market, so avoiding the business risks is the choice for each corporation that need to continue. What are the elements of the risks? Which it could find safe for the corporations and focusing on these elements, and in this study chosen the human resource based on thinking it is a one of the elements which it can support the corporation and find the awareness factor inside it as planning, decisions, processing, outcome, performance, control, and readiness for any risks and circumstances around.

This paper mentions that there are many factors inside and outside the company which they influence on the company performance and the presence as well. And the human resource considered one of the factors which it helps in the corporation to push it up and keeping the balance for its business. And this study heading to identify the size of influence the educated, skilled, experts' human resources on the risk management, are they increasing the readiness for the risk management. During this research paper and for the readers, there are some concepts needed to be known which makes the understanding and the harmonizing with the research topic easier. The relation between HRM and performance is not yet fully understood even after fast growth in human resource management [2-4].

The first concept is the risk management

Risk management is an important subject especially now because of the ongoing financial crisis, surveys done on the subject shows the need for risk management and how important it is to business, to increase the effect of risk management we must create a set of critical success factors to have a successful risk management [5].

The human resource

The human whom they are pillar of the corporations as the worker and manager, and those people who control the production processing and all of the corporation outcomes and results which it must be checked by the human resource (human) and have influence on this progress, of course it's controlled by the human resource [6]. So always they must oversee each particular small thing even some of the authors they called it performance management which it means and show the huge turn for the human resource on the performance, it considered the engine for the transactions, decisions, controlling, organizing, operations, hiring, organizations as all, and the organizations culture [7].

The educated employee

The company workers those whom they have advance certificate and those whom they are keeping on touch with the technology and development and they are knowing about the modern manners to treat the crisis and risk may it will face the business based on science, knowledge, and education.

The skilled employee

The employee whom they are discovering and created employee they can exploit their skills to work so well, and run the company by their notions and make differentiate value for the company so we need them to find the solution when we face a trouble, they can find it during short time and by simple tools. As mentioned by Clutterbuck and Hirst [8], a sign of a competent leader or a manager is his ability to communicate, being good at communication will enable such manager to have a better understanding of the objectives, expectations and goal. Team members whom communicate will have a better understanding of what they want to be and where they at.

The experts' employee

The existence of the experience for the employee is so important for decision making and supporting the company plans based on the last years circumstances and situation, and find the optimal plans and solutions almost, because they have background about the same status before, they can defend about the company market share and growth rate as well as when they know the alternative and available resources for them company, so they can control and manage the environmental factors surround.

UNDERPINNING THEORIES

According to Wright and Snell, [9] for the corporations to be a competitive advantage creator, they suppose to invest in the human capital, combine and employ their most important strength which its (skills, knowledge, and experience). Recently managers as well as have been seriously attempting to employ and manage the real competitive advantage- human capital- to more effective and efficient.

To develop the company we have to change the corporation vision and develop the knowledge which it must mix with culture to work together and change the process to reach the company for the objective and cover all the corporation needs. The human resource management by whole or its aspect as the strategies, practices, role, political and the impact it studied often in large entities. The human resource risk management service line leader in the United States of America (USA) they agree and support that huge importance for the risk management during the human resource stage, and its effected matter for the international executives [10]. The not sure happen occur is what we called it the risk management so it's an experience taken through previous happens to be used to support the future, so it's still unhappy and probably it will have bad impact and prevent the corporation from covering the goals [11].

The human resource staff must have and gather data base about the persons whom in charge for the governance, the acquiescence matters and the risk. Even the human resource managers have to show the corporation managers with whole statements of human research acquiescence and the processing risks. In addition the bespoke works, and agrees with the duty of deducting them. The human resource can offer help for the committee in same or near field like supporting the development committee and management services, and improving the rewarding committee too [12].

According to Deloitte, mentions for the human property as a most huge capital for any corporation and its merit the significant, and their conducts almost the most significant and hugest sources for the business risk. And the people risks must be as main risk in the corporation future plan. The human resource work in many aspects, to do facing the external risks if there are strong sources in the company, while it will be one of the corporation risks and weakness some other times, in which the 42% of the corporation expenses spent it in the readiness of the human resource and process workforce concern. For ready and stronger organization in the future, and avoid any trouble lead the company to be unable to face and avoid the future risks. The management theory is supporting the research and planning it. This research is matching between the readinesses of the human resource and influenced that on the risk Management, and how that does can happen? When you have strong human resource and qualified means you can face any risk, and that's what is managing the risks to get more safety and comfortability.

CONCEPTUAL FRAMEWORK

This research connecting between two different parties in the business, what it means have many elements can influenced on both of them as workers skills, if it helps the corporation to keep stand always, the size of the risk has huge impact on how and what we would face it and some of the risks can avoid it. And circumstances its behind the size of the risk but it is being defend depend on what the mechanism and the system you are following and how you did for like these surprising occurs.

The source of the risk is one of the most important variables for this research. Which based on from where the company get and suffer with this risk? is it from inside the corporation or outside as well as if it's from inside so you have weakness and problem in the corporation and if it's from outside so what you have to do, is you have to check your plan if you expect that before and did you have alternative plan for that?.

And the general education level for the all corporations is important to support its in the risk management, because the risk management need for awareness and mature people and that's mean also the knowledge consist in the organizations, what it guide the boarder to ride the right trails, Because the based on knowledge and knowledge based on scientific study and investigate, what it gives rational outcomes.

The paper has basic contains based on in the framework shows the main elements for the study, in this paper took only one aspect to focus more on, this in the independent factors and in the dependent factor it's the risk management.

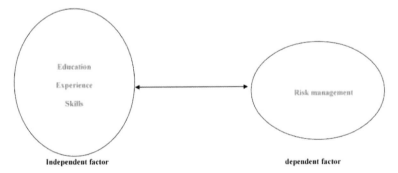

Figure 1: Independent factor.

This paper goal is testing the relationship between both of the framework aspects while the hypothesis said there is positive relationship between them as shown in Figure 1.

Finally these variables are effecting on the human resource and the function in the risk management how it is working by duality way to make harmonization between both of them (the risks, and human resources). In fact between many variables related with this study and this topic but in this study want to know exactly, how the human resource qualifications (educated), skills, and the experiences its effecting on the risk management so these variables seem as related with qualitative but actually what is targeting it is how that's effecting not the size of the qualifications. Simply studying the heading to how and what is the consequence for the workers qualifications, skills, and experiences not the size of its. So is it positive or negative relationship, and follow the steps what it is helping to make the completed cycle for these process.

HYPOTHESIS

The hypothesis would be tested are:

H1: the skilled stuff has appositive impact with the risk management.

H2: the education qualified worker or educated employee they have positive relationship with the risk management performance.

H3: the experts members in the risk management they have the highest capability to increase the quality of risk management performance.

Now need to test that if the hypothesis its right or wrong, have to choose sample in proper environment to make the survey for these hypothesis.

Measures and instrumentation In this descriptive research which it describe the managers education level, experience, and skills specifically and how they are effecting on the risk management and they have turn to organize, expect and control the risk and the data was collected by using the questionnaire. Which the education aspect will measure the level of the education diploma, bachelor, and master. And measure the different impact for that level on the performance for the risk management; secondly measure the experience years, type (major) which it's identify the impact of the experience factor on the risk management and managers. Thirdly measure the skills if its mind (manager), hand (IT, software) skills to know the type of the skills and the impact on the risk management performance, and measure the plan, solutions and experience for the risk managers how the independent factors can effect on.

Population and sample

The sample is the 35 educated, experts, professional managers in university as education organization from university science Islamic Malaysia (USIM). Al-sakran mentioned that the research test 30-300 sample is valid for the scientific research and the results able to be acceptable. This study as mentioned before selected the managers and the three classifications from them which they are educated, expert, and the skilled managers in (USIM). Additionally, this study will be use SPSS 17.0 to clarify the relationship between independent and dependent variables. The scanning process as explained by Raes et al. and Roe is detecting discontinuities in the environment. This procedure is the activities practiced by top management and middle manager to change the current strategy to new situation by analyzing and filter information from the external context [13].

Hypotheses testing-regression

The study proposes three hypotheses to test the relationships between the four factors (educated, experts, skilled) human resource on the risk management. The mean values of variables within the constructs or factors were calculated and regression analysis was conducted on these values.

The coefficient of determination (R^2) measures the proportion of the total variance of the dependent variable about its mean that is explained by the independent or predictor variables. The higher the value of R^2, the greater the explanatory power of the regression model. It is found that the regression model R^2 value for the dependent variable risk management is 0.522, meaning that 5.22% of the total variance in students' risk management are explained by the regression model. This value is considered high and thus the power of the regression model is good. This implies that the model is statistically significant (F=11.263, p<.001). The values of the regression coefficients and their significance determine the factors included in the model.

In short, referring to the data in Table 1, the regression model supports the following hypotheses:

• H1: skills --- risk management there is a positive relationship between skills and risk management

(SIG= 0.033<0.05).

H2: education --- risk management there is a positive relationship between service quality and risk management (SIG =0.028<0.05).

The three factors got results but we found the experience factor has the highest significant, and the experience years has influence to judge the impact for the labors on the risk management performance, and sometime the experience even help to measure the skills because it's effected by the years of work to acquire more skills.

Table 1: Regression coefficients

Coefficients[a]						
Model 1	Unstandardized Coefficients			Standardized Coefficients	t	Sig.
	B	Std. Error		Beta		
(Constant)	2.961	0.925			3.201	0.003
Education	0.27	0.117		0.384	2.313	0.028
Experience	0.124	0.16		0.127	0.773	0.005
Skills	0.006	0.179		0.006	0.035	0.033

[a]Dependent variable: Riskmang

Based on the previous study (Experience can be helpful to the project managers and project team in identifying specific risks on the corporations, expanding the thinking of the team as well. The past experience of the project team, project experience within the company, and experts in the industry can be valuable resources for identifying potential risk on a project). Once the Project Team identifies all of the possible risks that might jeopardize the success of the project, they must choose those which are the most likely to occur. They would base their judgment upon past experience regarding the likelihood of occurrence, gut feel, lessons learned, historical data, etc. [14]. Moreover, in case any gap isn't exactly identified by the managers would be filled by the experienced teammate [15].

The education makes the workers behavior more safety, rational and build all the decision on basic and principle, clear for the future plan. The employees should be educated, as well involved in exercises and training, to increase the capabilities being strengthened facing any potential risks, [16].

According to Thomas and Allen [17], the individual education for the corporation members able to find the knowledgeable and educated corporation, as well the ability to learn is builder by the learning corporations, what is figuring out that the human capital structural value could interpret as the learning corporation structure.

The past studies find the knowledge loss effects negatively on, and deducts the general corporations outcomes, the knowledge which it's unique or difficult to imitate. As well as the skills, mentioned the effective integration of risk management and human resource management requires that managers have certain skills. Most important are: leadership, communication, training, motivation, conflict management, and evaluation.

People and risk are as integral to farming as are weather, prices And technology, Human resources must have careful attention and a full understanding the sources of risks and their solutions for handling risk.

According to Bontis, one of the term three sub-constructs is human, and mentioned that the way to generate the wealth is IC (intellectual material) which it's knowledge, information, intellectual property, and experience. And they are all found in the company human capital.

The results for the three hypothesis it were positive that's give it accepted from the sample and approved, which means in brief the educated members in the company generally and in the risk management especially have impact on the risk management and that's reflect on the whole performance in the corporation and the business or service outcomes, about the skilled members so they are the mind of the company and the notions resources as well as the guideline for the company which they are using many ways to follow the best and easiest trail in the business and avoid any crisis especially during this era have many obstacles for any business, finally for the experts employee they are the language of the corporation what it can ask them help to speech with the past current and the future circumstances and express about what are the reoperation procedures to do.

In this respect, Wei and Lau [18-23] and Wei, Liu, Zhang and Chiu [24-30] show that organizational culture influences the way top managers perceive human resources in organizations.

CONCLUSION

This study come out with how the company can organize and utilize from the human resource inside the company, which need to hire the experts' employee in the risk management department, to ensure existence of the skills in the workers qualifications certificate, In other words, the corporation members have to be experts in the specific major for the company to keep the company firm balanced. its necessarily of the educated stuff to comply the modern manner in the science and technology, and focusing on the human resource in the risk management more than anything else because it's the decisions sources, and offer them the continues training which it's important for them to be in touch with them newcomer to perform their tasks [31-34]. The company performance development is based on selecting employees with highly specialized skills and on developing their skill base through off-the-job trainings whenever they need it. The educated, skilled, experts committee for the risk management has the heavy weight to impact on the performance; Give the risk management strong force if it has the qualified, skilled, experts' human resources. This study starts with a description of the research problem, research questions, research objective, and its significance. The literature reviews of literatures are discussed to support the research carried out. The research model and the hypotheses were developed based on the inputs from preliminary study, previous research, and theories, during this stage the hypothesis tested already and got the results which it were position [35,36]. In brief, the experts, educated, and the skilled managers are impacting on the risk management department in the company which it's improving the company performance at all.

REFERENCES

1. Lengnick-Hall ML, Lengnick-Hall CA, Andrade L, Drake B (2009) SHRM: the evolution of the field. Human Resource Management Review 19: 64-85.

2. Paauwe J (2009) HRM performance: achievements, methodological issues and prospects. Journal of Management Studies 46: 129-142.

3. Guest DE (2010) Human resource management and performance: still searching for some answers. Human Resource Management Journal 21: 3-13.

4. Wright PM, McMahan GC (2011) Exploring human capital: putting human back into strategic human resource management. Human Resource Management Journal 21: 93-104.

5. Al-Tamimi H, Al-Mazrooei FM (2007) Banks risk management: a comparison study of UAE national and foreign banks. The Journal of Risk Finance 8: 394-409.

6. Deloitte (2008) Consulting. Midtown: Manhattan.

7. Companies. Cape Town: Double Storey.

8. Clutterbuck D, Hirst S (2002) Leadership communication: A status report. Journal of Communication Management 6: 351-354.

9. Wright PM, Storey J, Snell SA (2009) The Routledge companion to strategic human resource management, Routledge, London pp: 345-356.

10. Ernest, Young (2009) The 2009 Ernest & Young Business Risk Report.

11. Naidoo R (2002) Corporate Governance: An essential guide for South African Juta and Company Ltd, South Africa.

12. Deloitte (2008) Taking the Reins: HR's opportunity to play a leadership role in Governance, risk management and compliance. CHRO Strategist and Steward Series.

13. Raes AML, Heijltjes MG, Glunk U, Roe RA (2011) The interface of the top management team and middle managers: a process model. Academy of Management Review 36: 102-126.

14. Stanleigh M (2010) PMO Global Study: How a Project Management Office Can Improve Organizational Effectiveness.

15. Zeynep T, Huckman RS (2008) Managing the Impact of Employee Turnover on Performance The Role of Process Conformance. Organization Science 19: 56-68.

16. Phillips RA, McNaught C, Kennedy G (2012) Evaluating e-learning: Guiding research and practice. Routledge, New York.

17. Reeves, Thomas C (1993) Pseudoscience in computer-based instruction: The case of learner control research. Journal of Computer-Based Instruction 20: 39-46.

18. Wei LQ, Lau CM (2005) Market orientation, HRM, importance and competency: determinants of strategic HRM in Chinese enterprises. The International Journal of Human Resource Management 16: 1901-1918.

19. Wei LQ, Liu J, Zhang Y, Chiu RK (2008) The role of corporate culture in the process of strategic human resource management: evidence from Chinese enterprises. Human Resource Management 47: 777-794.

20. (2015) According to a survey of risk management executives performed by The Conference Board.

21. Bernard LE (2013) Department of Agricultural, Environmental and Development Economics the Ohio State University.

22. Burkhardt H, Van den AJ, Gravemeijer K, McKenney S, Nieveen N (2006) From design research to large scale impact: Engineering research in education. Educational design research pp: 121-150. Abingdon, UK.

23. Edelson DC (2002) Design research: What we learn when we engage in design. Journal of the Learning Sciences 11: 105-121.

24. Flyvbjerg B (2007) Five misunderstandings about case-study research, Sage publications, London.

25. International ISO 31000:2009; Risk Management Principles and Guidelines ©ISO 2009.

26. McMillan JH, Schumacher S (2000) Research in Education: A Conceptual Introduction, (2nd edn): Longman, London.

27. Niss M (2006) The Concept and Role of Theory in Mathematics Education. Paper presented at Norma, Trondheim, Norway.

28. Orna E (2000) Practical Information Policies, (2nd edition), Gower, Aldershot.

29. Rowe HAH (1996) IT is failing to revolutionize the curriculum, because to date we have failed to evaluate its benefits in context, Australian Computers in Education Conference, Canberra.

30. Salomon G (1991) Transcending the qualitative-quantitative debate: The analytic and systemic approaches to educational research. Educational Researcher 20: 10-18.

31. (2008) Project Management for Instructional Designers.

32. Risk management (2011).

33. (2010) HR's Role in Effective Enterprise Risk Management.

34. (2015) Risk management.

35. (2015) Human Resource Management.

36. (2015) Australasian Journal of Educational Technology

10

CHAPTER

THE CONTRIBUTION OF HUMAN RESOURCE STRATEGIES TO THE ORGANIZATIONAL SUCCESS; A CASE OF COMMERCIAL BANKS IN KISII COUNTY

Dr. Charles Kombo Okioga

Kisii University, Kenya

ABSTRACT

Strategic Human Resource Management is the linkage between strategic management and human resource management; it is the set of managerial decisions and actions that determine the long term performance of an organization. It entails environmental scanning, strategy formulation, implementation, evaluation and control. Strategic Human Resource Management offers a competitive advantage by building critical capabilities of Human Resources, strategic management in the organization facilitates strategy formulation and in policy implementation by providing competent human resources and competitive intelligence. Strategic human resource planning introduces the aspect of a strategic plan; an important tool in determining whether an organization will have the skills and knowledge in place when it needs them. An effective strategic Human Resource management program will assist employees in using and developing skills and knowledge that will benefit the organization, the growth and self-esteem of its employees. Thus, Human Resource management is a vital tool in avoiding technological obsolescence. With a heightened competition for customers and offering quality service commercial Banks in Kenya are searching for strategies to implement so as to align business objectives with employees. If such alignment is successful, an organizational can accelerate workforce adaptation to change, improve cost-effectiveness of human resource decisions, and increase retention of the organization top achievers and this will go along way to assist in the general organizational performance.

Citation: Charles Kombo Okioga, 2013, The contribution of Human Resource strategies to the Organizational Success; a case of Commercial Banks in Kisii County", ISSN 2222-2839

INTRODUCTION

Strategic human resource management has emerged as a major paradigm among scholars and practitioners in many parts of the world. This is apparent from the recent literature on international human resource management as well from recent reviews of trends in the U.S. (Kochan et al 1994) and the U.K (Lundy, 1994). Strategic Human resource management is spreading popularity owing much to an explicit promise of enhanced organizational effectiveness which can be achieved according to the dominant models, by developing internally consistent bundles of human resource management practices which are properly matched or linked to the extent and organizational contexts, most notably business strategies. Watson Richard (1985) argues that the management of Human Resources has now assumed strategic importance in the achievement of organizational growth and excellence. As globalization advances and organization move into the information age, organizations need to adapt to the changes in technology and the changing issues in management of people. Some critical issues have clearly emerged in organizations' human resource planning, acquisition and development of human resources strategies, responding to the demands of the work place and, above all, evolving a strategy of dealing with industrial conflict. As a management practice, it covers all the conventional areas of personnel management and industrial relations, as well as the relatively new areas such as communication, counseling, training and development, and job enrichment (Watson Richard, 1985). The organization has to develop its physical resource strategies, financial management strategies and its human resource strategies. Human Resources Strategies are therefore central to the delivery of the strategic objectives that has been developed covering the innovation in the delivery of all organization activities, externally focused on the markets and customers, commercially astute and growth driven. Arthur, J. (1994) observes that flexible and integrated promotion services equipped with responsive and efficient organizational structures, to achieve financial sustainability. This requires a strategic approach to organizational development, a clear integration between strategic goals and employee's values, beliefs and behaviours and strategic interventions focused clearly on the leadership and management of change.

Commercial banks are profit making financial institutions that play a significant role in the financial sector. Commercial banks offer a wide range of corporate financial services that address the specific needs of public/private enterprise. They provide deposit, loan and trading facilities and service investment activities in financial markets. The term commercial bank is used to differentiate day today profit oriented banks from investment banks, which are primarily engaged in the financial markets. Commercial banks are also differentiated from retail banks that cater to individual customers only (Kochan, et al. 1994). Commercial banks in Kenya play a number of roles in the financial stability and cash flow of the country's private sector. They process payments through a variety of means including telegraphic transfer, internet banking and electronic funds transfers. They also issue bank cheques and drafts, as well as accept money on term deposits. They act as moneylenders, by way of installment loans and overdrafts. Loan options include secured loans, unsecured loans and mortgage loans. In today's competitive banking environment, exemplary customer service is one of the distinguishing characteristics that commercial banks can exploit to establish a competitive edge. Since most of the commercial banks offer comparable promotions and services, they continually search for a competitive advantage that will attract new customers and help them retain existing ones. They, therefore, endeavor to develop innovative programs and initiatives to maintain superior customer service levels while remaining profitable. These has led to commercial banks either downsizing or rightsizing themselves while continuously restructuring their operations in order to develop more cost effective and efficient operations (Lawler Edwards, 1992).

STATEMENT OF THE PROBLEM

In today's intensely competitive and global financial marketplace, maintaining competitive advantage over other organization, organizations must recognize its financial position and create the capacity to invest in the delivery of human resource Strategy. The employees and managers face challenges in balancing delivery of operational plans, employing the best Human Resource strategy is an investment in the organizational capability which will contribute directly to the delivery of the organizational strategic objectives and heavy premium on having a highly committed or competent workforce. When the human resource strategy is not applied to the whole organization and does not supports a general approach in the organization and is not concerned with longer term people issues and macro concerns about structure, quality, culture, values, commitment and matching resource to future needs. The strategy becomes obsolete in itself and application. The commercial banks in Kenya have introduced strategic Human resource management in the quest to retain highly qualified employees and have a high customer base. The study aims to investigate the contribution of strategic human resource management in the organizational success in the commercial banks in Kisii County.

LITERATURE REVIEW

Schuler Randy et al. (1993) observes that Strategic Human Resource Management sets out the general direction the Organization will follow to secure and develop its human resources to deliver a sustainable and successful Organization. Human Resource issues are becoming central to all strategic decision making level in the organization, the development of a culture that encourages all employees to be highly committed to the organization and its continuous improvement of trust, team working and willing cooperation making close supervision unnecessary with a consequential flattening of structural hierarchies. Managing organizational change will require putting people at the top of the agenda, planning for enhanced employees performance must be a key element of the Human Resource Strategy, line managers play a pivotal role in winning hearts and minds.(Begin James, 1991) concurs that there needs to be a clear commitment from the top of the organization to engage and equip line managers in helping them to ensure their employees are committed to the change program, Communication with employees can be mechanical. Communication has to be meaningful as it is through 'conversations' something new is created and change is addressed. Strategic objectives have been identified for each theme and will be delivered through a number of supporting strategies some of which have been developed and others which will be formalized in accordance with an agreed plan. The human resource strategic themes are attracting and recruitment, reward and recognition, learning and development, leadership, management of performance and employees engagement (Begin James, 1991).

Betcherman et al (1994) argues that Human Resource strategies are core in maximizing the potential talent of the employees, Human Resource strategies are interlinked and facilitate the delivery of the organizational goal and enhance organizational performance and Operational Plans. Organization and workforce must embrace strategic human resource planning in order to deliver the organizational success. Given the unique organizational profile and the challenges in attracting and developing the employees profile, Understanding the talent and their potential within the current employees when trying to recruit and select 'high flyers', Expanding the recruitment base to include the developing structured training programmes to support 'growing their own talent' Developing excellent Human Resource progression opportunities as a means of attracting and retaining key employees. (Betcherman et al. 1994) Developing appropriate strategies for the development of high potential individuals like the identification of talent pools. Using succession planning to identify future potential leaders for key positions and develop them accordingly also ensuring that equality and diversity is embedded in all stages of the talent management process.

Walton Richard (1985) observes that the competition for high quality middle and senior skills is likely to increase as organizations focus on communication, coaching and leadership skills as well as professional and technical skills. A human resource strategy should assist in developing succession planning policies that identify and develop employees to fill these roles. This needs to be linked to the leadership and management. Human Resource progression policies support the development and retention of key employees, the Organization needs to consider the identification of talent pools and develop tailored development polices to support that particular group. An increasingly diverse workforce with independent views about their lifestyles, requires well developed polices on work life balance.(Lundy olive,1994) The flexible Working Strategy provides the opportunity to balance operational and individual requirements to enhance corporate performance through reduced absenteeism rates and increase employees motivation and job satisfaction. The leadership and management challenges of a flexible working environment are also recognized.

Lawler Edward (1992) argues that Organization need to develop a greater understanding of the markets and how to widen the potential pool of applicants. Aligning the recruitment and selection processes with Organization strategies and Organizational plans. Changing the resourcing policies to recruiting flexible pools of employees recognizing that some jobs will always require specialists, identifying and developing groups of jobs to enable potential successors to be identified for a variety of roles in developing talented administrators, each of whom is adaptable and capable of filling a number of roles. Developing long term work force planning models that inform recruitment and deployment plans. The development of strategies and policies to promote the Organization as an employer of choice and Human Resource progression policies that support flexible employee deployment. Schuler, Randy & Jackson Susan (1987) defines Performance management strategies as a holistic process which brings together many of the elements that go to make up the talent management pipeline. The management of performance in the Organization needs therefore to be strategic and integrated with all other elements of the human resource Strategy and Organization operational plans. The Organization will develop its human resource information systems to support efficient performance management tools which are appropriate to the scale of the Organization's operations. The ability to invest at appropriate levels in the implementation of the Human Resources Strategy is linked to achieving the Organization's income growth targets and creating the capacity for investment. Failure to deliver that investment capacity will inhibit the Organization's ability to support delivering the changes in culture, skills, competencies and behaviours needed to achieve its strategic growth objectives.

Why strategic Human Resource Management

Recruitment of right person on right job is a critical issue in domestic as well as marketing for the organization. In an organization, human resource manager is fully responsible for recruitment of right person. Because of different culture and religion, it is difficult to provide the required training and development programs to the employees at global level (Preffer Jeffrey, 1994). Managing talent is also a critical issue to address at international level due to high competition. Cultural change at global level create complication to manage skills and talent of diversify workforce to implement the strategies and plans in order to achieve organizational goals and objectives; It also affects the training and development programs of organization.

Presently, managing globalization is also a critical issue for human resource manager. Due to globalization and regular changes in technological and social environment, liberalization of trade policies and regulations, etc. it has become critical for human resource managers to cope with the competitive environment that affects the performance of organization at domestic as well as global platform. Managing demographic workforce is also an emerging issue for the organization and human resource department. At domestic and global level, there are many policies and regulation that affects the recruitment policy of an organization to manage people specially, aging workforce. Company's pension plan, retirement benefits for aging people are affected by the governmental policies (Lawler Edward, 1992). This is a very important and difficult challenge for human resource managers in recent times.

Managing organizational changes and culture at global level also creates the issues for organization and human resource department. In most of the time, organizational changes create conflicts between employees and management team that affects the culture of the organization (Kochan et al. 1994). So change management is an important emerging issue for the human resource managers. A best practice in strategic human resource management has invoked a great deal of interest among Human Resource professionals. Companies that are currently under-performing in the human resource area can learn and adopt some of the best practices from organizations that have acquired some mastery over the good practices in human resource. In the era of liberalization, the competitive scenario in the business environment has changed a lot. Consequently, human resource practices have also changed phenomenally. The performance of the employees determines the failure or the success of an organization. Arthur Jeffrey, (1994) indicates that Multi-cultural workforce congregations have become today's workplace realities. The cross-border market terrorism spared by multi-national corporations evoked counter-insurgency and strategic warfare from domestic businesses. Partnering people in this race is vital for success in the market place. Workplaces have increasingly symbolized multi-cultural villages, resulting in a growing need for cross-cultural intelligence (Arthur Jeffrey, 1994) the future competitiveness of corporations will depend on their ability to attract and manage diverse talents effectively. Cross-cultural training will give managers on international assignments the cultural understanding essential to accomplish their tasks. Cross-cultural differences are the cause of failed negotiations and interactions, resulting in losses to the firms. The strategic role of human Resource Management in strengthening and sustaining corporate growth has assumed paramount significance, the world over.

Promotions and process alone can't help organizations to sustain loyal customers. They also need highly-motivated, dedicated and involved employees who are very passionate about their work and their organization; in short, they need "engaged employees". But, nurturing engaged employees requires a lot of effort and skill on the part of human resource managers and calls for a different human resource philosophy in the organization.

Lundy Olive (1994) states that the employee engagement to serve as a core competency of an organization that would provide sustainable competitive advantage. employee engagement towards their work, human Resource few test "symptoms", feeling of creating value, having a direction to follow, an air of trust, creating engaged employees human Resource top management endorsement, a work environment to cherish, innovative leadership and clear growth trajectories, 'one step up from commitment'. Employee engagement is the new buzzword. A successful business is directly linked to the commitment of its employees. Employee engagement ensures the successful execution of any business strategy.

The challenge before human resource professionals today is to create an enabling organizational climate for the employees, For this, they need to examine relevant issues such as training and development, performance appraisal and Human Resource planning in the organization. Selection and recruitment of personnel is an important responsibility of the human resource department (Walton Richard, 1985) the recruitment policy provides competitive remuneration as per industry norms, maintains high standards for selection of recruits, and encourages lateral induction to infuse fresh ideas and new skills in the organization.

Arthur Jeffrey (1994) insists that after successful selection and recruitment of manpower, it is essential that all employees undergo specific training programmes that help in maximizing their potential. Today's need is to place training and development at the heart of a business strategy. Training should be a continuous process keeping in view the changing market demands, the environment and the organizations' own culture. The role of a trainer, on the other hand, should be that of a mentor, facilitator and change agent. Assess the training needs of individuals who will be undergoing training, to avoid a mismatch with training programme. Provide a questionnaire to help the participants analyze their own capabilities. This includes their knowledge, skill, aptitude and attitude. Bring out the latent potential in people and channelize it towards the common goal of the organization. Design training programmes. Ensure that the programme covers behavioral and cognitive leaning, focuses on up gradation of skills and encourages group participation. Include the real world programmes to solve the real life problems.

Performance appraisal is a process of assessing the capabilities, both known and hidden, of employees, so that their strengths and weaknesses can be determined for increasing the organizational effectiveness. The appraisal is for identifying, whether the employee is: Due for a promotion or reward or an increase in salary (Begin James, 1991) Capable of handling additional responsibilities or needs future training and development to upgrade their skills. Incapable of meeting the requirement and is, thus, dispensable. 360° feedback appraisal system is the formal performance appraisal system. In this system, the employee receives feedback from his manager, supervisor, peers and others, that he comes in contact with. It helps in increasing employee participation, makes the person feel more committed, increases his sense of ownership for company policies, and allows alignment of personal expectations with organizational goals; it helps in assessing the employee strengths and weaknesses (Begin James, 1991).

RESEARCH STRATEGY

The study adopted a survey research design of all commercial banks in Kisii County to evaluate the contribution of strategic human resource management on service delivery. This type of study design enabled the researcher to single out a specific group of bank users to find out their view on the quality of service they receive from the commercial banks. The study was carried out among all the commercial banks in Kisii County. The study targets 300 bankers and customers in Kisii County which has nineteen (19) commercial banks. The target population for each commercial bank consisted of general manager, tellers, operation manager and the customers. A sample comprising of 30% of the total population was taken. According to Kothari (2008) 30% is appropriate sample for descriptive studies. Thus with the target population of 500 respondents the researcher chose 150 calculated at a confidence level of 95%. Since the population of study was not homogeneous population, the researcher employed stratified random sampling technique to select respondents. The strata comprised of the 19 commercial banks with different populations. Kothari (2008) mentions that stratified sampling technique were generally applied in a heterogeneous population in order to obtain a representative sample. Consequently, since the researcher intended to collect data from all the commercial banks within the area under study, each bank happens to have a different number of customers who are served by them. The following formula was used to sample the population used for the study. The representative ration of each group was calculated to settle on the sample population in the study. This helped the researcher to distribute the target population representatively among the banks under study. This is indicated in the table below:

Banks	Total Population	Sample
1. KCB	59	18
2. Barclays Bank	47	14
3. K-Rep Bank	8	2
4. Equity Bank	74	22
5. Cooperative Bank	35	10
6. National Bank	24	7
7. Eco Bank	8	2
8. DTB Bank	11	3
9. SCB Bank	6	2
10. Family Bank	17	5
11. CFC Bank	14	4
12. Equity Keroka branch	56	17
13. KCB Keroka branch	42	13
14. Cooperative bank Keroka branch	16	5
15. KCB Nyamira branch	16	5
16. Equity Nyamira Branch	25	9
17. Family Bank Nyamira Branch	11	3
18. Cooperative bank Nyamira Branch	14	4
19. Barclays bank Nyamira	17	5
Total	500	150

The data collection instrument used in this study was a questionnaire and an interview schedule. The questionnaire designed by the researcher consisted of close and open ended items. The close ended section evaluated the quality of strategic human resource management shown by services provided by the bank and the open ended section solicited to find respondents views on the possible ways of improving the quality of strategic human resource management to meet customers need. The interview schedule consisted of items administered among the banking personnel in charge of strategic human resource management in all the commercial banks in Kisii County.

To ascertain the validity of the instrument, questionnaire designed to tap information from the respondents' content validated by relevant the experts in research to test the Suitability of items and appropriateness of language will also be determined.

To ascertain the reliability of the instrument, the researcher carried out a pilot study by using a test-retest method on 10 respondents from K-Rep Bank Kisii Branch. This population was not involved in the actual study. After the two administrations of the questionnaire, data collected from the field was analyzed through a Statistical Package for Social Sciences (SPSS, 11.5). Acceptable reliability was accepted at Alpha Coefficient of 0.5 and above. Relevant adjustment was made on the instrument by adjusting some questions which might seem ambiguous to the respondents and not giving a clear picture of the survey.

The data was collected coded, keyed into SPSS (Version 11.5) computer software database, organized and checked for any errors that could have occurred during data collection. The data was analyzed with the aid of the SPSS and Microsoft Excel 2007 computer software. Descriptive statistics were adopted for data analysis and presentation, total percentages, frequencies, bar graphs, pie chart to describe the data while chi-square and bringing in weighted average scale technique were used to analyze and interpret the data.

RESEARCH FINDINGS AND DISCUSSION

Respondents on Years worked in the organization

Most of the employees have worked in this organization for 0-2 years with 64% and the least 36% having worked for 3-10 years revealing that most employees have not worked in this organization for long.

Table 1

Years worked	Frequency	Percentage
0 – 2 yrs	96.0	64%
3 – 5 yrs	24.0	16%
6 – 10 yrs	15.0	10 %
Over 10 yrs	15.0	10 %
Total	150.0	100%

Respondents on Integration of Human Resource strategies

The research findings showed that the commercial Banks have integrated the Human Resource Strategies in their work place well indicated by 58 % because the organization knows the importance of the human Resource strategies.

Table 2

Response	Frequency	Percentage
Very well	33.0	22.0
Well	87.0	58.0
Average	30.0	20.0
Total	150.0	100.0

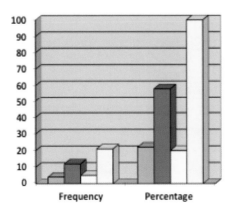

The above table reveals that, 58% of the respondents suggested that the organization is using its strategies well to improve organizational performance, 22% said that the organization has been using the strategies very well. The least, 20% revealed that they averagely used the Human Resource strategies.

Extent of management's involvement in HR Strategies Implementation

Respondents on the Level of management's participation in Human Resource strategies Implementation. The extent to which the management are involved in Human Resource strategies implementation in the organization the respondents showed 82 % were of average and 3 % were of very High extend and 17.6% were of low extend revealing majority of the respondents were saying it has an average effect on service delivery.

Table 3: Extent of management's involvement in HR Strategies Implementation

Response	Frequency	Percentage
High extent	3.0	2%
Average	123.0	82 %
Low extent	24.0	16 %
Very low extent	0.0	0.0%
Total	150.0	100%

The above table reveals that, the existence of the mechanism in Human Resource strategies implementation that is all inclusive favoured by many respondents since activities that borders on Human strategies implementation like staff engagement rather than organizational, have a great impact on organizational performance, with majority response indicating that they were averagely involved in human resource strategy implementation with 82 % and the least with 2%. Indicated they were highly involved in implementation.

Respondents on the Strategies which are used to deal with Non conformity with Human Resource Strategies

Table 4

Response	Frequency	Percentage
Warning	114	76
Suspension	30	20.0
Dismissal	6	4
Total	150.0	100.0

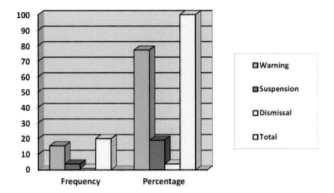

It shows that the organization have been frequently using warning as a way of correcting non conformity to human resource strategies that the commercial banks introduce so that it can improve it performance. This is obtained by 76 % of the respondents view. Unless on serious occasions the suspension of employees is done on rare occasion when the organization has no otherwise to deal with non conformity the employees are dismissed it is equivalent to 20 % of the respondents view.

Table 5: Model Summary

R	R square	Adjusted R square	Std. error of estimate	Change statistics				
				R square change	F change	Df1	Df2	Sig F change
.918(a)	.843	.805	.51038	.843	1.242	4	36	.000

Predictors: (Constant), Strategic review, market strategy, Promotion strategy, Investment strategy Dependent Variable: Commercial Bank competitiveness.

As shown in Table 5, none of the predictor variables had coefficient of correlation between themselves more than 0.5; hence all of them were included in the model. The analysis also indicated high correlation between the response and predictor variables. The Analysis shows that the coefficient of determination (R2) equals 0.843, that is, Strategic review, market strategy, Promotion strategy, Investment strategy explain 84.3 percent of Human resources competitiveness leaving only 15.7 percent unexplained. The P- value of 0.000 (Less than 0.05) implies that the model of Human resources competitiveness is significant at the 5 percent level of significance.

Table 6

	Sum of squares	Df	Mean squares	F	Sig
Regression	.852	4	.213	1.242	.000
Residual	6.173	36	.171		
Total	7.024	40			

Predictors: (Constant), Strategic review, market strategy, Promotion strategy, Investment strategy Dependent Variable: commercial bank Performance

A multiple regression model has been used to describe the relationship of Human Resource strategy and commercial bank competitiveness (Y) which depends on Market strategy (X1), Promotion strategy (X2), Investment strategy (X3) and Strategy review (X4). This is given by the equation;

$$Y = \beta_0 + \beta_1 X_1 + \beta_2 X_2 + \beta_3 X_3 + \beta_4 X_4 + e_i, \text{ where } e \text{ is the error term}$$

Findings (P- value of 0.00) shows that there is correlation between the predictor's variables (Strategic review, market strategy, Promotion strategy, Investment strategy) and response variable (commercial bank competitiveness) the estimated multiple linear regression equation was found to be: $Y = 0.260 + 0.131X_1 + 0.170X_2 + 0.051X_3 + 0.048X_4$

Model Elasticity Constant = 0.260, shows that if Strategic review, Market strategy, Promotion strategy, Investment strategy were all rated as zero, Commercial Bank competitiveness would be 0.260. $X_1 = 0.131$, shows that one unit change in Market strategy results in 0.131 units increase in Commercial Bank competitiveness. $X_2 = 0.170$, shows that one unit change in Promotion strategy results in 0.170 units increase in Commercial Bank competitiveness. $X_3 = 0.051$, shows that one unit change in Investment strategy results in 0.051 units increase in Commercial Bank competitiveness. $X_4 = 0.048$, shows that one unit change in Strategic review results in 0.048 units increase in Commercial Bank competitiveness.

Table 7: Coefficients of regression equation

		Unstandardized Coefficients		standardized Coefficients	t	sig
		B	Std Error	Beta		
Constant		.260	.460		0.565	.231
Marketing strategy	X1	.131	.048	.254	2.729	.001
Promotion strategy	X2	.170	.045	-.300	3.778	.0000
Investment strategy	X3	.051	.023	.113	2.217	.0002
Strategy review	X4	.048	.022	.093	2.182	.0000

CONCLUSION

The study used regression analysis to investigate the association between Human Resource strategies on the commercial bank performance, Promotion strategy, Market strategy, Investment strategy, Strategic review and Commercial Bank competitiveness which was found significant (with R2, 84.3). It was established that the relationship between Commercial bank competitiveness and Promotion strategy was strong at 75.2; moderately strong with Marketing at 53.6; moderately weak with Investment strategy at 46.7 and weak with the Strategic review at 30.7. The R 2 of 84.3. All the independent variables were found to be linearly related with the dependent variable thus a model of four predictor variables could be used to rate Commercial Bank competitiveness. The significant relationship that was established between Commercial bank competitiveness and the strategies under investigation, which was similar to findings by other scholars such as Kochan et al (1994) the traditional functions of Human Resource Manager now need to be strategically directed towards developing and sustaining organizational capabilities, human resource activities that overlap with traditional business functions such as finance, marketing, and non-traditional activities, such as knowledge management. Human resource strategies play a virtual role and help the communications process in the organization. Most importantly, organizations can hire and retain the top performers, improve productivity and enhance job satisfaction of the employees. Human Resource Management has the responsibility to maximize efficiency and profit, but in the emerging scenario, the role of human resource manager is changing rapidly due to changes in government policies, unions, labour legislations and technology. The trends have taken place in the organization, human resource planning, job design, motivation, and recruitment and skill development and employee relations.

REFERENCES

1. Arthur, Jeffrey. "Effects of Human Resource Systems on Manufacturing Performance and Turnover". Academy of Management Journal, Vol. 37, No. 4, 1994, pp. 670-687.

2. Begin, James. Strategic Employment Policy: An Organizational Systems Perspective (Englewood Cliffs, NJ: Prentice-Hall, 1991).

3. Betcherman, Gordon, McMullen, Leckie, Norm, and Caron, Human Resourcing. The Canadian Workplace in Transition (Kingston, Ontario: Industrial Relations Centre Press, Queen's Organization, 1994).

4. Kochan, Thomas and Osterman, Paul. The Mutual Gains Enterprise (Boston, MA: Harvard Business Organization Press, 1994).

5. Kothari, C.R. (2008) Research Methodology; Methods and Techniques, (5ft Ed) New Age International LTD, New Delhi.

6. Lawler, Edward E. III. The Ultimate Advantage: Creating the High Involvement Organization (San Francisco, CA: Jossey-Bass, 1992).

7. Lundy, Olive. "From Personnel Management to Strategic Human Resource Management". The International Journal of Human Resource Management. Vol. 5, No. 3, 1994, pp. 687-720.

8. MacDuffie, John Paul. "Human Resource Bundles and Manufacturing Performance: Flexible Promotionion Systems in the World Auto Industry. Industrial and Labor Relations Review, in press, 2000.

9. Pfeffer, Jeffrey. Competitive Advantage Human Resource People (Boston, MA: Harvard Business Organization Press, 1994).

10. Schuler, Randy. "Strategic Human Resource Management: Linking the People With the Strategic Needs of the Business". Organizational Dynamics, summer 1992, pp. 18-31.

11. Schuler, Randy, Dowling, Peter, and De Cirri, Helen. "An Integrative Framework of Strategic International Human Resource Management". Journal of Management.

Vol. 19, No. 2, 1993, pp. 419-459.

12. Schuler, Randy and Jackson, Susan. "Linking Competitive Strategies with Human Resource Management Practices". Academy of Management Executive, Vol. 1, No. 3, 1987, pp. 207-219.

13. Walton, Richard. "From Control to Commitment in our Workplace". Harvard Business Review, March-April 1985, pp. 77-84.

EFFECTIVE HUMAN RESOURCE MANAGEMENT AS TOOL FOR ORGANIZATIONAL SUCCESS

Anthony Igwe[1], J. U. J Onwumere[2], Obiamaka P. Egbo[2]

[1]Department of Management, University of Nigeria, Enugu Campus, Enugu, Nigeria

[2]Department of Banking and Finance, University of Nigeria, Enugu Campus, Enugu, Nigeria

ABSTRACT

Human Resource is a very important input in the production matrix. Other seven inputs include materials, money, time, energy, knowledge, information and infrastructure. These inputs are transformed by the process to get the output with feedback and control. It is also an input of the Leontief's model. In this model, there are three elements, namely; inputs, transform and output, all of which need human resource to galvanize them to be productive. Management involves the design and provision of an environment within groups and organizations so that the individuals and the groups and organizations can achieve their objectives by utilizing both human and material resources. Human resource management is one of the functional areas of management. The others are finance, marketing, production, research and development and innovation. Human resource management consists of personnel management, industrial relations management and employee welfare management. So the early founders of production management are also the founders of human resource management such are Rountria, Robert Owen, and Henry Fayol. Today, most organizations prefer to use the term human resource management to designate such funsctions as recruitment, section, placement, induction, orientation, training and development, wage administration and motivation. Today, human resource management has

Citation: Anthony igwe, J. U. J onwumere,Obiamaka P. Egbo, Effective ,2014, Human Resource Management As Tool For Organizational Success, ISSN 2222-2839

become very important as a tool for organizational success. For an organization to succeed, it has to first of all breakeven, when total revenue equals total cost and even to have units produce beyond breakeven point as well as survive and still perform well. To perform well, it has to achieve its objectives and goals. It has to satisfy the demands of stakeholders and staff and the regulatory authorities. It is against this background that this study undertakes a theoretical review of human resource management as a tool for organizational success.

INTRODUCTION

A major contributory area to organizational success is the management of workers in organizations. Business success in a market economy is dependent on the optimal utilization of relevant resources such as the financial resources, material resources, and human resources. It is through the combination of these resources that the attainment of the goal is achieved. However the most significant and complex component for the attainment of organizational success is the human resource.

The concept of human resource, according to Udo-Udoaka (1992: 45), refers to the managerial, scientific, engineering, technical, craft and other skills which are developed and employed in creating, designing and developing organization and in managing and operating productive and service enterprise and the economic institution. Human resource is composed of individual working for an organization, employed these days as temporary staff or contracted staff but collectively making up the most important of organizational resources. Therefore, an organization must have the right number and types of employees who must be managed in such a way that they will be able to achieve their personal and organizational objectives.

Since the early 1980s, the field of human resources management has been in a state of rapid transition. As the world continues to experience profound changes, different sets of changes are revolving. Today, most managers are comfortable with the term "Human Resources" but a few still prefer to refer to "people", "Employee" or "staff" and to use the term "personal management". Cowling (1998;35) argues at one level that terminology 'may be deemed to be less important, because it is practice that really counts. However, at another level, he argues that it does matter because ways of managing people at work have come a long way in the last fifteen years, and a refusal to use the modern term "human resources" can be an indication of a failure to recognize and utilize recent development.

Human resource management (HRM) involves practices that ensure that employees' collective knowledge, skills, and abilities contribute to business outcomes (Huselid, Jackson, & Schuler, 1997). The traditional conceptualization of HRM focused on managing, measuring, and controlling organization's workforces. Tactical (Whitner, 1997) or technical (Huselid, et al., 1997). HRM includes selection testing, training, performance measurement and administration of benefits (Whitener, 1997). Huselid, et al (1997) have identified empirically a second dimension of HRM activities: strategic HRM whih involves employee participation and empowerment, communication, team based work design, and development of managers of the organization. Arthur

(1994) identified two types of human resource systems similar to those found by Huselid et al (1997): Commitment and control. The human resource system that is based on commitment is focusing on the psychological links between organizational and employee goals. It is associated with higher involvement in managerial decision, participation, providing training and rewards. A human resource system that is based on control focuses on directly monitoring and rewarding employee behavior or the specific outcomes of that behavior (Arthur, 1994).

The theoretical literature suggests that HMR practices increase productivity by increasing employees' skills and motivation. Moreover, HRM practices contribute to business objectives through strategic innovation or technical competence. Recent empirical studies on larger companies supported the basic assumptions of HRM theory (Arthur, 1994; Huselid, 1995; Huselid et al., 1997). Does this theory apply to small-scale enterprises as well? HRM also carries costs and they might neutralize the positive effects of HRM in small-scale enterprises. HRM is an investment, and thus, it costs time and/or money. The current performance of employees may even be decreasing because of the time spent on training. Moreover, HRM can only have effects when employees stay in the company for a certain period of time. Otherwise, the company suffers a loss because of the investments in HRM. Thus, the benefits of HRM must exceed costs invested in HRM. Since small-scale enterprises have limited financial resources it is very well possible that large investments in HRM do not pay off. This paper, therefore, reviews human resource management as a tool for organizational success. It is divided into six sections. Section one is the introduction. Section two examines the perspectives of human resource management and the human resource function with section three looking at the importance of personnel and human resource management. Section four x-rays current challenges, issues and trends associated with HRM. Section five shows some results of human resource management contributions in business success while section six contains our conclusion.

PERSPECTIVES OF HUMAN RESOURCE MANAGEMENT AND THE HUMAN RESOURCE MANAGEMENT FUNCTION

There are numerous definitions of the term human resource management as there are many experts in the field and it is called by different names for example, in certain public enterprises it may be called personnel administration, employee relations or manpower. Human resource management is concerned with the proper use of human factors in business. Byers and Rue (2000:75) are of the opinion that human resource management is that part of management that is designed to provide for and coordinate the employees in the organization. Plants, equipment and all others that a modern firm uses are unproductive except for the effort and direction by human resource.

According to Obikoya (2002 :6), "human resource management process is that part of mangement process that specializes in the management of people in the work organization". To Randal S Schuler and Landra L. Hummer (1993: 48), human resource management can be defined as the use of several activities to ensure that human resources are managed effectively for the benefit of the individual, society and the business. According to (Cole, 2002 : 44) human resource management is that part of management which is concerned with people at work and with their relationship within an enterprises and it seeks to achieve both efficiency and justice.

Human resource management has to do with various operative functions of recruiting, maintaining and utilizing a labour force in such a way that objectives for which the company was established are attained economically and effectively. In sum, human resource management can simply be defined as an effective and efficient utilization of human element at work.

Human Resource Management Function The personnel/human resource department programme of each organization is unique and personnel activities will vary somewhat from firm to firm yet trends clearly indicate that the scope personal responsibilities in increasing in organizations of all sizes. Personnel/Human resource management functions can be described as follows;

- Job analysis and design
- Recruitment and selection
- Appraisal Training and Development
- Compensation and wealth
- Employee relations

(1) Jobs Analysis and Design

For an employee to perform satisfactorily, his or her skills, abilities and motives to perform the job must match the job requirements. A mismatch may lead to poor performance, absenteeism, turnover, and other problem. Through a process called job analysis, the skills and abilities to perform a specific job are determined when scientific management was popular, jobs were created to be simple and routine so that unskilled works could be quickly learned. A primary assumption to such job design was that the average workers had no need to gain satisfaction from work and had neither the skill nor the inclination to participate in work decisions, no doubt many assumptions about turn to the century workers were valid. But through employee needs, the motives have experienced many changes since the formative years of industrialization. Job design in many organizations skill resembles that of scientific management. Organizational research shows that employees are not only demanding more satisfying and rewarding work but also demonstrating that their involvement in decision making can enhance rather than impair organizational effectiveness.

(2) Recruitment and selection

To a great degree, organizational effectiveness depends on the effectiveness of its employees. Without a high quality labour force, an organization is destined to mediocre performance. For this reason, the recruitment of human resource is a acritical personnel function. Recruiting and selecting a quality labour force involves a variety of personnel activities, including analysis at the labour market, long term planning, interviewing, and testing.

(3) Appraisal, Training and Developments

Organizational growth is closely related to the development of its human resources. When employees fail to grow and develop in their work, stagnant organizations most likely will result. A strong employee development programme does not guarantee organizational success, but such a programme is generally found in successful, expanding organizations.

One important development function is the appraisal of employee performance. During an appraisal process, employees become aware of any performance deficiencies they may have and are informed of what they must do to improve and be promotable. For many organizations, the heart of the development process is composed of on the job and off the job activities that teach employees new skills and abilities. Because modern managers recognize the benefits derived from the training and development process, expenditures for employee education are at an all time high. The rise in employee education has been accompanied by growing professionalism in the training field and a demand for competent, quality trainers.

(4) Compensation and Health

The issue of compensation has long posed problems for the personnel manager. How should job be evaluated to determine their worth? Are wages and salary levels competitive? Are they fare? Is it possible to create an incentive compensation system tied to performance? Techniques for evaluating the financial worth of jobs and other issues pertaining to the design of pay will not be discussed in this paper. An increasingly important part of compensation is employee benefits and because the cost of benefit for many organization is now averaging 40% of total pay roll cost, employees are trying to control benefit costs without seriously affecting the overall compensation program. The kinds of benefit that employees may offer and the considerations that should be given to planning a total benefit package are of various types and these benefits can be monetary and nonmonetary.

(5) Employee Relation

Labour unions exert a powerful force upon employees and influence personnel policies and programs for union employees. Because union participation in personnel decision making may have great impact on the economic condition of the firm, managers must understand a union's philosophies and goal and explore ways in which a cooperative rather than an adversarial relationship may be achieved. Many personnel problems are costly and impede on organization's productivity rate. Modern personnel administrators must create strategies to resolve these problems and to do so, they must posess a complete understanding of the research process. How to conduct research and development stragtegies, how to strengthen the personnel programmes.

Organizing the Human Resource Department

In organizing the human resource department, two major questions can be adressed.

Where are the human resource decisions made?, Who is responsible for those human resource decisions?

Centralizaton and decentralization

Centralization means that essential decision making and policy formulation are organized and done at one location (at the headquaters) while decentralization means that essential decision making and policy formulation are organized and done at several locations(in the division or department in the organisation).

How human resource departments are organized differs widely from one company to the other, not only because of differences in type of industry, but also because of differences in the philosophy, culture and strategic plans of the organization for purpose of illustration. It is useful to compare the centralized human resource structure with the decentralized resource structure. In the centralized human resource structure, large specialized corporate human resource staffs formulate and design human resource strategy and activities which are then communicated to the small human resource staff of the operating units for implementation. High consistency and congruence with corporate goals are attained. In the decentralization models, small corporate staff manage only the human resource system for executives and act as advisers only to operating units. Here, there tend to be wider divergence in human resource practice and flexibility for operating to address their human resource concern as effectively as possible.

Because of the rapidly changing and highly competitive environment, the trend seems to be towards greater decentralization and delegation of human responsibilities to lower human resource level and to the operating units and managers themselves. Along with this is the trend toward less formalization of human resource policies. These conditions give the human resource department and organization the flexibility for coping with the more rapidly changing environment. The diminished bureaucratization of the function of human resource department can lead to a greater openess in the human resource perspective and method used. Of course, activities such as fair employment issues and compensation matters mayhave to be centralized because of legal requirements and the sake of consistency, nevertheless the general trend is for less formalization and less centralization. Along with this is the need for everyone to be responsible for managing human resources.

The human resources manager, staff and line Managers

Managing human resources effectively is the task of individuals who have specialized in it and are primarily responsible for human resource management. Human resource managers comptrisestaff and line managers (those in charge of the employees who are producing the products and delivering the services of the company). These two sets of managers are interdependent in the management of human resources. Increasingly, they work together. Thus, chief executive officers (C.E.O), human resource managers, and all levels of senior management will be involved in managing human resources. Amidst other senior executives, the human resource leader will be indistinguishable from others, in concern for and understanding of the needs of the business, likewise the staff of the human resource department will appear indistinguishable from their counterparts in the firm, sharing in the human resource function, line managars, human resource staff, and non managerial employees together will forge and implement human resource activities, structure, roles, policy, goals and practices. The Employees:- Employees are also taking a role of human resource management. For example, employees may be asked to appraise their own performance or that of their colleagues. It is no longer common for employees to write their own job description. Perhaps most significantly, employees are taking a more active role in managing their own careers, assessing their own needs and values, and desingning their own jobs. Nevertheless, the human resource department must help guide this process to these ends, but must be staffed with qualified individuals.

Role of the Human Resource Department

The primary task of personnel department is to ensure that the organisation's human resources are utilized and managed as effectively as possible to acquired and retain an organisations human resources, personnel administrators perform four critical roles, create and implements policy, offer advice, provide services and control personnel programs and procedures.

1) *Creates and Implement Policy*: Policies are guides to management thinking and they help management achieve the organisational objectives. The top personnel officials are generally responsible for policy making. The policy should not be formulated alone but must also be implemented into the organisation and this function is also carried out by the personnel department.

2) *Advice*: Over the past several decades, management has become increasingly complex. A restrictive legal environment, sophisticated technologies, knowledgeble labour force, and demand by labour and societal groups for more "socially responsible activities" as a few of the pressures felt by managers. To cope with complex issues, managers often turn to experts for advice and counselling. All staff members have an obligation to ensure that their advice is sound, objective, and fair and will contribute to the goals of the organization.

3) *Services*: The services provided by the personnel department generally are the permanent human resource programmes and activities that aid line managers and administrators in performing their jobs. Separating services from other personnel responsibilities is difficult. On the other hand, the personnel department like each staff unit exist to serve other organisation units and practically all personnel activities may be broadly labelled as some form of service on the other hand, these personnel function are clearly services.

*   Recruitment, selection and placement
*   Training and development
*   Personnel research
*   Company recreation programs etc.

4). Control: Like the quality control department in practically every manufacturing concern, the personnel department performs important control functions for the management of human resources. For example, a written policy on equal employment opportunity is ineffectual unless executives are aware of the policy and adhere to it. Personnel administrators are responsible for monitoring personnel goals and guidelines to ensure their achievement.

Role of the Human Resource Leader

For the human resource department to perform all it roles effectively, it needs to have a leader who is knowledgeable in the human resource activities. Increasingly the human resource leader must also be familiar with the needs of the business and be able to work side by side with line management as partner in topics such as mergers and acquisitions, productivity and quality enhancement efforts. This is the essence of the focus on research. New key roles and responsibilities for personal leader include.

1). Business Person

- Shows concern for bottom line.

- Understands how money gets made lost and spent.

- Knows the market and what the business is about.

- Has long term vision of where the business is leaded.

2). Shaper of Changes in Accordance with Business

- Can execute change in strategy

- Can create sense of urgency

- Can think conceptually and articulates thoughts

- Has sense of purpose, a steadfast holding a definite value system.

3). Consultant to Organisation/Partner to line

- Has ability to build commitment into action

- Responds to organisation needs

- Recognises importance of teamwork

- Is capable of relationship building

4). Strategy/Business Planner

- Knows plan of top executives

- Is involved in strategy formulation of executive is not an afterthought.

- Develops and sells own plans and ideas and able to get needed resources

- Has three to five years focus.

5). *Talent Manager*

- Sees the movement from an emphasis on strictly numbers or bodies needed to the type of talent and skill

- needed in the organisation

- Sees the emphasis on talent needed for the executing future strategies as opposed to today's needs

- Is capable of educating management

- Knows high potential people and anticipates their concerns

6) Human Resource Asset Manager/Cost Controller

- Initiatives and does not work for others to call attention to need for action

- Can educate and self-management.

- Can creatively measure effectiveness in own areas of responsibility and other areas of organisation

- Can use automation effectively.

IMPORTANCE OF PERSONNEL AND HUMAN RESOURCE MANAGEMENT

Now, more than ever before, human resource management is recognised as being critical to the survival and success of organisations. In 1991, IBM and the internationally recognised consulting firm of towers Perrin jointly conducted a worldwide study of nearly three thousand senior personnel and human resource management leaders and chief executive officers. Results indicate that about seventy percent of human resource managers see the human resource function as critical to the success of organisations. By the year 2000, more than ninety percent expect the human resource department to be active while the human resource respondents here perhaps a bit more positive about this trend. The Chief executive officers were very close behind. While serving the very success of the business can certainly be regarded as an important goal of personnel and human resource management.

External Influence on Human Resource Management

The external factors are those factors that affect the organisation, which the personnel manager exerts little control over. Personnel administration must understand the nature and importance of the external environment and recognise its impact upon current and future personnel activities. Some of these external factors are:

Laws

The legal environment within which modern business organisations operate is a far cry from the lassiez – faire environment. Adam smith advocated 200 years ago in his classic work "The health of nations" personnel programs that not only satisfy the needs of both the organisation and employee, but they must also satisfy innumerable legal requirements. Increasingly legislative acts are helping to shape personnel programs, helping personnel administrators to study the various laws, to know how they are to be interpreted and to understand how they affect the firm.

Labour Unions

A union can have a profound impact on an organisation's effectiveness which may be viewed as a positive or negative. A Wall Street journal George Gallup study found a wide divergence in attitudes toward unions among 782 top corporate executives. Although the executives often spoke of unions in positive terms, most thought union here is detriment to organisational effectiveness. On the positive side, union here was praised for aiding in labour management, communication, co-operating in attempts to increase productivity,helping in reducing labour cost and co-operating withmanagement. On the negative side, unions were condemned for hurting productivity, meeting inflexibility in work rules, making excessive wage demands, and causing inflation. Regardless of the attitudes of managers, most agree that influence of the union is felt in practically every personnel policy, programme and activity designed for the union employee.

Labour Market

A recurring problem for personnel managers is the recruitment and selection of qualified, motivated people at reasonable wages or salaries. Labour market conditions which are heavily influenced by the supply and demand for labour, determine if an organisation can satisfy its objectives. Like the legal environment, the labour market conditions are quite variable and sometimes unpredictable; the labour market often adds an element of frustration and uncertainly to a variety of personnel activities. The federal government often publishes labour market information to assist the personnel specialist in the collection and analysis of labour market date.

Society

To great extent societal values, attitudes and benefits influence what workers want from their jobs. In contrast to workers demand more than a "fair day's wage" and a safe and healthy place of work. Many enjoy a greater involvement in their jobs and seek increased attention by management to their particular work problems and needs such demands are likely to intensify in the coming years as workers aspirations rise with increases in their educational levels.

Technology

An organisation's technology is the method and technique it uses to produce its goods and services and it attracts the skills and abilities that organisations' employees must possess. Considering the computer, as computers became common in the 1960's many bookkeeping and clercal skills were no longer marketable, keying, programming and systems analysis were in demand. But in 1980's, data entry technology eliminated the need for keypunching skills. Similar effects are expected to result from an increasing trend orwards robotics, the operation of programmable robots to perform routine assembly operations. Although the use of robots will increase productivity, employee resistance is sure to result particularly from those employees whose jobs will be eliminated by robots.

Current Challenges, Issues and Trend

To a large extent, the personnel department's newfound yet well deserved prestige is the result of the enormous responsibilities undertaken by personnel managers. Today, many problems and issues that have traditionally been the responsibility of the personnel department remain so. Examples are the recruitment, selection, orientation and training of high quality personnel, job analysis and job evaluation, labour relations and employee appraisal systems. Current problems and issues have created a new era of professionalism in personnel management. Some of these problems and issues are productive improvements, the quality of working life, safety and health, equal employment opportunity and the increase in computer usage.

1. Productive improvement

Despite the comparisons of productivity among nations, the United States still leads the rest of the world in total output yet in recent years, productivity output per hour of work has remained steady in the United States while it has increased in other countries, such as Japan and China. The crisis in productivity arose for a number of reasons; poor labour management relations, and often hostile relationship between business and government, out dated plants and equipment and lack of capital for plant modernization. In addition, the management of human resources is increasingly being recognized as having an important bearing on unemployment and productivity. Many companies report that the implementation of modern practices of personnel management has led to greater output and improved quality. Because research has shown that a sound personnel management programme can make a difference in a firm's rate of productivity, personnel role in productivity improvement should increase in the years ahead.

2. Quality of working life

Sociologists have spoken of the quality of life. Behavioural scientists have also begun using the related term, quality of working life (QWL). The quality of working life refers to the extent to which employees personal needs are met through their work. One's quality of working life improves as one's work meets more and more personal needs, such as security, responsibility and self esteem. Many organizations consider that producing a good quality of work life to employees is both a social and ethical responsibility each firm must bear. But there are strong indications that improvement in quality of work life favourably affects organization performance.

3. Safety and health

Creating a work environment which minimizes the likelihood of an accident or injury has long been a goal of both personal specialists and operating managers. In the modern work place, a number of safety and health issues have proved difficult to resolve in both manufacturing and service industries. First there is evidence that some work environments are responsible for cancer, infertility, lung disease, and other illness. Unlike an accident or injury occupational injuries, some are difficult to detect and often they remain undetected until it is too late for remedy. More and more, the work place is being labeled as hazardous to one's long term health. Secondly, job stress can be just as hazardous as an unsafe work place unlike accidents and injuries which are at most concern in construction, manufacturing, mining, and transparent industries. Job stress can be a problem in any kind of firm in any job, whether it be blue collar, clerical, managerial, or professional. Extreme stress can lead to ulcers, heart failure, nervous conditions and other psychological stress on job. Managers are now beginning to recognize potential personal and organization job stress and reduce the problem.

Thirdly, many employees suffer from some form of chemical dependency. About one in every ten employees suffers from a drinking problem that negatively affects performance. In the past, an alcoholic employee was either ignored or fired. But because such solutions fail to rehabilitate the sufferer, a growing number of firms have implemented employee assistance programs (EAP), whereby troubled employees (mostly alcoholic employees) are recognized, counseled, rehabilitated and placed back on the job. Not every employee assistance programme is said to enjoy up to 70% success rate. Most employee assistance programmes are administrated within the personnel or human resource.

4. Equal employment opportunity

Creating an environment in which equal employment is reality rather that popular slogan is no doubt one of the personnel managers toughest jobs. Much like the plant foreman who is often referred to as the "man in the middle" between labour and upper management, the personnel manager has the federal government pushing for compliance to the law while the operators press for greater autonomy in personnel decisions. There has also been the discrimination of womem at occupying managerial positions in organisations because of the believe that woman cannot make effective and some very crucial decisions

5. Increased use of computer

Computers are not new to the personnel department, though in the past, their use was primarily limited to payroll task and record keeping. Few organizations applied computer technology in ways that actually enhanced the personnel decision making process, but will the advent of desktop, micro computers and an array of personnel, related software packages in the early 1980s, the use of computers in the personnel department has increased significantly. The advantages of computerization are speed, flexibility and on-line capability. With the aid of desktop computers and even laptops, a manager can quickly retrieve a vast amount information about an employee's job status or a personnel activity, skills inventory or attendance record can obtained in a matter of seconds, flexibility is achieved through the computers ability to generates a wide variety of special reports and documents. They enable the user to build security into an information system which is not normally possible with the conventional file system. Managers and personnel administrators are able to use desktop computers (when connected to a main computer) in a variety of functions and activities. Examples include multifunctional payroll system, salary and performance reviews, and skills inventory.

Some Results of Human Resource Management in Business Success

Without the assurance that HR does make a distinction, HR professionals will not, and cannot, be encouraged to develop HR measures that drive business performance. Fortunately, in the last few years, several research studies have reported some important findings regarding the relationships between HR and business performance (Arthur, 1994; Huselid, 1995; MacDuffie & Krafcik, 1992; Ostroff, 1995; Pfeffer, 1994; U.S. Department of Labor, 1993). Several reliable themes emerge from these commendable studies of the HR–business performance relationship. First, HR practices certainly make a difference in business results, particularly the use of HR practices that build employee commitment. Second, all of these studies examine the HR system as a whole rather than individual HR practices. The synergy and resemblance among HR practices have an important impact on business performance. Third, these studies are quite robust as they examine sample firms within an industry [e.g., the auto industry (MacDuffie & Krafcik, 1992), the steel minimill industry (Arthur, 1994)] and across multiple industries (Pfeffer, 1994), both within a region (Huselid, 1995) and across the nation (Ostroff, 1995).

To develop significant HR measures, a structure is needed to outline how HR can impact business performance. Based on the experience of Eastman Kodak, this article proposes an integrative framework that builds upon a balanced scorecard framework (Kaplan & Norton, 1992, 1993) and a strategic HR framework (Ulrich & Lake, 1990). While the balanced scorecard framework defines what a business should focus on, the strategic HR framework offers specific tools and paths to identify how a firm can leverage its HR practices in order to succeed. In this section, we will first briefly review the balanced scorecard framework, then the strategic HR framework, and finally the integrative framework. If HR practices can impact business accomplishment through building up organizational capabilities, improving employee satisfaction, and shaping customer satisfaction, new HR measures should be developed to drive business performance. As succinctly argued by Kaplan & Norton (1992, p. 71): "What you measure is what you get." Unless HR measures are realigned to drive the activities and behaviors of HR professionals and line managers, HR practices can hardly be expected to demonstrate any impact on the bottom line.

Dramatic changes in HR measures are urgently required to refocus the priorities and resources of the HR function. Instead of being HR-driven (what makes sense to HR professionals), the next generation of HR measures needs to be business-driven (how HR can impact business success). Instead of being activity-oriented (what and how much we do), new HR measures should be impact-oriented (how much we improve business results). Instead of looking backward (what has happened), innovative HR measures should be forward looking, allowing managers to assess and diagnose the processes and people capabilities that can predict the future success of corporations (Kaplan & Norton, 1992). Finally, instead of focusing on individual HR practices (the performance of staffing practices, training and development practices, etc.), future HR measurement should focus on the entire HR system, taking into account the synergy existing among all HR practices.

CONCLUSION

The issue of human resource management as a tool for achievement of goals and objectives of any organisation cannot be over- emphasized.It is imperative, therefore, that for human resource managers to fully achieve the goals and objectives of any organisation, both the organisation and the employees must come to terms with regard to what would be beneficial to both. Since an organisation does not exist in vacuum, it has to employ personnel to achieve its set objectives and this is what human resources management is all about. Management involves working with and through people to accomplish organisational goals and objectives. The head of management is concerned with systematic co-ordination of affairs.It is aimed at utilizing available resources to attain the goals and objectives of the organisation. Of all resources available to the organisation, human resources enjoy primacy of position because without it, all other resources will remain idle. From this research study, it can be deduced that human resource department must be seen as a pivotal unit in facilitating competitive advantage. It is imperative that the human resource department serves as a communication link between the stakeholders, management and employees in a business organisation. It should be managed by well trained human resource managers.

REFERENCES

1.   Arthur, J. (1994). Effects of human resource systems on manufacturing performance and turnover. Academy of Management Journal, 37, 670–687.

2.   Byars and Rues (2000), Human Resource Management, United States of America, New York.

3.   Cole G. A. (1999), Personnel Management: Theory and Practice, London, Ashford Colour Press

4.   Huselid, M. (1995). The impact of human resource management practices on turnover, productivity, and corporate financial performance. Academy of Management Journal, 38, 635–672.

5.   Huselid, M. A., Jackson, S. E., & Schuler, R. S. (1997). Technical and strategic human resource management effectiveness as determinants of firm performance.

Academy of Management Journal, 40(1), 171–188.

6.   MacDuffie, J.P. & Krafcik, J.F. (1992). Integrating technology and human resources for high-performance manufacturing: Evidence from the international auto industry. In Kochan, T. & Useem, M. (eds.), Transforming organizations. New York: Oxford University Press.

7.   Michael R. Carrel and Frank.K.K. (1996), Personnel Managements. USA, New York.

8.   Obikoya J. (2002), The Foundations of Human Resource Management, First edition, Ijebu-ode, pius Debo (Nigeria) Press

9.   Obisi.C. (1996), Personnel Management.First Edition Nigeria, Ibadan; Jacbod Enterprises.

10. Ojo F. (1997), Human resource management, Nigeria Yaba, Ement Company.

11. Ostroff, C. (1995). Human resource management: Ideas and trends in personnel, June 21, Issue number 356, CCH Incorporated.

12. Pfeffer, J. (1994). Competitive advantage through people: Unleashing the power of the work force. Boston, MA: Harvard Business School Press.

13. Ulrich, D. (1989b). Assessing human resource effectiveness: Stakeholder, index, and relationship approaches. Human Resource Planning, 12, 301–315.

14. Rick Bottler. (2004), Personnel Management and Human Resource, Second edition USA, New York. R.R. Donnelly and son's Company.

15. Randall S. S. and Landra L. H. (1993), Human Resource Management, U.S.A New York

16. Sinclair A. (1994), Human Resource Management, Third Edition. U.S.A, McGraw-Hill.

17. Whitener, E. M. (1997). The impact of human resource activities on employee trust. Human Resource Management Review, 7, 4, 389–404.

12
CHAPTER

ACHIEVING ORGANISATIONAL OBJECTIVES THROUGH HUMAN RESOURCE MANAGEMENT PRACTICES

Rukevwe Juliet Ogedegbe

Ajayi Crowther University, Department of Business Administration, Ogbomosho Road, Oyo .Oyo State, Nigeria

ABSTRACT

The concerns of human resource management in the organization, is to optimize organizational performance through planned employees satisfaction. Thus achieving organisation's objectives depends largely on employees' attitude and behaviours. In this study, relations between selected human resource management practices and organizational objectives were investigated among 201 employees of the Nigeria brewery. Various statistical analytical procedures were applied to validate the samples and address the study's objectives. Results show that HRM practices is significantly associated with achieving organizational objectives. It also shows that, improving the quality of work induces certain behaviours in the employee who is a source of competitive advantage for the organization.

INTRODUCTION

Contemporary economy is changing rapidly. It is characterized by phenomena, such as globalisation and deregulation of markets, changing customer demands and increasing competition (Becker & Gerhart, 1996). Most companies' failure to reach their goals in these turbulent and volatile periods is due to excessive focus on technical problems at the expense of human resources (Cross and Isrealit, 2000). Explaining the impact of human

Citation: Rukevwe Juliet Ogedegbe, 2014, Achieving Organisational Objectives through Human Resource Management Practices, ISSN 2222-2839

resource management (HRM) activities on organisation's performance has dominated discussions and research interest in the last decades (Becker and Huselid, 2006). March and Sutton (1997) stated that explaining organizations' performance variations remain one of the most enduring subjects of study. This has prompted research to be directed towards explaining and understanding of the relationship between human resources management practices and firm performance. As the personnel is the crux to resolve management problems of an enterprise, an effective human resource system ensuring that personnel in the organization are optimally motivated and committed to the aims of the organization is a pivot success (Ulrich, 1998). Little and Nel, (2008) opined that when employees are guided to achieve their performance potentials, this ultimately leads to organizations' success. Thus, success of the organizations depends on the amount of commitment bought in by the individual employee operating in a highly competitive environment which will be complemented by the organizations. Improved quality and productivity linked to motivation can be achieved through training, employee involvement and extrinsic and intrinsic rewards. The growing interest in the compensation geared to performance and skills reflects one aspect of the increasing significance of HRM in realizing management goals and objectives. Therefore the study will be focusing on the following selected HRM practices (training and development, recruitment and selection, performance appraisal, compensation,) performed by the HR department, to influence the attainment of organization's objectives.

LITERATURE REVIEW

Human resources are part of a firm's total resources, so their management must align with the firm's strategy (Baron & Kreps, 1999).Traditionally, human resources has been seen to be the highest operating cost in the organization that mangers logically find ways to minimize (Becker & Gerhart, 1996). It shows therefore, that companies consider people as variable cost rather than as asset. According to Bratton and Gold (2007), strategic human resource management is "the process of linking the human resource function with the strategic objectives of the organization in order to improve performance". People are the assets who create value use for gaining competitive advantage over rivals. People and their collective skills, abilities and experience, coupled with their ability to deploy these in the interests of the employing organization, are now recognized as making a significant contribution to organizational success and as constituting a significant source of competitive advantage (Armstrong and Baron, 2002). Also, as stated by Baird and Meshoulam (1988) that "business objectives are accomplished when human resource practices, procedures and systems are developed and implemented based on organizational needs, that is, when a strategic perspective to human resource management is adopted." Results of several researches, has confirmed that employee skills, attitudes and behaviors play a mediating role between HR systems and firm outcomes. Khatri (2000) found that in his study of 194 Singaporean companies from different industries, there's a strong direct influence of HR practices on firm profitability. According to him, HR function in Singapore companies still remains secondary. The effect of organizational strategic variables regarding HRM and the source of competitive advantage of 138 Korean firms was examined by Bae and

Lawler (2000). They found that firms with high-involvement HR strategies had better performance. Batt (2002) examined the relationship between human resource practices, employee quit rates, and organizational performance in the service sector. His findings confirm that, firms emphasizing high skills, employee participation in decision making and in teams, and human resource incentives such as high relative pay and employment security, have lower quit rates and higher performance (sales growth).

Paul and Anantharaman (2003) tested the causal model linking HRM with organizational performance. They found that practices like training, job design, compensation and incentives had a direct effect on the operational performance parameters. Sing's study (2003) tested and showed that there exists a significant relationship between strategic HR orientation of Indian firms and their performance. HR orientation was conceptualized as the alignment of HR planning, selection, evaluating, compensating, developing and staffing practices with the business strategies of the firm.

Wattanasupachoke (2009) examined the relationship between HR strategies and the performance of 124 Thai companies and found that the extra pay and profit sharing is the only factor group that has a statistically important correlation with the companies' financial performances such as sales, profits and liquidities. The results of these studies have thus confirmed the dependency of an organizational achievement on the caliber of its employees and how effectively the companies manage the human resource practices to influence positive objectives.

Selected HRM Practices in Organisations

Recruitment and Selection

A major concern of human resource management is the recruitment and retention of valued employee (Davenport, 2000). A recruitment campaign usually identifies a number of applicants who can potentially meet the requirements of particular jobs or roles. The hiring managers then select, among the candidates with the aid of a competency profiles (knowledge, skills, abilities and other attributes) in this selection pool, those that would add the highest value to the firm. The importance of managing the employment relationship such that is generates value added knowledge for the organization has an obvious link to recruitment and retention of staff (Ulrich and Lake, 1990; Wayland and Cole, 1997)

Training and Development

Training is a key factor related to the achievement of organisational objectives. The individual plays a more active role in defining his/her own training objectives, and attempts to match them to company objectives. The focus of human resource training is placed on developing people who are capable of tapping internal and external information and turning it into useful organizational knowledge. Thus, leadership, management change and company mission and values are reinforced through training (Yahya and Goh, 2002). Companies intending to gain a sustained competitive advantage should help their employees raise their skills by receiving continuous training so that they can learn new things needed to ensure quality improvement of the products and services of the company. A clear understanding of the company's mission and values would help ensure a right direction for goal attainment.

Performance Appraisal

The measurement of employees' performance allows the company to provide compensation fairly to the deserving individuals according to certain predetermined criteria like employee competency, teamwork ability, initiative, soft skills and ethics. Organizations can monitor the development of desired employee attitudes and behaviors through the use of the appraisal mechanisms. This appraisal-based information could be used for changing the selection and training practices to select and develop employees with the desired behaviors and attitudes. However, the effectiveness of skilled employees will be limited unless they are motivated to perform their jobs.

Compensation System

Firms can affect the motivation of employees in several ways. They can use performance-based compensation to provide rewards to employees for achieving the specific goals and objectives of the firm. A substantial body of work has provided evidence that incentive-based compensation has an impact on firm performance (Milkovich and Boudreau, 1998).

Thus, the following hypotheses were proposed for the study:

1. Training and development, recruitment and selection, performance appraisal and compensation will jointly and independently predict organizational objectives.

2. There will be a significant relationship between recruitment and selection and organizational objectives.

3. There will be main and interaction effect of performance appraisal and compensation on organizational objectives

4. There will be a significant differences between training and development on organizational objectives

5. There will be main and interaction effect of training and development and recruitment and selection on organizational objectives.

METHODOLOGY

0The research design for this study is survey design. The study made use of primary data gathered with the help of questionnaire comprising of three sections. The first section contained 7 background questions and second section contained 23 statements about the human resource management practices. The third section contained 3 statements related to organisational objectives. However, in this study only second section was covered i.e. related to human resource management practices (23 statements) along with first part i.e. related to general statements. The respondents were asked to rate statements on a five point rating scale where one indicated that respondents strongly agree, two meant for agree, three for neutral, four indicated disagreeing and five meant strongly disagree about what was described in the statement. The scale use was developed by Mourad Mansour with Cronbach alpha coefficient of 3.56. These 23 statements can be seen through exhibit 1.The questionnaire was administered to 450 respondents of the Nigerian Brewery. Only 201 (44.6%) of the returned questionnaires were found suitable for final analysis and without any discrepancies. The data gathered was analyzed with the help of statistical tools like frequency counts and simple percentages for demographic information. Multiple regression, correlations, analysis of variances and the t- test were used to analyzed the hypothesis and assess the relationship of human resources management practices practiced in the brewery companies and standard deviations were calculated to understand the variations in data collected through responses.

The data collected were revalidated with Cronbach Alpha value calculated as: training and development 0.69, recruitment and selection 0.74, performance appraisal 0.67, compensation 0.82, organisaional objectives 0.76.

RESULTS OF FINDINGS

Table 1: Summary of multiple regressions showing the effect of training and development, recruitment and selection, performance appraisal and compensation on organizational objectives

Model	Sum of Squares	DF	Mean Square	F	Sig.
Regression	254.488	4	63.622	31.965	.000
Residual	390.109	196	1.990		
Total	644.597	200			

R = .628

R^2 = .395

Adj R^2 = .382

It was shown in the table above that the joint effect of Training and Development, Recruitment and Selection, Performance Appraisal and Compensation on Organizational Objectives was significant ($F(4,196)$ = 31.965; R = .628, R^2 = .395, Adj. R^2 = 0.382; P < .05). About 40% of the variation was accounted for by the independent variables while the remaining 60% was not due to chance.

Table 2: summary of multiple regression showing any effect of the independent variable -training and development, recruitment and selection, performance appraisal and compensation- on organizational objectives.

Model	Unstandardized Coefficient		Standardized Coefficient	T	Sig.
	B	Std. Error			
(Constant)	2.928	1.013		2.889	.004
Training and Development	-1.808E-02	.055	-.027	-.331	.741
Recruitment and Selection	.185	.078	.162	2.376	.018
Performance Appraisal	.249	.047	.431	5.261	.000
Compensation	5.180E-02	.032	.153	1.640	.103

The result above shows the relative contribution of each of the independent variables on the dependent: Training and Development (β = -.027, P >.05), Recruitment and Selection (β = .162, P .05), respectively. Hence, Recruitment and Selection, and Performance

Appraisal were found significant while Training and Development, and Compensation were not.

Table 3: Summary of Pearson correlation showing the relationship between organizational objectives and recruitment and selection

Variable	Mean	Std. Dev.	N	R	P	Remark
Organizational Objectives	13.0448	1.7953				
			201	.429**	.000	Sig
Recruitment and Selection	12.8458	1.5688				

** sig at .01 level

It is shown in the above table that there was significant relationship between Organizational Objectives and Recruitment and Selection($r = 429**$, $N= 201$, $P < .05$).

Table 4: Summary of analysis of variance showing the effect of performance appraisal and compensation on organizational objectives.

Source	Sum of Squares	DF	Mean Square	F	Sig.
Main Effect:	177.740	3	59.247	25.000	.000
Performance Appraisal	86.961	1	86.961	36.695	.000
Compensation	15.651	1	15.651	6.604	.011
2-Interactions:					
Performance Appraisal x					
Compensation	14.990	1	14.990	6.325	.013
	177.740	3	59.247		
Explained	466.857	197	2.370		
Residual	644.597	200			
Total					

In the table above, it was observed that there was significant difference in the Main effect of Performance Appraisal and Compensation on Organizational Objectives. The Interaction effect of Performance Appraisal and Compensation on Organizational Objective was significant ($F (3,197) = 6.325$, $P<.05$.

Table 5: T-test showing the organizational objectives and low and high training and development among respondents.

Organizational Objectives	N	Mean	Std. Dev.	Crit-t	Cal-t.	DF	P
Low	61	12.1311	2.1485				
				1.96	5.045	199	.000
High	140	13.4429	1.4557				

The above table showed that there was significant difference between Organizational Objectives and Low and High Training and Development among respondents (Crit-t = 1.96, Cal.t = 5.045, df = 199, P < .05 level of significance).

Table 6: Summary of ANOVA showing the main and interaction effect of Training and Development, and Recruitment and Selection on Organizational Objectives

Source	Sum of Squares	DF	Mean Square	F	Sig.
Main Effect:	209.490	3	69.830	31.616	.000
Training and Development	99.273	1	99.273	44.947	.000
Recruitment and Selection	100.284	1	100.284	45.405	.000
2-Interactions:					
Training & Developmen x	48.782	1	48.782	22.086	.000
Recruitment and Selection	209.490	3	69.830		
Explained	435.107	197	2.209		
Residual	644.597	200			
Total					

In the table above, it was observed that there was significant difference in the Main effect of Training and Development, and Recruitment and Selection on Organizational Objectives. The Interaction effect of Training and Development, Recruitment and Selection on Organizational Objective however, was significant (F $(3,197)$ = 22.086, P<.05.

DISCUSSION AND CONCLUSION

According the study, the HRM practices in the brewery industry in Nigeria exert significant influences on organizational achievement. Among the independent variables; the recruitment and selection and performance appraisal has the greatest effect. The training and development and compensation systems encounter certain problems. These systems are seemed as autonomous and at the instance of the management. The tradition of having to "hand-pick" who goes for training and gets a pay rise affect the moral of employee in their performance in achieving the organizations' goals and objectives. The better the recruitment and selection process the more effective is the work structure that enhances an appropriate performance appraisal for individual that fosters training and development. However, the rationale of this research is to enhance an understanding of the relationship between HRM practice in the brewery industry in Nigeria and the influence on organisational objectives. HRM practice competence takes time to develop, accumulate and cultivate and as such requires the support of other tangible factors such as infrastructure, organizational culture and management support.

REFERENCES

1.   Armstrong, M. and Baron, A. (2002) Strategic HRM: the route to improved business performance, CIPD, London.

2.   Bae, J. and Lawler, J.J. (2000) Organizational and HRM strategies in Korea: impact on firm performance in an emerging economy, Academy of Management Journal, 43(3), 502-517.

3.   Bae, J., Chen, S-J., Wan, T.W.D., Lawler, J.J., and Walumbwa, F.O. (2001) Human resource strategy and firm performance in Pacific Rim countries, International Journal of Human Resource Management, 14(8), 1308-1332.

4.   Baird, L. and Meshoulam, I. (1988) Managing two fits of strategic human resource

management, Academy of Management Review, 13(1), 116-128.

5. Batt, R. (2002) Managing customer services: human resource practices, quit rates, and sales growth, Academy of Management Journal, 45(3), 587-597.

6. Becker, B., and Gerhart, B. (1996) The impact of human resource management on organizational performance: Progress and prospects, Academy of Management Journal , 39, 779-802.

7. Becker, B., & Huselid, M. (2006) Strategic human resource management: where do we go from here? Journal of Management , 32, 898-925.

8. Bratton, J., and Gold, J. (2007) Human Resource Management: Theory and Practice, 4th Edition, Houndmills: Macmillan.

9. Baron, J.N. & Kreps, D.M. (1999). Strategic human resources. Hoboken: Lenigh Press. Cross, R. and Israelit, S. (2000): Strategic learning in a knowledge economy: Individual, collective and organizational process, in Robert, L., Cross, J. and Israelit, S.B. (Eds.) Strategic Learning in a Knowledge Economy: Individual, Collective and Organizational Learning Process, ButterworthHeinemann, pp. 69-90.

10. Davenport, T. (2000): Human Capital: What it is and why people invest in it. San Francisco: Jossey-Bass.

11. Khatri, N. (2000) Managing human resource for competitive advantage: a study of companies in Singapore, International Journal of human Resource Management, 11 (2), 336-365.

12. Milkovich, T.G., and W.J. Boudreau (1998). Human resource management, 8th Edition. Boston:Irwin.

13. Nel PS, Werner A, Haasbroek, GD, Poisat P, Sono T and Schultz HB (2008) Human resources Management, (7th Edn) Oxford University Press, Cape Town.

14. Paul, A.K. and Anantharaman, R.N. (2003) Impact of people management practices on organizational performance: analysis of causal model, International Journal of Human Resource Management, 14 (7), 1246-1266.

15. Sing, K. (2003) Strategic HR orientation and firm performance in India, International Journal of Human Resource Management, 14(4), 530-543.

16. Ulrich, D. (1998): A new mandate of human resources, Harvard Business Review, Vol. 41,No. 1, pp. 124-134.

17. Gómez-Mejía, L.R., Balkin, D.B. and Cardy, R.L. (2001): Dirección y gestión de recursos humanos, 3 edition.

18. Ulrich, D. and Lake, D. (1990): Organizational Capability: Competing from the Inside Out. New York: John Wiley.

19. Wattanasupachoke, T. (2009) Strategic human resource management and organizational performance: a study of Thai enterprises, Journal of Global Business Issues, 3(2), 139- 148.

20. Yahya, S. and Goh, W. (2002): Managing human resources toward achieving knowledge management, Journal of Knowledge Management, Vol. 6, No. 5, pp.457-468

13

CHAPTER

ANALYZING THE EFFECTS OF HR SYSTEM ON ORGANIZATIONAL PERFORMANCE

Salman Hussainm, Shah Muhammad, Zia-ur-Rehman Majed Rashid

AIOU, Islamabad, Pakistan

ABSTRACT

It is responsible for bringing people into the organization, helping them carry out their work, pay off them for their labors, and solving problems that arise. There are seven management functions of a human resources (hr) department that will be specifically addressed: staffing, performance appraisals, compensation and benefits, training and development, employee and labor relations, safety and health, and human resource research. The organizations should focus, promote and endorse the effective use of hr policies for the enhancement of pace of organizational performance. The management of performance can often involve tough decisions such as choosing who to let go, who to promote and who to hire. Keeping the decision making process behind closed doors is an ethical practice that breeds the least amount of contention possible.

INTRODUCTION

An organization is said to be as good or bad as its people. Successful organizations have competent and committed people. So an organization should develop such a system through which they can produce, develop and train highly motivated and utmost skilled personals and plan such activities to provide its members to meet current and future job

Citation: Salman Hussain Shah, Muhammad Zia-ur-Rehman ,Majed Rashid, Analyzing the Effects of HR System on Organizational Performance, European Journal of Business and Management. http://www.iiste.org/Journals/index.php/EJBM/article/view/20524

demands. The activities can cover the entire period of the employee career. This system should respond to job changes, and integrate its activities to the long-term plans of the organization.

Managing Human Resources is one of the key elements in the coordination and management of work organizations. Several new technologies are used to ensure the creation and delivery of services and goods in modern economies. Whatever means are used, the role of individuals and groups as employees and the ability of management to effectively deploy such a resource is vital to interests of both employee and organization alike. Research Questions or Problem Statement.

Following is a set of investigations that need resolution and findings for the study.

Research Questions

1. Whether HR department boosts the overall performance of the organization which can create satisfaction of the employees with their jobs?

2. Is an HR department cause for any organization to achieve its goals and remain effective for long term Basis in Business world?

Research Objectives

1) To develop such a system, which covers all the activities, related to the HR department?

2) To compare the performance of the organization after development and implementation of the proper HR system. 3) To examine that whether an HR system helps the organization to grow and move forwarded for long-term basis.

LITERATURE REVIEW

The existing literature is reviewed as;

HRM & Employee's Motivation

In the process of human resource management all activities are used for the retention, compensation and motivation of the employees of an organization. The old personnel has rigidity in all its processes while the new trend shows flexibility in all these activities and thus human resource management shows a behavior of motivation in the environment of the organization (Rao,S.P.2000). When the employees for an organization are recruited, trained and developed they are motivated in all these processes. In the same sense when the aggrieved employees are settled as a result of an effective process of grievance handling it will be a source of inspiration. Safety and health measures can also be a wide range of encouragement and motivate the people working in a safe and healthy environment (Louis T, 1987). Most important factor in the employment is the pay, compensation and reward system introduce by the management of any organization has the most attractive features in it. Employees work for money to take care of them and their families and to enhance their livelihood so it can be said that this factor is the largest part having source of motivation for the employees in any organization.

HRM and Organizational Performance

Human resource management is all about the supervision of the employees working in any organization. Every activity operating in the organization can be planned in such a way that the employees of that organization work efficiently and provide better services for the achievement of the goals of the organization (Cecil Bell 1973). They are fully management in the environment of competition provide pace to the organizational work. Every person works for the organization with full zeal and zest and of course managed and motivated employees can provide. To be successful in the automotive market, these companies needs a highly skilled, flexible and committed work force, a flexible and innovative management, the ability to retain developed talent, and a strong partnership between management and labor unions. To achieve these goals, the company needs a talented HR department (Wright P. & Snel, S.1991). Besides hiring the right people to manage and perform specific jobs, HR managers have to build up commitment and loyalty among the workforce by keeping them up to date about company plans, and laying out the implications for job security and working conditions.

HRM & Goals Achievement

Human Resource Management has brought to the fore a concern for maximizing the potential of employees. In the past, the HR function served only the interests of management. Today, some HR departments are close to the other end of the spectrum where they are concerned only with employee welfare. The general wisdom is that HRM should help balance the interests of the employees with those of the organization HR system plays a vital role for the success of any organization if its policies are implemented effectively (Welson R. 1990.). Humans are key assists of any organization that run the organization elegantly when they are fully motivated through planned HR policies. Therefore, we can say that human resource department is the heart of any organization and much can be done through effective use of HR policies for the betterment of the whole organization. The successful organization have familiar with the importance of human resource; they are a important factor in to management's strategic decisions, which guide the organization in its future procedures. Enterprises stay alive because of human resource's work and the ideas they generate (Spors 2007). HRM benefits the organization in every aspect. Fully trained, motivated and managed employees can prove their competence that results higher production and organization can achieve its goals. If human resources are acquired, retained, developed and motivated then the goals of any Organization can be achieved and there will be higher level of work efficiency and improve output in the every field of the organization.

RESEARCH METHODOLOGY

Methodology

First of all previous researches are summarized through content analysis. Then the current Research was conducted by using a questionnaire based on Likert scale. The questionnaire was personally distributed to all of employees working at Lahore head office and was mailed to the employees working in other branches out of Lahore city. The results received were summarized by using Mstat programme, by applying simple formulae of mean and standard deviation.

Subjects

Since our target population was purely government institution with minimum levels of hierarchy, so the sample can be classified in Executives and non Executives. Sections of the office are four, News Electronic media, Accounts section, Administration section & Technical Section. The data were collected from all of the six departments. Executives completed their questionnaire themselves and were also requested to help in the understanding of questions to the non- Executives. The Executives helped them in filling the questionnaire. But the focus was given on Executives to get proper results in the research. Participation in the research was voluntary and employees were assured of confidentiality in the data analysis. To complete this process, the questionnaires were mailed to respondents working at different sections of Head Office & Regional Offices out of the Lahore city. The responses were collected in the same way through mail. Un-complete questionnaires were again mailed with a request letter to complete the questionnaire and got complete responses to get proper results.

This research activity was a multi-method based. Previous research on this construct was also summarized through content analysis. The construct of the impact of the effects of HR system on organizational performance was measured through a questionnaire based research in a selected government institution that is Directorate General Public Relations, Government of the Punjab, Lahore.

For past perspective (i.e. to summarize previous research) Qualitative (content analysis), and for current perspective Quantitative (questionnaire Based) research was done.

Content Analysis of Qualitative Research

The effects of HR system on organizational performance are a famous topic, which has also been previously researched, so we can conduct content analysis of the effects of HR system on organizational performance. The construct of the effects of HR system is purely defined in terms of the selected organization, so we cannot find extensive researches about effects of HR system. Hence content analysis will be limited to the available researches. Previous quantitative findings about the effects of HR system will be summarized to get government Institution score by using the research technique of content analysis.

Procedures

The total population of the organization is 350 employees; seventy of them are below matriculation. Therefore they are ignored during research. Hundred people out of the remaining total population are considered our sample. Then the population is segregated into two groups, Executives and non-Executives which will be used during information collection based on questionnaire. The researcher then used the descriptive method to obtain information using the questionnaire as the source of the information.

Data Treatment

Data was collected from the questionnaire based on liker Scale i.e. The effects of HR system on organizational performance being perceived by the respondents from the attached questionnaire. Data analyzed by using MSTAT to apply specific formulae and find mean, standard deviation and variance etc.

Population

Overall 100 questionnaires were distributed and researcher was able to retrieve 86 questionnaires, and success rate was 86%. Some of the people were not willing to answer, some were unable to understand. In this regard, help was taken from the Executives to make understandability to the non-Executives. This success shows that the responses received from the respondents were complete, valid and understandable for the respondents and they were able to answer it accurately.

Sample

The questionnaire-based research covered Executives and Non Executives of employees serving in different branches in the selected organization. The perceived sample was consisted of around 100 employees of target population.

Instrumentation

Questionnaire consisted of three pages comprised of 27 questions based on Likert Scale. These questions comprise different dependant and independent variables and their effects on HR techniques.

Research Tools and Instruments

The data were classified in accordance with research variables and arranged as well as organized respective calculations in line with the sequence presented in the research questions. Data ere analyzed by using Microsoft Excel. The following statistical formulas were applied to make the interpretation of data even more comprehensive:

Percentile

This method is employed to present the relation of the part to a whole. In the study in hand, it was used for data presentation on the profile, and on the problems that were faced. The formula for percentage calculations is as under:

$$p = \frac{f}{n} * 100$$

Where

P = Computed percentage

f = Frequency of the scores

n = Number of respondents

Arithmetic Mean

This is a measure of central tendency, which was used by the researcher to determine the respondents' perceptions of work-related stress.

$$\bar{x} = \frac{\sum x}{n}$$

Where:

x = Arithmetic mean

$\sum$ = Symbol of summation

x = Scale value

n = No. of observations

Standard Deviation Standard Deviation was used as a measure of variance. This modus operandi was used by the researcher to examine the variation in the results that could possibly be due to differences in the population. The formula used for this measure is as under:

$$\sigma = \sqrt{\frac{\sum (\bar{x} - x)^2}{N}}$$

Where: $\sum$ = Symbol of summation

σ = Symbol of Standard Deviation

x = Mean value

X = Scale value

N = Total number of observations

DATA PRESENTATION, ANALYSIS & INTERPRETATION

The research was made to find effects of HR System on Organizational Performance which is the strategic and coherent approach to the management of an Organization's most valued assets - the people working there who individually and collectively contribute to the achievement of the objectives of the business. The terms "human resource management" and "human resources" (HR) have largely replaced the term "personnel management" as a description of the processes involved in managing people in Organizations. In simple sense, HRM means employing people, developing their resources, utilizing, maintaining and compensating their services in tune with the job and Organizational requirement. Synonyms such as personnel management are often used in a more restricted sense to describe activities that are necessary in the recruiting of a workforce, providing its members with payroll and benefits, and administrating their work-life needs.

It has been found during the whole research that humans are an Organization's greatest assets; without them, everyday business functions such as managing cash flow, making business transactions, communicating through all forms of media, and dealing with customers could not be completed. Humans and the potential they possess drive an Organization. Today's Organizations are continuously changing. Organizational change impacts not only the business but also its employees. In order to maximize Organizational effectiveness, human potential-individuals' capabilities, time, and talents-must be managed. Human resource management works to ensure that employees are able to meet the Organization's goals.

The objective of planning for HR system is to help an Organization to meet strategic goals by attracting, and maintaining employees and also to manage them effectively. The key word here perhaps is "fit", i.e. a HRM approach seeks to ensure a fit between the management of an Organization's employees, and the overall strategic direction of the company.

However, many HR functions these days struggle to get beyond the roles of administration and employee champion, and are seen rather as reactive as strategically proactive partners for the top management. In addition, HR Organizations also have the difficulty in proving how their activities and processes add value to the company. Only in the recent years HR scholars and HR professionals are focusing to develop models that can measure if HR adds value. Different questions related to Human relations and business, HRM & Organizational Performance, Role of HR System, Benefits of HRM, Organization without HRM, HRM Heart of Organsiation, Training & Development, Recruitment & Selection, Effective Selection & Organizational Performance, Training & Employee's Professional Carrier, Investiment on Training, Schedule for Training, HR Department & Strategic Decision Making, Orientation & Satisfaction of Employees, Orientation Reduces Employee Turnover, Reward Mechanism, Salary Increment & Promotion, HR Departments & Employees performance, Effective HR System, Grievance Handling Procedure, Purpose of Discipline, Effective Disciplinary Process, Employees Safety, Job Analysis, Performance Appraisal, Organizational Development, Downsizing were analysied and presented the information.

Departmental Distribution

Frequency Table Department (Table 4.1A)

		Frequency	Percent	Valid Percent	Cumulative Percent
Valid	Accounts	17	19.8	19.8	19.8
	Admin	21	24.4	24.4	44.2
	E. Media	21	24.4	24.4	68.6
	Technical	27	31.4	31.4	100.0
	Total	86	100.0	100.0	

Descriptive Statistics (Table 4.1 B)

	N	Minimum	Maximum	Mean	Std. Deviation
Department	86	1	4	2.67	1.121
Valid N (listwise)	86				

(Graph 4.1C)

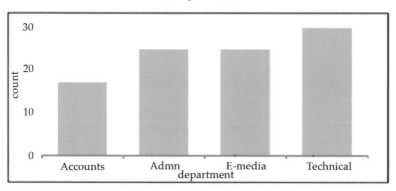

These tables and graph show that the research respondents were 86 in total. From 86, 17 respondents belong to the Accounts department, 21 respondents from Admin department, 21 from E-media department and 27 belong from Technical department. Therefore all the departments are given a valid percentage. Therefore the results are totally represents an average of the views of people belonging to the every department. The results have a mean average of 2.67 with a standard deviation of 1.121.

Experience Wise Distribution

Experience (Table 4.2A)

		Frequency	Percent	Valid Percent	Cumulative Percent
Valid	1-5	51	59.3	59.3	59.3
	5-10	27	31.4	31.4	90.7
	10-15	8	9.3	9.3	100.0
	Total	86	100.0	100.0	

Descriptive Statistics (Table 4.2B)

	N	Minimum	Maximum	Mean	Std. Deviation
Experience	86	1	3	1.50	.664
Valid N (listwise)	86				

(Graph 4.2C)

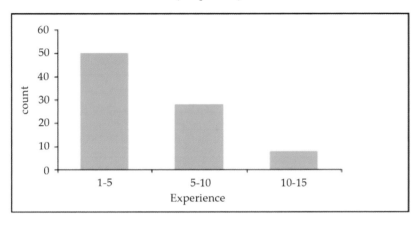

These figures represent the average experience of the people who were the respondent. Definitely the work experience of 1-5 years experience person is greater. This is very good in the sense that they are young and energetic and wants to make a place in the market. They want to stay in the organization. Therefore they can very good give us the details how they will be retained. What are the policies of the organization, which are good for the employees and vice versa? The results show average mean of 1.5 and a standard deviation of .664.

Age Wise Distribution

Age (Table 4.3A)

		Frequency	Percent	Valid Percent	Cumulative Percent
Valid	21-30	48	55.8	55.8	55.8
	31-40	30	34.9	34.9	90.7
	41-50	8	9.3	9.3	100.0
	Total	86	100.0	100.0	

Descriptive Statistics (Table 4.3B)

	N	Minimum	Maximum	Mean	Std. Deviation
Age	86	1	3	1.53	.663
Valid N (listwise)	86				

(Graph 4.3C)

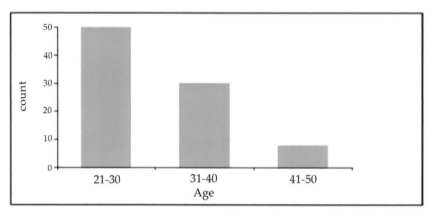

This table represents the frequency distribution of age of respondents. People from the age of in between 21-30 are more than 50 %, Therefore young and energetic people are greater in the organization. They can shape the profit of the organization, but if they are retained. Therefore the researcher is trying to find from them what is the thing that will inspire them to stay with the organization. The results show an average mean of 1.53 and a standard deviation of .663.

Gender Wise Distribution

Gender (Table 4.4A)

		Frequency	Percent	Valid Percent	Cumulative Percent
Valid	Male	73	84.9	84.9	84.9
	Female	13	15.1	15.1	100.0
	Total	86	100.0	100.0	

Descriptive Statistics (Table 4.4B)

	N	Minimum	Maximum	Mean	Std. Deviation
Gender	86	1	2	1.15	.360
Valid N (listwise)	86				

(Graph 4.4 C)

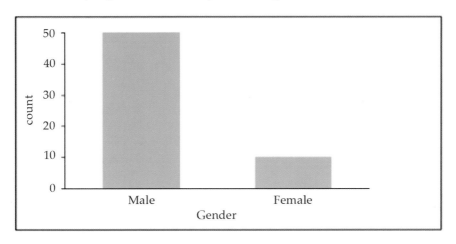

These figures represent the frequency distribution of gender. Definitely the male respondents are greater in quantity, and as the researcher also belongs from male segment, therefore the biasness towards gender will be present in the results, which show an average mean of 1.15 and standard deviation of .36.

Business & Human Relations

Human Relations (Table 4.5A)

		Frequency	Percent	Valid Percent	Cumulative Percent
Valid	Strongly Agree	62	72.1	72.1	72.1
	Agree	9	10.5	10.5	82.6
	Neutral	13	15.1	15.1	97.7
	Disagree	2	2.3	2.3	100.0
	Total	86	100.0	100.0	

Descriptive Statistics (Table 4.5B)

	N	Minimum	Maximum	Mean	Std. Deviation
Business & HRM	86	1	4	1.48	.836
Valid N (listwise)	86				

(Graph 4.5 C)

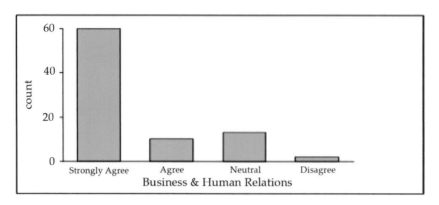

This table represents the responses of the respondents about the Business & Human relations. If we see the results then we will come to know that 62 %, means more than 50% strongly agree that there should be a well defined relationship between the Business and Human relations. Therefore my organization has a strong relationship between Business and Human relations. The results show an average mean of 1.48 and a standard deviation of .836.

HRM & Organizational Performance (Table 4.6A)

Organizational Performance		Frequency	Percent	Valid Percent	Cumulative Percent
Valid	Strongly Agree	2	2.3	2.3	2.3
	Agree	12	14.0	14.0	16.3
	Neutral	32	37.2	37.2	53.5
	Disagree	17	19.8	19.8	73.3
	Strongly Disagree	23	26.7	26.7	100.0
	Total	86	100.0	100.0	

Descriptive Statistics (Table 4.6 B)

	N	Minimum	Maximum	Mean	Std. Deviation
HRM & Org. Performance	86	1	5	3.55	1.102
Valid N (listwise)	86				

(Graph 4.6 C)

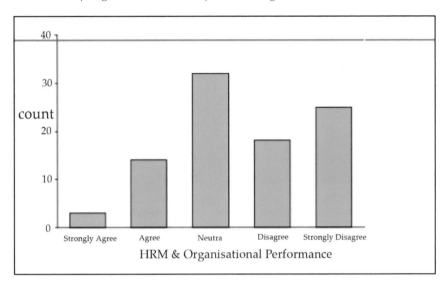

These figures represent the responses about HRM & Organizational growth of the employees. Everyone thinks that HRM plays a vital role in Organizational performance. But if we see the results of the research, we will come to know that only two respondents strongly agree with this argument. While others not, thus HRM is not important for Organizational growth. Therefore what is the important? Let us know about the other results. The results show an average mean of 3.55 and a standard deviation of 1.102.

Role of HR System

HR Role (Table 4.7A)

		Frequency	Percent	Valid Percent	Cumulative Percent
Valid	Strongly Agree	45	52.3	52.3	52.3
	Agree	15	17.4	17.4	69.8
	Neutral	9	10.5	10.5	80.2
	Disagree	5	5.8	5.8	86.0
	Strongly Disagree	12	14.0	14.0	100.0
	Total	86	100.0	100.0	

Descriptive Statistics (Table 4.7B)

	N	Minimum	Maximum	Mean	Std. Deviation
HRM Role	86	1	5	2.12	1.459
Valid N (listwise)	86				

(Graph 4.7 C)

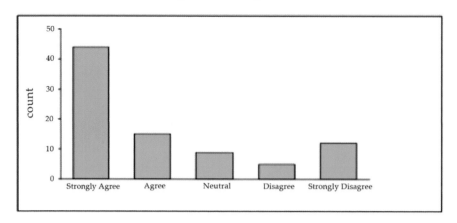

The figures show about the responses about role of HR system in Organsiational performance Majority of the respondents give their opinion that their should be a well defined HRM system for the management of the employees of any organization. People do work well for the better productivity and success if their HR system is effective. The results show an average mean of 2.12 and a standard deviation of 1.459.

Benefits of HRM: (Table 4.8A)

		Frequency	Percent	Valid Percent	Cumulative Percent
Valid	Strongly Agree	29	33.7	33.7	33.7
	Agree	27	31.4	31.4	65.1
	Neutral	17	19.8	19.8	84.9
	Disagree	7	8.1	8.1	93.0
	Strongly Disagree	6	7.0	7.0	100.0
	Total	86	100.0	100.0	

Descriptive Statistics (Table 4.8B)

	N	Minimum	Maximum	Mean	Std. Deviation
Benefits of HRM	86	1	5	2.23	1.205
Valid N (listwise)	86				

(Graph 4.8 C)

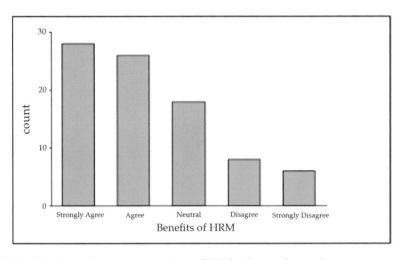

This table shows that a proper system of HR for the employees is very necessary for the business prospect, if the employees of any business are properly managed through HR policies they will make their best efforts for the development of the business and the business will definitely grow better as the results of the respondents tell us about this regard, that is more than 50% respondents agree about it. The results show an average mean of 2.23 and a standard deviation of 1.205.

Organizations without HRM

Organizations without HRM (Table 4.9A)

		Frequency	Percent	Valid Percent	Cumulative Percent
Valid	Strongly Agree	23	26.7	26.7	26.7
	Agree	26	30.2	30.2	57.0
	Neutral	21	24.4	24.4	81.4
	Disagree	9	10.5	10.5	91.9
	Strongly Disagree	7	8.1	8.1	100.0
	Total	86	100.0	100.0	

Descriptive Statistics (Table 4.9 B)

	N	Minimum	Maximum	Mean	Std. Deviation
Organization without HRM	86	1	5	2.43	1.223
Valid N (listwise)	86				

(Graph 4.9 C)

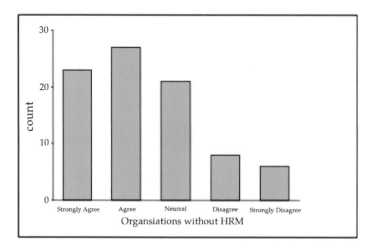

Growth of the Organization is very difficult without the use of HR policy and most of the respondents are agreed with the statement. Every one works for the better future if he is well managed through a well defined system of HR, so every employee will stick to the Organization. Therefore, the organizations of today focus on the management of the employees and if the rigid personal policies of the past are followed then there should be many hurdles and problems for the improvement in Organizations. The results show an average mean of 2.43 and a standard deviation of 1.223.

HRM, Heart of Organization

Heart of Organsiation: (Table 4.10A)

		Frequency	Percent	Valid Percent	Cmlt. Percent
Valid	Strongly Agree	28	32.6	33.3	33.3
	Agree	19	22.1	22.6	56.0
	Neutral	21	24.4	25.0	81.0
	Disagree	12	14.0	14.3	95.2
	St. Disagree	4	4.7	4.8	100.0
	Total	86	100.0	100.0	

Descriptive Statistics (Table 4.10 B)

	N	Minimum	Maximum	Mean	Std. Deviation
HRM Heart of Org.	86	1	5	2.35	1.217
Valid N (listwise)	86				

(Graph 4.10 C)

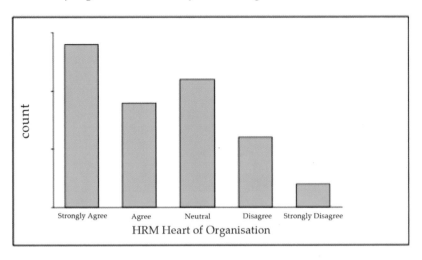

These diagrams represent the responses of employees that almost all the employees of the organsiations are trained, managed and polished through the effective system of HRM and such motivated employees work for the well being of their Organization and country. Some employees were focusing on this point and some were opposing this point. The results show an average mean of 2.35 and a standard deviation of 1.217.

Training & Development

Training & Development: (Table 4.11A)

		Frequency	Percent	Valid Percent	Cumulative Percent
Valid	Strongly Agree	27	31.4	35.1	35.1
	Agree	15	17.4	19.5	54.5
	Neutral	18	20.9	23.4	77.9
	Disagree	5	5.8	6.5	84.4
	Strongly Disagree	12	14.0	15.6	100.0
	Total	77	89.5	100.0	
Missing	System	9	10.5		
Total		86	100.0		

Descriptive Statistics (Table 4.11 B)

	N	Minimum	Maximum	Mean	Std. Deviation
Training & Development	77	1	5	2.48	1.429
Valid N (listwise)	77				

(Graph 4.11 C)

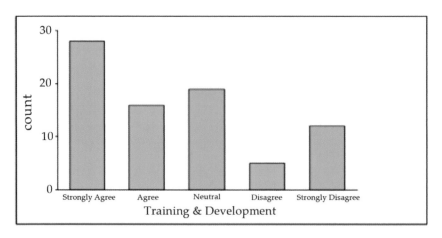

These depictions show that technological developments and Organizational change have gradually led some employees to the realization that success realize on the skills and abilities of their employees. And this means considerable and continuous investment in training and development programs. But some remain neutral and some give no response in this regard which shows that something like fifty 50 percent response was present in this regard. The result shows an average mean of 2.48 and a standard deviation of 1.429.

Recruitment & Selection

Recruitment & Selection: (Table 4.12 A)

		Frequency	Percent	Valid Percent	Cumulative Percent
Valid	Strongly Agree	39	45.3	47.0	47.0
	Agree	29	33.7	34.9	81.9
	Neutral	10	11.6	12.0	94.0
	Disagree	5	5.8	6.0	100.0
	Total	83	96.5	100.0	
Missing	System	3	3.5		
Total		86	100.0		

Descriptive Statistics (Table 4.12 B)

	N	Minimum	Maximum	Mean	Std. Deviation
Recruitment & Selection	83	1	4	1.77	.888
Valid N (listwise)	83				

(Graph 4.12 C)

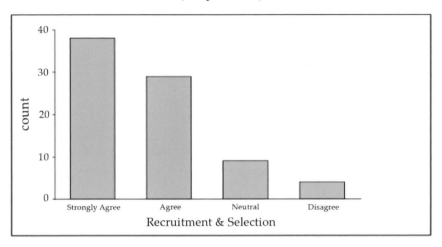

Recruitment & Selection

Effective process of recruitment and selection of the employees can be a successful tool for the betterment of any organization. The right people on the right work places can generate better results as compare to irrelevant persons doing that jobs. Therefore it is a best point for the wellbeing of the employees and growth of the business. The results show an average mean of 1.77 and a standard deviation of .888.

Effective Selection & Organizational Performance

Effective Selection (Table 4.13 A)

		Frequency	Percent	Valid Percent	Cumulative Percent
Valid	Strongly Agree	32	37.2	38.6	38.6
	Agree	30	34.9	36.1	74.7
	Neutral	17	19.8	20.5	95.2
	Disagree	2	2.3	2.4	97.6
	Strongly Disagree	2	2.3	2.4	100.0
	Total	83	96.5	100.0	
Missing	System	3	3.5		
Total		86	100.0		

Descriptive Statistics (Table 4.13 B)

	N	Minimum	Maximum	Mean	Std. Deviation
Effective Selection	83	1	5	1.94	.954
Valid N (listwise)	83				

(Graph 4.13 C)

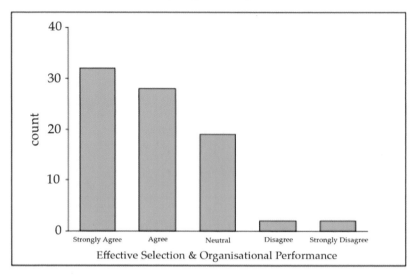

Effective Selection & Organisational Performance

The effective methods of selection not only provide more information about the candidates but information that is relevant, useful and comparable between candidates. And this whole process can bring fruitful results for the organsiational performance. Majority of the employees agree with this point of view which is shown from the table that more than 70% of the employees are in the favor of the effective process of selection. The results show an average mean of 1.94 and a standard deviation of .954.

Training & Employee's Professional Carrier

Training & Employee (Table 4.14A)

		Frequency	Percent	Valid Percent	Cumulative Percent
Valid	Strongly Agree	42	48.8	51.9	51.9
	Agree	12	14.0	14.8	66.7
	Neutral	21	24.4	25.9	92.6
	Strongly Disagree	6	7.0	7.4	100.0
	Total	81	94.2	100.0	
Missing	System	5	5.8		
Total		86	100.0		

Descriptive Statistics (Table 4.14 B)

	N	Minimum	Maximum	Mean	Std. Deviation
Training & Professional Carrier	81	1	5	1.96	1.209
Valid N (listwise)	81				

(Graph 4.14 C)

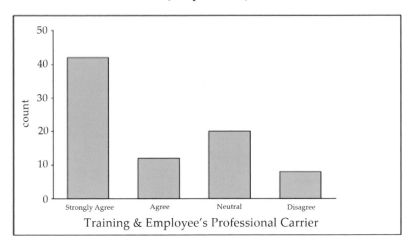

Training & Employee's Professional Carrier

New employees are in some respect, like other raw materials –they have to be processed to become able to perform the task of their job adequately and to fit into their work group and into the Organization as a whole. Majority of the employees like it but 21 respondents were neutral and 5 respondents remain silent in this regard which shows that it is important but for some respondents it is not. The results show an average mean of 1.96 and a standard deviation of 1.209.

Investment on Training

Investment on Training: (Table 4.15A)

		Frequency	Percent	Valid Percent	Cumulative Percent
Valid	Strongly Agree	25	29.1	29.1	29.1
	Agree	26	30.2	30.2	59.3
	Neutral	17	19.8	19.8	79.1
	Disagree	11	12.8	12.8	91.9
	Strongly Disagree	7	8.1	8.1	100.0
	Total	86	100.0	100.0	

Descriptive Statistics (Table 4.15 B)

	N	Minimum	Maximum	Mean	Std. Deviation
Investment on Training	86	1	5	2.41	1.259
Valid N (listwise)	86				

(Graph 4.15 C)

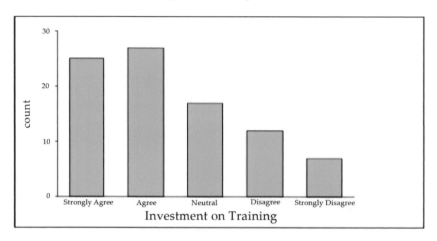

A careful use of training method can be very cost effective instrument; however it has often been found that organsiations usually used inappropriate methods which can be both costly and time wasting and bring very little improvement in the performance of employees. Therefore most of the respondents are willing in this regard and give their vote that organizational culture should support the employee. If the employee is satisfied with the organizational culture he will stay longer with the organization. The results show an average mean of 2.41 and a standard deviation of 1.259.

Schedule for Training

Schedule (Table 4.16 A)

		Frequency	Percent	Valid Percent	Cumulative Percent
Valid	Strongly Agree	30	34.9	34.9	34.9
	Agree	18	20.9	20.9	55.8
	Neutral	14	16.3	16.3	72.1
	Disagree	15	17.4	17.4	89.5
	Strongly Disagree	9	10.5	10.5	100.0
	Total	86	100.0	100.0	

Descriptive Statistics (Table 4.16 B)

	N	Minimum	Maximum	Mean	Std. Deviation
Training Schedule	86	1	5	2.48	1.395
Valid N (listwise)	86				

(Graph 4.16 C)

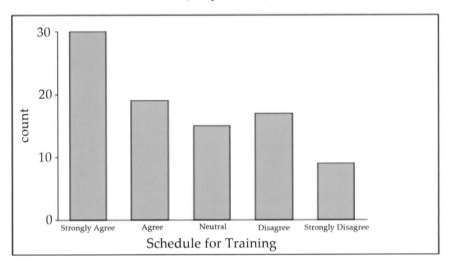

Schedule for Training

This table shows that almost all the organsiations have proper schedule for employees training programs. They believe that employees are trained by these programs and work more efficiently and produce better results for the organsiation. The results show an average mean of 2.48 and a standard deviation of 1.395.

HR Department & Strategic Decision making

Strategic Decision making: (Table 4.17 A)

		Frequency	Percent	Valid Percent	Cumulative Percent
Valid	Strongly Agree	37	43.0	45.7	45.7
	Agree	31	36.0	38.3	84.0
	Neutral	10	11.6	12.3	96.3
	Disagree	3	3.5	3.7	100.0
	Total	81	94.2	100.0	
Missing	System	5	5.8		
Total		86	100.0		

Descriptive Statistics (Table 4.17 B)

	N	Minimum	Maximum	Mean	Std. Deviation
Strategic Decision Making	81	1	4	1.74	.818
Valid N (listwise)	81				

(Graph 4.17 C)

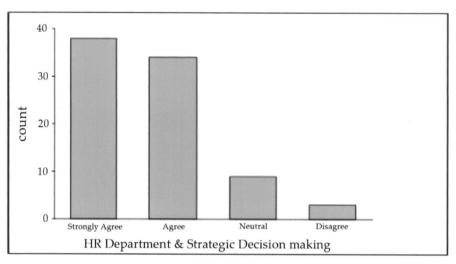

HR Department & Strategic Decision making

The rationale of strategic decision making rests on the perceived advantage of having an agreed and understood basis for developing approaches to manage people in the long term in an organsiation. It also contains the belief that declarations of intent in human resource management should be integrated with the needs of both the Organization and the people in it. Many people agreed with this statement during the survey. The results show an average mean of 1.74 and a standard deviation of .818.

Orientation & Satisfaction of Employees:

Satisfaction of Employees (Table 4.18A)

		Frequency	Percent	Valid Percent	Cumulative Percent
Valid	Strongly Agree	38	44.2	46.9	46.9
	Agree	19	22.1	23.5	70.4
	Neutral	10	11.6	12.3	82.7
	Disagree	9	10.5	11.1	93.8
	Strongly Disagree	5	5.8	6.2	100.0
	Total	81	94.2	100.0	
Missing	System	5	5.8		
Total		86	100.0		

Descriptive Statistics (Table 4.18 B)

	N	Minimum	Maximum	Mean	Std. Deviation
Orientation	81	1	5	2.06	1.268
Valid N (listwise)	81				

(Graph 4.18 C)

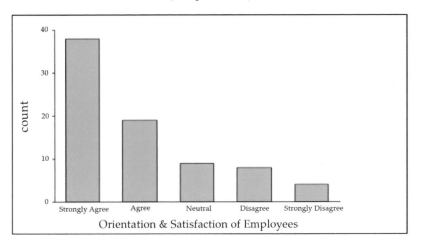

Orientation & Satisfaction of Employees

Valuable and useful process of orientation reduces the start up costs for the new employees, reduces the amount of anxiety and hazing new employee's experiences and also reduce employees turnover rates. All these things provide high level of satisfaction for new employees. The results of the respondents show an average mean of 2.06 with a standard deviation of 1.268.

Orientation Reduces Employee Turnover

Employee Turnover: (Table 4.19 A)

		Frequency	Percent	Valid Percent	Cumulative Percent
Valid	Strongly Agree	39	45.3	48.8	48.8
	Agree	25	29.1	31.2	80.0
	Neutral	8	9.3	10.0	90.0
	Disagree	5	5.8	6.2	96.2
	Strongly Disagree	3	3.5	3.8	100.0
	Total	80	93.0	100.0	
Missing	System	6	7.0		
Total		86	100.0		

Descriptive Statistics (Table 4.19 B)

	N	Minimum	Maximum	Mean	Std. Deviation
Employee Turnover	80	1	5	1.85	1.080
Valid N (listwise)	80				

(Graph 4.19 C)

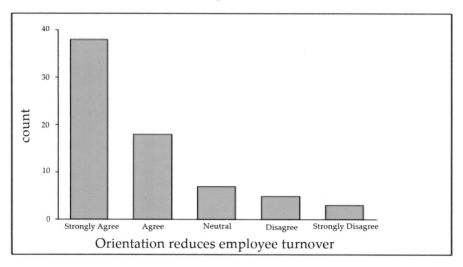

Orientation reduces employee turnover

Organizations having a success and proper orientation process have low turnover rate of the employees. As compare to the other organsiations who have not proper orientation process, people leave such organsiations frequently. The results show an average mean of 1.85 with a standard deviation of 1.080.

Reward Mechanism & Employees Motivation

Employees Motivation Reward Mechanism (Table 4.20 A)

		Frequency	Percent	Valid Percent	Cumulative Percent
Valid	Strongly Agree	21	24.4	25.3	25.3
	Agree	34	39.5	41.0	66.3
	Neutral	17	19.8	20.5	86.7
	Disagree	2	2.3	2.4	89.2
	Strongly Disagree	9	10.5	10.8	100.0
	Total	83	96.5	100.0	
Missing	System	3	3.5		
Total		86	100.0		

Descriptive Statistics (Table 4.20 B)

	N	Minimum	Maximum	Mean	Std. Deviation
Reward & Motivation	83	1	5	2.33	1.201
Valid N (listwise)	83				

(Graph 4.20 C)

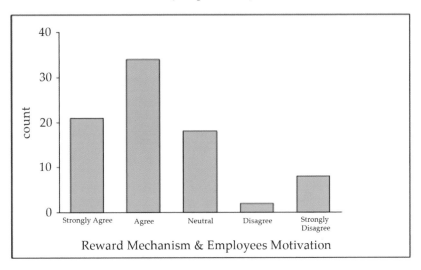

Reward Mechanism & Employees Motivation

Reward Mechanism plays a very vital role for the encouragement & motivation of the employees of an organization. Better reward mechanism encourages employees for hard work and competition and it results better productivity and improvement in employee's performance. Large amount of people is agreed with this opinion. The results show an average mean of 2.33 with a standard deviation of 1.201.

Salary Increments & Promotions

Increments & Promotions (Table 4.21 A)

		Frequency	Percent	Valid Percent	Cumulative Percent
Valid	Strongly Agree	43	50.0	50.0	50.0
	Agree	14	16.3	16.3	66.3
	Neutral	8	9.3	9.3	75.6
	Disagree	12	14.0	14.0	89.5
	Strongly Disagree	9	10.5	10.5	100.0
	Total	86	100.0	100.0	

Descriptive Statistics (Table 4.21 B)

	N	Minimum	Maximum	Mean	Std. Deviation
Increments & Promotions	86	1	5	2.19	1.443
Valid N (listwise)	86				

(Graph 4.21 C)

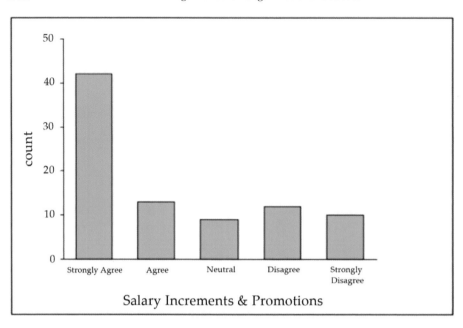

The process of basic salary increments & promotions is different in different Organization. Government & Private sectors have entirely different methods and systems for salary increments and promotions of the employees. During the survey most of the respondents are agreed from this phenomena. The results show an average mean of 2.19 with a standard deviation of 1.443.

HRM & Employees Satisfaction

Employees Satisfaction (Table 4.22 A)

		Frequency	Percent	Valid Percent	Cumulative Percent
Valid	Strongly Agree	58	67.4	67.4	67.4
	Agree	8	9.3	9.3	76.7
	Neutral	12	14.0	14.0	90.7
	Disagree	3	3.5	3.5	94.2
	Strongly Disagree	5	5.8	5.8	100.0
	Total	86	100.0	100.0	

Descriptive Statistics (Table 4.22 B)

	N	Minimum	Maximum	Mean	Std. Deviation
Employees Satisfaction	86	1	5	1.71	1.187
Valid N (listwise)	86				

(Graph 4.22 C)

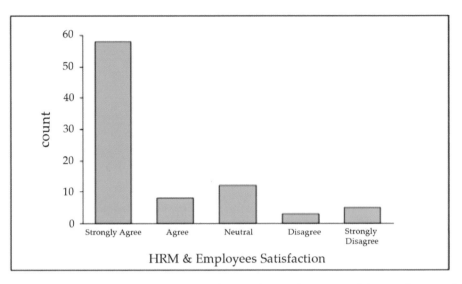

HRM & Employees Satisfaction

Large number of Survey respondents reflected that performance of the employees of any Organization is directly related to effective HR department's policies implemented by HR personnel's. Employees work in managed and gentle manners to run their activities for the good of Organization. The results show an average mean of 1.71 and a standard deviation of 1.187.

HRM & Goals Achievement

Goals Achievement (Table 4.23 A)

		Frequency	Percent	Valid Percent	Cumulative Percent
Valid	Strongly Agree	35	40.7	40.7	40.7
	Agree	25	29.1	29.1	69.8
	Neutral	13	15.1	15.1	84.9
	Disagree	3	3.5	3.5	88.4
	Strongly Disagree	10	11.6	11.6	100.0
	Total	86	100.0	100.0	

Descriptive Statistics (Table 4.23 B)

	N	Minimum	Maximum	Mean	Std. Deviation
Goal Achievements	86	1	5	2.16	1.318
Valid N (listwise)	86				

(Graph 4.23 C)

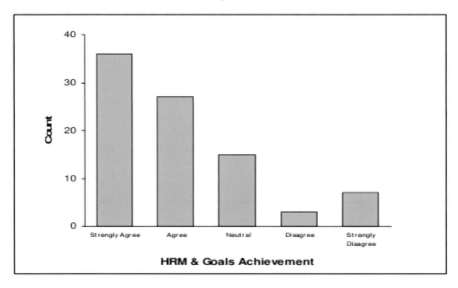

HRM & Goals Achievement

Effectual and efficient use of HR policies is a useful instrument for an Organization to achieve its future goals and objectives. It increases the pace of escalation of the organization. Employees work elegantly as they are managed and incorporated with their HR department. The results show an average mean of 2.16 with a standard deviation of 1.318.

Grievance Handling Procedure (Table 4.24 A)

		Frequency	Percent	Valid Percent	Cumulative Percent
Valid	Strongly Agree	46	53.5	53.5	53.5
	Agree	17	19.8	19.8	73.3
	Neutral	15	17.4	17.4	90.7
	Disagree	2	2.3	2.3	93.0
	Strongly Disagree	6	7.0	7.0	100.0
	Total	86	100.0	100.0	

Descriptive Statistics (Table 4.24 B)

	N	Minimum	Maximum	Mean	Std. Deviation
Grievance handling	86	1	5	1.90	1.198
Valid N (listwise)	86				

(Graph 4.24 C)

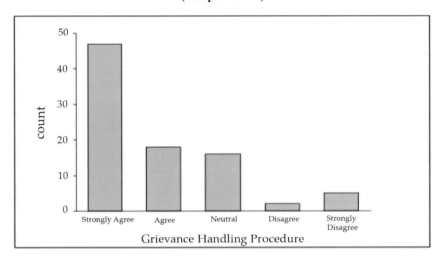

Grievance Handling Procedure

A very large member of respondents expressed that a proper grievance handling procedure is a key element to reduce dissatisfaction among the employees of any Organization. People of that organsiation will be more satisfied and motivated if their grievances are managed and handled efficiently. The results have an average mean of 1.9 with a standard deviation of 1.198.

Purpose of Discipline

Discipline (Table 4.25 A)

		Frequency	Percent	Valid Percent	Cumulative Percent
Valid	Strongly Agree	40	46.5	46.5	46.5
	Agree	18	20.9	20.9	67.4
	Neutral	12	14.0	14.0	81.4
	Disagree	16	18.6	18.6	100.0
	Total	86	100.0	100.0	

Descriptive Statistics (Table 4.25 B)

	N	Minimum	Maximum	Mean	Std. Deviation
Purpose of Discipline	86	1	4	2.05	1.167
Valid N (listwise)	86				

(Graph 4.25 C)

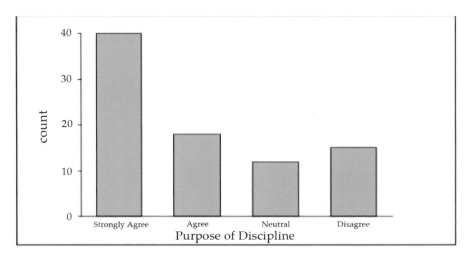

The people, who don't follow established standards of job performance, they can't bring desirable results for their Organization. Similarly, when the management is dissatisfy with the employee, disciplinary action is initiated to correct the situation. No one strongly disagree with this comment. Therefore the results have an average mean of 2.05 with the standard deviation of 1.167.

Effective Disciplinary Process

Disciplinary Process (Table 4.26 A)

		Frequency	Percent	Valid Percent	Cumulative Percent
Valid	Strongly Agree	15	17.4	18.1	18.1
	Agree	25	29.1	30.1	48.2
	Neutral	23	26.7	27.7	75.9
	Disagree	6	7.0	7.2	83.1
	Strongly Disagree	14	16.3	16.9	100.0
	Total	83	96.5	100.0	
Missing	System	3	3.5		
Total		86	100.0		

Descriptive Statistics (Table 4.26 B)

	N	Minimum	Maximum	Mean	Std. Deviation
Effective Disciplinary Process	83	1	5	2.75	1.314
Valid N (listwise)	83				

(Graph 4.26 C)

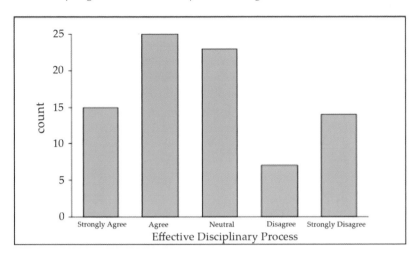

If the people of any Organization are trained and handled by a course of corrective action, they will be able to produce better results as compare to the people who are less managed having a weaker disciplinary process. Most of the people are agreed from this statement but many respondents were neutral in this regard. Therefore the results have an average mean of 2.75 with a standard deviation of 1.314.

Employees Safety

Safety (Table 4.27 A)

		Frequency	Percent	Valid Percent	Cumulative Percent
Valid	Strongly Agree	36	41.9	42.9	42.9
	Agree	18	20.9	21.4	64.3
	Neutral	21	24.4	25.0	89.3
	Disagree	9	10.5	10.7	100.0
	Total	84	97.7	100.0	
Missing	System	2	2.3		
Total		86	100.0		

Descriptive Statistics (Table 4.27 B)

	N	Minimum	Maximum	Mean	Std. Deviation
Employees Safety	84	1	4	2.04	1.058
Valid N (listwise)	84				

(Graph 4.27 C)

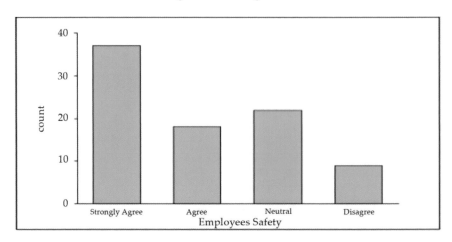

Rational of the employee's safety is to ensure so far as possible every working man and women in the Organization is safe in all the working conditions and it is the duty of their managers that safety measures are successfully put into action for the welfare of the employees. Therefore the results have an average mean of 2.04 with a standard deviation of 1.058.

Job Analysis

Job Analysis (Table 4.28A)

		Frequency	Percent	Valid Percent	Cumulative Percent
Valid	Strongly Agree	45	52.3	52.3	52.3
	Agree	15	17.4	17.4	69.8
	Neutral	9	10.5	10.5	80.2
	Disagree	5	5.8	5.8	86.0
	Strongly Disagree	12	14.0	14.0	100.0
	Total	86	100.0	100.0	

Descriptive Statistics (Table 4.28B)

	N	Minimum	Maximum	Mean	Std. Deviation
Job Analysis	86	1	5	2.12	1.459
Valid N (listwise)	86				

(Graph 4.28 C)

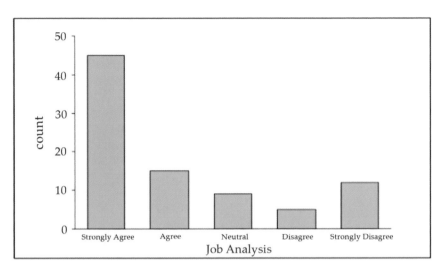

Job Analysis

This table represents the responses about the information that is being provided by the job analysis method related to different jobs. This method has influenced jobs, employers are continuously on the lookout for employees with requisite knowledge, skills and ability to perform adequately. Most of the people in the research are strongly agree in this regard. The results show an average mean of 3.55 and a standard deviation of 1.102.

Benefits of Performance Appraisal

Performance Appraisal: (Table 4.29A)

		Frequency	Percent	Valid Percent	Cumulative Percent
Valid	Strongly Agree	29	33.7	33.7	33.7
	Agree	27	31.4	31.4	65.1
	Neutral	17	19.8	19.8	84.9
	Disagree	7	8.1	8.1	93.0
	Strongly Disagree	6	7.0	7.0	100.0
	Total	86	100.0	100.0	

Descriptive Statistics (Table 4.29B)

	N	Minimum	Maximum	Mean	Std. Deviation
Performance Appraisal	86	1	5	2.23	1.205
Valid N (listwise)	86				

(Graph 4.29C)

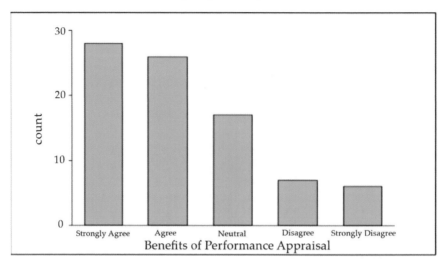

Benefits of Performance Appraisal

This table shows that information gathered from job analysis is used to prepare for performance appraisal which are used to evaluate employees performance. It tells us about the strengths and weakness of the employees of any organisaton and thus helps to take corrective actions for improvement. The results show an average mean of 2.23 and a standard deviation of 1.205.

Organizational Development

Organizational Development (Table 4.30 A)

		Frequency	Percent	Valid Percent	Cumulative Percent
Valid	Strongly Agree	32	37.2	38.6	38.6
	Agree	30	34.9	36.1	74.7
	Neutral	17	19.8	20.5	95.2
	Disagree	2	2.3	2.4	97.6
	Strongly Disagree	2	2.3	2.4	100.0
	Total	83	96.5	100.0	
Missing	System	3	3.5		
Total		86	100.0		

Descriptive Statistics (Table 4.30 B)

	N	Minimum	Maximum	Mean	Std. Deviation
Organizational Development	83	1	5	1.94	.954
Valid N (listwise)	83				

(Graph 4.30 C)

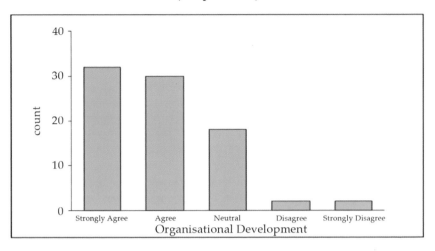

Organizational Development is a method that is aimed at changing the attitudes, values and beliefs of employees so that the employees can identify and implement the technical changes such as reOrganizations, redesigned facilities, and the like that are required, usually with the aid of an out side change agent or consultant. Most of the people in the research are agreed with this phenomenon that this method can bring revolutionary results in the organization. The results show an average mean of 1.94 and a standard deviation of .954.

Downsizing

Downsizing (Table 4.31 A)

		Frequency	Percent	Valid Percent	Cumulative Percent
Valid	Strongly Agree	37	43.0	45.7	45.7
	Agree	31	36.0	38.3	84.0
	Neutral	10	11.6	12.3	96.3
	Disagree	3	3.5	3.7	100.0
	Total	81	94.2	100.0	
Missing	System	5	5.8		
Total		86	100.0		

Descriptive Statistics (Table 4.31 B)

	N	Minimum	Maximum	Mean	Std. Deviation
Downsizing	81	1	4	1.74	.818
Valid N (listwise)	81				

(Graph 4.31 C)

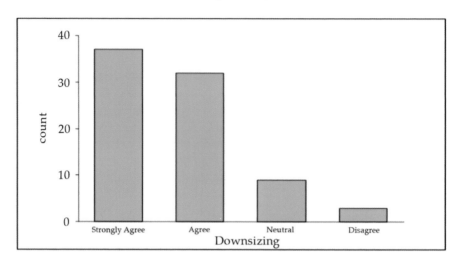

The Organization can rid its self of excess employees through a variety of methods sum of which allow employees to leave voluntarily or through systematic elimination. The restructuring associated with downsizing brings Organizational eliminating a product or service or a departmental function. Majority of the respondents during the research found to be strongly agree with this statement. The results show an average mean of 1.74 and a standard deviation of .818.

Findings

The findings of the research are as under: 1. Use of effective HR system has emerged as a major function in enterprises and Organizations. It is the focus for a wide-ranging debate concerning the nature of the contemporary employment relationship in many market economies. 2. New expertise is used to certify the conception and distribution of services and goods in modern economies. Whatever means are used, the role of individuals and groups as employees and the ability of management to effectively arrange such a resource is vital to interests of both employee and organization alike. 3. Effective HR system and organizational performance are very closely interconnected with each other. If the polices of HR system are examined and implemented successfully they can give us the fruitful results. Therefore all the organizations should plan for a reasonable, effective and progressive course of action to acquire, retain, develop and motivate their employees through a vigorous HR system.

CONCLUSION AND RECOMMENDATIONS

The nature of the employment relationship has experienced a series of important changes and adaptations over the past decade. These are both significant in themselves and will provide the basis for further development in future. Through the effective HR system the employees of an Organization can meet the challenges faced by such changes and adaptations. The responses of the employees to the factors in all the variables of research throw light on their ideas how they can be acquire, retain, develop and motivate through the effective HR system. There responses show that they need motivation and encouragement for the implementation of an effective, successful and progressive HR system for an organization to achieve its goals. Overall, effective HR system ultimately results in the slowly and steadily pace in performance of the organization. Growth only be attained if the employees are satisfied with the organization and employer. If there is not a healthy progress put into practice in the field of management then there will be complexity to attain desirable results in the business world. Now after seeing the results of the research researcher would like to propose that Human Resource Management is responsible for how people are treated in Organizations. It is responsible for bringing people into the Organization, helping them perform their work, compensating them for their labors, and solving problems that arise. The organizations should focus on strategies that promote and endorse the effective use of HR policies for the enhancement of pace of Organizational performance.

Some recommendations are given as:

1. The organization should formulate strategies through the help of HR department to asses that which areas of the organization need attention & care of HR policies to be implemented for the Organizational performance and progress to target future objectives.

2. Then organization should develop a HR system that helps to all the departments so as to make that Organization able to meet the challenges of diversity & changing environment of the modern age because it is the need of the hour for the survival and improvement of the organization.

3. Then Organization will have to assess that how much its policies are successfully implemented and brought out desirable results for its goal achievement. If there is need of any improvement then execution should be carry out after refinement for better results.

4. Rationale of implementation of HR system and its policies will bring improvement in all areas of organization for the betterment of productivity, enhancement of efficiency and motivation of its human assets as a result of managing their performance.

5. There should be proper plan to ensure consistency in the implementation of HR policies and generation of desirable objectives for the progress and improvement of organizational performance.

6. The Research was made by taking a very little sample, therefore to get accuracy of results it should be made by taking a big sample rounding to 2000 to 3000 employees.

7. Research was limited to available researches due to time factor, therefore it is suggested that it should be made by taking a wider aspect so that it can help the managers to develop HR system by focusing on true factors.

REFERENCES

1. Beardwell, I& Holden L. 1994. Human resource management: a contemporary perspective. London: Longman Group UK Ltd.

2. Beer, M. Specter, P.R. Mills D.Q & Walton, R.E. 1985. Managing human assets, part I:A general manager's perspective. Personnel Administrator, 30, 60-69.

3. Belbin, E., & Belbin, R.M. 1972 Problems in adult retraining. London: Heinemann.

4. Bethanis, Susan J.:1999 "Creating a Culture People Want to Work In: How to Recruit and Retain Top Talent." Prepared for the Multimedia Summit, San Francisco.

5. Booth News,: 2003. Long term labor, skills shortages ahead. Booth News, January, 2003

6. Brendler, B. Why isn't every ceo addressing this question? CRM Today, (n.d.).

7. Burke Incorporated.: 2005. Employees can make the difference! Retrieved

8. Cadrain, D.:2002 An Acute Condition: Too Few Nurses. HR Magazine, Dec 2002

9. Cameron KS. 1(994) Strategies for successful Organizational downsizing. Human Resource Management, 33: 477-500.

10. Cascardo, D. C. :2002 Worker shortage continues to plague healthcare industry.

11. Catlette, B. & Hadden, R.: 2000. Prepare employees for their next job and they'll stick

12. Cowling, A. & Walters, M. 1990. Staffing planning- Where are we today? Personnel Review 19(3).

13. Cummings, T. G., Worley, C., :1997. Organizational development and change.

14. David Shadovitz: editor in chief of human resource executive magazine in his article employee retention strategy.

15. Dessler, G. 2001. Human resource ranagement, 7th Ed. New Delhi: Prentice-Hall of India Private Ltd.

ORGANIZATIONAL SUPPORTING BY HUMAN EMPOWERMENT

Nasser Fegh-hi Farahmand

Department of Industrial Management, Tabriz Branch, Islamic Azad University, Tabriz, Iran PO box 6155, Tabriz, Iran

ABSTRACT

A discussion about a review on Human Resources System (HRS) in workplace has received relatively little attention from organizational behavior researchers. The first of the themes to be addressed concerns the relationship between emotion and rationality. There has been a longstanding bifurcation between the two with emotions labeled in pejorative terms and devalued in matters concerning the workplace. The form and structure of an organization's human resources system can affect employee motivation levels in several ways. Organizations can adopt various Human Empowerment (HE) practices to enhance employee satisfaction. Recognizing the importance of human empowerment in achieving flexibility in an international context expands the types of research questions related to the role of human empowerment functions in organizational performance, such as selection of human resources, training, and compensation and performance appraisal. This paper considers the value of workers as an important intangible asset of an organization. The strategic importance of workers is discussed and their interaction, as an asset, with other important organization assets. The basic methodologies for valuing workers are then explained and their limitations are considered. A significant finding from this study and own experience is that many issues remain unrecognized for far too long after they are first identified. Valuing intangible assets, in particular workers-related intangibles, is clearly not a straightforward exercise. These values are

Citation: Nasser Fegh-hi Farahmand, 2011, Organizational Supporting by Human Empowerment, http://www.iiste.org/Journals/index.php/EJBM/article/view/656

not as robust as we would hope, it is certainly better to attempt to attribute value to intangible assets than classifying everything as goodwill.

INTRODUCTION

Are the approaches applied by accountants and the resulting values, however, equally valid for strategic planning and performance measurement or simply numbers to satisfy the information requirements of investors and efficient tax planning? Continuous training, employment security, performance appraisal and alternative compensation systems can motivate skilled employees to engage in effective discretionary decision making and behavior in response to a variety of environmental contingencies. A discussion about a review on Human Resources System (HRS) in workplace has received relatively little attention from organizational behavior researchers. The first of the themes to be addressed concerns the relationship between emotion and rationality. There has been a longstanding bifurcation between the two with emotions labeled in pejorative terms and devalued in matters concerning the workplace. The next theme explored centers around the theoretical grounding of emotion. Emotion is often described either in psychological terms as an individualized, intrapersonal response to some stimulus, or by contrast, a socially constituted phenomenon, depending upon the disciplinary perspective one adopts. This study has reviewed how organizations, as powerful culture eating institutions, have applied normative expectations and established boundaries for the acceptable expression of emotion among human resources system through tactics such as applicant screening and selection measures, employee training, off-the-job socialization opportunities, organizational rewards and the creation of rituals, ideologies and other symbols for indoctrinating the newly hired into the culture of the organization.

There is no doubt that valuing acquired intangibles such as brands, patents and workers lists makes a lot of sense rather than placing these organization critical assets in the accounting black hole known as goodwill.

Modern approaches recognize that selection of Human Empowerment (HE) is a complex process that involves a significant amount of vagueness and subjectivity. Tangible assets as such machinery, building, stocks and shares are pretty straightforward to value, their visible and corporeal nature makes them relatively easy to define and in most cases there is an active market from which value can be derived. In contrast, intangible assets are not so easily defined while it is rare that they are actively traded. Consequently, any intangible valuation exercise must start with 'What?' and 'Why?' before considering 'How?'

ORGANIZATIONAL WORKERS

Capturing the wrong Organizational Workers (OW) information, unclear goals, inappropriate selection and use of technology, inability to integrate workers and processes and use of misleading metrics or improper measurement approaches are the major barriers in implementing and managing human empowerment projects systems that seek to identify individuals with the ability to learn and adapt to new situations and markets can provide a firm with competitive advantage. Human empowerment of organizational workers is defined as a complex feeling state accompanied by physiological arousal and overt behaviors. These words in essence, imply motion. Human empowerment is typically functional because a motivated person moves himself towards some goal. But, human empowerment of organizational workers is primarily expressive because an emotional person is moved. Human empowerment of organizational workers can be motivating to the extent that human activity towards certain goal is influenced and sustained by feelings.

Forever, international organizations can adopt various practices to enhance employee skills s follows:

1)   Efforts can focus on improving the quality of the individuals hired, or on raising the skills and abilities of current employees, or on both. Employees can be hired via sophisticated selection procedures designed to screen out all but the very best potential employees. Indeed, research indicates that selectivity in staffing is positively related to firm performance.

2)   Organizations can improve the quality of current employees by providing comprehensive training and development activities after selection. The more we understand people and their total environment, the more their needs are likely to be met. When we talk about valuing workers relationships, the scope of definition is expansive. On the one hand, it is simply the value that workers generate for the organization. On the other hand, it is purely the value of the relationship. Neither definition is more correct than the other; however, the purpose and approach for valuing each are different.

A positive experience throughout the workers cycle should foster trust and develop loyalty, therefore allowing an organization to generate more revenue for less incremental expenditure.

For example:

1)   Happy existing workers are more willing to operation or services and try new operation or service offerings.

2)   Making empower workers aware of operation and the cost of operation existing workers can be lower and, operation predicted.

HUMAN EMPOWERMENT AND DEVELOPMENT

Employees are one of the most valuable resources and organizations have to remain competitive. Modern organizations might achieve this by using organic Human Empowerment and Development (HED) that promote the development of a human capital pool possessing a broad range of skills and that are able to engage in a wide variety of behavior. Human empowerment and development can be managed through conscious practices.

This definition comes from an inter actionist approach, where, human empowerment are expressed in and partially determined by, the social environment. The human empowerment consists of four dimensions:

a) Frequency of interactions,

b) Attentiveness

c) Variety of human empowerment required,

d) Human empowerment dissonance.

Human empowerment dissonance was discussed as a state where, in the emotions expressed are discrepant from the human development felt. Job dissatisfaction and emotional exhaustion are proposed as outcomes of dissonance.

This definition of emotional labor includes the organizational expectations for employees in their inter actions with customers. According to human development regulation proposed the individual can regulate emotions at two points. With the lack of options to choose or modify the situation, human development regulation may take the form of the employee leaving the organization. In short, service employees for human development may not have the breadth of situation modification that is available outside of a work role. Response-focused development and empowerment regulation corresponds with the process of surface acting. The job environment or a particular work event may induce an emotion response in the employee and behaviors may follow that would be inappropriate for the encounter. Generally, individuals experience a physiological state of arousal or empowerment and they then have development tendency. The arousal state from emotions informs them and gets them in a bodily state to respond to the situation. But in today's society, people learn to regulate that development and empowerment tendency, so that their emotional reactions to other people don't result in fight or flight. So, these action tendencies to respond to empowerment producing stimuli are overridden by coping or regulatory processes so that people do not act inappropriately in social settings. One way of considering how workers relationships create value is within the framework of Porter's value chain. In according with Porter organizational activities categories to support and main as Table 1, we know that organizational goal attachment depend on all of them.

Table 1. Strengthening of Organization activities

Organizational support activities	Infra Structure (IF)				
	Human Empowerment and Development (HED)				
	Technology Development (TD)				
	Organizational Resources Procurement (ORP)				
Organizational primary activities	Input Activities	Process Activities	Output Activities	Marketing Activities	Services Activities

The chain of activities gives the products more added value than the sum of added values of all activities. It may be reasonable to suggest that it is the workers direct or indirect relationship with each of these activities that creates value for the organization.

Human empowerment and development as organizational support activities, organizations tend to be highly decentralized and use informal means of coordination and control. The reasons have to do with human bounded rationality. Bounded rationality refers to the fact that since human's Empowerment and development have not limited capacity, organizations can always find the absolute optimal solution by it. In contrast, there are operation drivers that cannot be attributed to the brand but can have a significant influence on the workers relationship with a organization. For example, inertia is considered to be the single biggest driver of workers retention in the banking industry; clearly, this is not attributable to brand and therefore could be considered as part of the workers relationship value. Many organizations are becoming aware of the need to provide continued hands-on training rather than just pre-departure awareness training.

In contrast to pre-departure training, post-arrival training gives global managers a chance to evaluate their stressors after they have encountered them. Documentary and interpersonal training methods have additive benefits in preparing managers for intercultural work assignments.

HUMAN EMPOWERMENT AND DEVELOPMENT AND STRENGTHENING OF ORGANIZATION

Human empowerment is often described either in psychological terms as an individualized, intrapersonal response to some stimulus, or, by contrast, a socially constituted phenomenon, depending upon the disciplinary perspective one adopts. The experiences of competition and domination likewise produce emotions in male s such as elation when they win and anger when their hegemonic position in the hierarchical structure is challenged. Organizational actors quite rationally draw upon their emotions to evaluate their circumstances. This ensures that members will behave in ways that are consistent with their self-interests. Hence, according to this perspective, Human empowerment underwrites rational decision making and enables employees to behave in ways that are rational for them. The behaviors of leaders and decision makers have been described as psychologically defensive reactions to unconscious fears and anxieties and unresolved early life experiences. Other defensive posture s adopted by leaders in response to unrecognized and unconscious fear, anger, or envy may include coalition building, influence tactics or divide and conquer forms of control.

STRENGTHENING OF ORGANIZATION BY HUMAN EMPOW-ERMENT AND DEVELOPMENT STRATEGY

The functions of human empowerment and id can be considered to have a major impact on organizational behavior. By assuming individuals as pleasure seeking organisms, it is argued that ego searches for pleasure producing experiences in order to human empowerment drives and this process gives birth to defensive, intellectual-cognitive and executive human empowerment and development. Specifically, human empowerment and development can be examined as a part of the id that adapts and adjusts to those conditions residing in the external world. Additionally, human empowerment and development covers unconscious behaviors of individuals who make sense of the world around them through conscious awareness found in strengthening of organization by human empowerment. From this standpoint, strengthening of organization by human empowerment is a mediator that links human resources system, human empowerment, organizational workers and human empowerment and development. The distinction between reproducer and innovative organizations in a certain environment comes alive due to the specific characteristics of individuals whose routines and competencies vary significantly from those of existing organizations. The relationship between human resources system, human empowerment, organizational workers, human empowerment and development could be associated with strengthening of organization by human empowerment. As defense mechanisms enable strengthening of organization by human empowerment to inhibit feelings of discontent, a tension between human empowerment and organizational workers occurs. The main argument here remains that human empowerment and organizational workers purpose is to acquire perfection under the circumstances the individual faces, postulates those occasions which is in direct opposition.

Capturing achievements and perfection strengthens human empowerment and organizational workers and at the same time, human empowerment cracks may come into existence because of the weakening role of human empowerment and development.

The meaning of human empowerment and development and founding of a new organization is closely related to each other. As a result, the relation between human empowerment and organizational workers and the environment becomes the fundamental issue of entrepreneurship through displaying characteristics of the need for achievement which may be associated with the harmony among these constructs.

Conceptually, argued that human empowerment and development exhaustion best captures the core meaning of burnout. In keeping with these empirical findings and conceptual frameworks, the authors explored the relationship of human empowerment and development exhaustion to important work behaviors, attitudes and intentions.

Impact of strategic planning on organizational performance and survival reported. Based on the findings from the study the following recommendations are made.

Having discovered that organizational performance and survival is a function of strategic planning, Organizations should accord priority attention to the elements of strategic planning for example:

a) Having a documented mission statement,

b) A future picture and vision of the organization,

c) Organizations should establish core values i.e., organization's rules of conduct, set realistic goals, establishment of long term objectives,

d) The development of action and strategic plans,

e) Implementation and adequate follow-up.

f) Since it was discovered that environmental factors affect strategic planning intensity,

g) Organizations should make adequate environmental analysis both the internal and external analysis; this can be done through the SWOT analysis which indicates the organization's strengths, weaknesses, opportunities and threats.

The concept of workers value discussed above for strategic purposes is very different from the accepted definitions applied by those involved in carrying out technical valuations for financial reporting. Classifies intangible assets into four categories:

1) Workers related

2) Marketing related

3) Technology based

4) Empower workers

Fewer employees work under individual incentive plans while greater numbers of individuals work under some type of group incentive system. A substantial body of evidence has focused on the impact of incentive compensation and performance management systems on group performance. For financial reporting, an intangible asset should be recognized as an asset apart from goodwill if it arises from contractual or other legal rights.

Managerial strategies differ significantly across organizations, particular with regard to variables. Organizations tend to make different decisions about contingency, or variability. In general organizations implement incentive compensation systems that provide rewards to employees for meeting specific goals. An intangible asset may also be recognized only if it is separable, that it is capable of being sold, transferred, licensed, rented or exchanged.

STRENGTHENING OF ORGANIZATION BY HUMAN EMPOW-ERMENT AND DEVELOPMENT MANAGEMENT

Effective performance feedback is timely, specific, behavioral in nature, and presented by a credible source. Performance feedback is effective in changing employee work behavior and enhances employee job satisfaction and performance

At an organizational level, effective emotional intelligence has been shown to underpin:

1)   A work team's capacity to identify and ascribe to attitudinal and behavioral norms related to more effective patterns of interacting employees capacity to recognize,

2)   Understand and navigate boundary and role confusion between work teams, departments,

3)   Divisions and the organization within the broader market context and a sense of organizational accomplishment and trouble free operation,

4)   Development of vertical trust, organizational support and general workplace wellbeing. At an individual and leadership effectiveness level, Human Empowerment and development human empowerment and development management intelligence is related to a leader's capability to show:

a) Sensitivity and empathy towards others;

b) Build on other work colleague's ideas;

c) Influence others to accept alternative points of view;

d) Demonstrate integrity and; act according to prevailing ethical standards by remaining consistent with one's words and actions

Human empowerment and development management feedback is essential in gaining the maximum benefits from goal setting. Without feedback, employees are unable to make adjustments in job performance or receive positive reinforcement for effective job behavior.

The common approaches for valuing intangible assets, including workers-related intangibles, are as follows. Each method is based on strong, rational theory and yet, in practice, each method may produce starkly different values:

1)   Effective approach; the historic cost is distorted by the time value of money and evolvement of the competitive environment. How much did it cost to create the asset or how much it would cost to replace it? Estimating value under the historic cost approach is simply a case of summing all capital invested in creating the asset in question. In the case of a workers base, the historic cost could be considered as equivalent to the total amount of marketing investment expended.

2)   Management approach; the amount paid for the asset or similar assets. In a new product or service market with relatively few competitors, economic theory suggests that workers acquisition costs should be relatively low before gradually increasing as the market for new workers becomes more competitive, forcing companies to capture market share from rivals in order to realize growth.

3)   Strengthening approach; the present value of future cash flows, that is, how much income the asset will generate throughout its useful life, accounting for the time value of money and associated risk.

At all hierarchical levels and across all departments in a modern organization effective human empowerment and development means managing the above activities successfully in an international context. The strengthening of organization by human empowerment and development management functions is essential to a human resources manager job.

The strategic areas and unit's level:

a)   Where decisions are made by the general manager of the official organization unit and the other top organization leaders,

b)   Measures undertaken concerning the entire particular official organization and especially the future competitiveness of the organization and management of the whole organization system are addressed. Very often in corporations there are different official organization areas that may be at different development stages.

RESULT

The principal weakness of the multiple excess earnings approach is that it is complicated to carry out. Furthermore, correctly identifying all the value drivers operating functions and intangible assets employed and calculating their respective functional returns and present values is open to distortion and inaccuracy due to the sensitivity of the valuation to key assumptions and source data. In the case of an acquisition, the excess returns will also include the value of any synergies resulting from the organization combination. Different organizations have different priorities and varying amounts of funding to invest in SOHE. Many of these organizations have sustained their strengthening of organization by human empowerment systems focus over time, although these investments may or may not be considered part of a long-term strengthening of organization by human empowerment strategy. For example, one major international bank defines its SOHE systems as the marketing databases and campaign management and considers distribution channels to be a separated systems investment area.

CONCLUSION

Managers have too many successful measures, and a simplified set with fewer yet more important metrics would lead to superior successful. Successful management systems are hindered by too many low-level measures. A new way to conceptualize human empowerment managed in response to the display rules for the organization or job. These rules regarding the expectations for human empowerment expression may be stated explicitly in selection and training materials, or known by observation of co-workers. Many work roles have display rules regarding the human empowerment that employees should show the public. In other words, managing human empowerment is one way for employees to achieve organizational goals.

Dramaturgical perspective offered two main ways for actors to manage human empowerment:

a)   Through surface acting where,

b)   One regulates the emotional expressions and through deep acting where,

c)   One consciously modifies feelings in order to express the desired emotion,

d)   One of major tenets is that this management of emotions requires effort.

The key issue is whether the firm wants to make use of these relationships in the way it manages customers or not, and whether a given customer wants to be an actively managed relationship with the service provider, or not. Organizations compete with the quality level of their operations. An organization, which cannot manage operations competition, will have problems surviving. In order to be able to do this successfully, the organization has to view its business and its customer relationships from a service existence. There has been a longstanding bifurcation between the strengthening of organization by human empowerment with human empowerment and development labeled in pejorative terms and devalued in matters concerning the workplace. The human empowerment and development explored centers around the theoretical grounding of emotion. Human empowerment and development is often described either in psychological terms as an individualized, intrapersonal response to some stimulus, or by contrast, a socially constituted phenomenon, depending upon the disciplinary perspective one adopts. This study has reviewed how organizations, as powerful human empowerment and development eating institutions, have applied normative expectations and established boundaries for the acceptable expression of emotion among employees through tactics such as applicant screening and selection measures for:

a) Strengthening of organization by human empowerment,

b) Organizational workers job socialization opportunities,

c) Organizational rewards,

d) Creation of human resources system,

e) Creation of ideologies and other symbols for indoctrinating the newly hired into the culture of the organization,

f) Creation of human empowerment for indoctrinating the strengthening of organization by human empowerment.

A significant finding from this study and own experience is that many issues remain unrecognized for far too long after they are first identified. Valuing intangible assets, in particular human empowerment is clearly not a straightforward exercise.

Each strengthening of organization by human empowerment method prescribed by accountants has different strengths, weaknesses and complexities and yet none are able to provide an indisputably accurate and reliable value. Although these values are not as robust as we would hope, it is certainly better to attempt to attribute value to intangible assets than classifying everything as goodwill.

Strengthening of organization by human empowerment orientation is suggested to have a robust effect on individuals who endeavor to overcome the constrained commonplace conditions and deliver worthy achievements like social stability and world peace.

The ability of the strengthening of organization by human empowerment to provide the needs of human empowerment effect on pleasure and satisfaction experiences for those individuals. In this view, strengthening of organization by human empowerment encounter more accomplishments throughout organizational workers and their tendency to seek more of empowerment and growth can become increasingly.

REFERENCES

1. Aldrich HE (2005). Entrepreneurship. In N. Smelser, R. Swedberg (Ed.), Handbook of Economic Sociology, 451-477. Princeton, NJ: Princeton University Press

2. Bjerke, B., Hultman C. (2002). Entrepreneurial marketing: The growth of small firms in the new economic era. UK: Edward Elgar

3. Boussouara, M., Deakins, D. (1999). Market-based learning, entrepreneurship and the high technology small firm. International journal of entrepreneurial behavior and research, 5(4), 204-223

4. Bruderl, J., Preisendorfer, P., Ziegler R. (1992). Survival chances of newly

founded business organizations. American Sociological Review. 57, 227-242

5.   Carson, D., Cromie, S., McGowan, P., Hill, J. (1995). Marketing and entrepreneurship in SMEs. An innovative Approach. New Jersey: Princeton Hall

6.   Crawford, V. (1982), Strategic Information Transmission, Econometrical, p50.

7.   Feghhi Farahmand, Nasser (2001), Executive Management Process, Islamic Azad University, Tabriz Branch, Iran, pp 19-23.

8.   Feghhi Farahmand, Nasser (2003), Permanent Management of Organization, First edition, Frouzesh Publication, Tabriz, Iran, 105-322.

9.   Feghhi Farahmand, Nasser (2003), Strategic Structure of Organization Management Process, Forth edition, Islamic Azad University, Tabriz Branch, Iran, 10-25.

10. Feghhi Farahmand, Nasser (2005), Strategic Management of Organization, First edition, Frouzesh Publication, Tabriz, Iran, 114.

11. Feghhi Farahmand, Nasser (2009), Organization Strategic Plan compilation, First edition, Frouzesh Publication, Tabriz, Iran, 31-104.

12. Feghhi farahmand, Nasser (2011), Active and Dynamic Management of Organization, Second edition, Frouzesh Publication, Tabriz, Iran, 122-130.

13. Feghhi Farahmand, Nasser (2011a), Technology Management of Organization, Second edition, Frouzesh Publication, Tabriz, Iran, 21-25.

14. Gilligan, T. (1987), Collective Decision-Making, Journal of Organization, 112-118.

15. Glenn H. (2002), The application of QFD to Design a course in TQM, QFD Institute, USA, 35-39.

16. Gopinath, R (2011), Employees' Emotions in Workplace, [Online] Available: http://scialert.net/fulltext/?doi=rjbm.2011.1.15&org=10

17. Harris, M. (2007), A Theory of Board Control and Size, Review of Financial Studies, pp 61-77.

18. Hartmann, H. (1981). Essays on ego psychology: Selected problems in psychoanalytic theory. New York: International University Press

19. Hartmann, H., Kris, E., Loewenstein, R. (1964). The function of theory in psychoanalysis. Psychological Issues, 4, 117-143

20. Homans, G. (1950), The Human Group, New York: Harcourt, Brace, Jovanovich, 52-87.

21. Jain, R., Jain, S. and Dhar, U. (2007) 'CUREL: A scale for measuring customer relationship management effectiveness in service sector', Journal of Services Research, Vol. 7, No. 1, 39–51.

22. M. Miral Ural and Mustafa M. Gokoglu (2009), The Relationship between Entrepreneurial Success and Growing Ego Needs, Baskent University IIBF, Baglica, Ankara

23. Mintzberg, H. (1973), The Nature of Managerial Work, New York: Harper and Row, 51-74.

24. Payne, A. and Frow, P. (2005). A strategic framework for customer relationship management, Journal of Marketing, Vol. 69, 36–81.

25. Payne, A. and Frow, P. (2006) 'Customer relationship management: From strategy to implementation', Journal of Marketing Management, Vol. 22, 147–154.

26. Perls, F.S., Heffenline, R.F., Goodman, P. (1989). Gestalt therapy. Excitement and growth in the human personality. New York: Julian Press

27. Raman, P., Wittmann, C. M. and Rauseo, N. A. (2006) 'Leveraging CRM for sales: The role of organizational capabilities in successful CRM implementation', Journal of Personal Selling & Sales Management, Vol. 26, No. 1, 84–98.

28. Rapoport, D. (1951). Organization and pathology of thought. New York: Columbia University Press

29. Rubin, J.B. (1998). A psychoanalysis for our time: Exploring the blindness of the seeing I. New York: New York University Press

30. Schmitz, J. and Platts, K. W. (2004) 'Supplier logistics performance measurement: Indications from a study of the automotive industry', International Journal of Production Economics, Vol. 89, No. 2, 215–284.

INDEX